Volunteer ENGAGEMENT 2.0

Ideas and insights changing the world

EDITED BY
ROBERT J. ROSENTHAL

Cover image and design: VolunteerMatch

Published by John Wiley & Sons, Inc., Hoboken, New Jersey.
Published simultaneously in Canada.

For general information on our other products and services or for technical support, please contact our Customer Care Department within the United States at (800) 762-2974, outside the United States at (317) 572-3993 or fax (317) 572-4002.

Wiley publishes in a variety of print and electronic formats and by print-on-demand. Some material included with standard print versions of this book may not be included in e-books or in print-on-demand. If this book refers to media such as a CD or DVD that is not included in the version you purchased, you may download this material at http://booksupport.wiley.com. For more information about Wiley products, visit www.wiley.com.

Library of Congress Cataloging-in-Publication Data:

Volunteer engagement 2.0 : ideas and insights changing the world / edited by Robert J. Rosenthal.
pages cm
Includes index.
ISBN 978-1-118-93188-2 (paperback); ISBN 978-1-118-93190-5 (ebk); ISBN 978-1-118-93189-9 (ebk)
1. Voluntarism–United States. 2. Voluntarism. I. Rosenthal, Robert J., 1972-
HN90.V64V643 2015
302'.14–dc23

2015001923

Printed in the United States of America

10 9 8 7 6 5 4 3 2 1

This book is for everyone who dreams of a better world—and especially for those who help achieve it.

Contents

About the Book

The volunteer engagement field is filled with textbooks showing how to model our programs on those of others. In contrast, the purpose of this publication is to help us *think differently* about what's possible—for ourselves, for our work, and for the many challenges that will rise up ahead on our journey. It's meant to be a collection of ideas and insights to help you find the way on your own path in social change.

From 2009 to early 2014 I was lucky to lead the communications team at VolunteerMatch, where, among other things, we produced thought-leadership and education programs for our network of millions of nonprofit professionals, volunteers and corporate social responsibility teams. The inspiration for *Volunteer Engagement 2.0: Ideas and Insights Changing the World* was our series of free webinars, which presented to nonprofit audiences a diverse range of thinkers who might have otherwise not been heard by those who work with volunteers. Some of the contributors to this book, in fact, first introduced their ideas to volunteer engagement audiences during those webinars, and today thousands of volunteer coordinators are putting to work what they learned there.

Nonprofit staff, volunteers, and corporate social responsibility teams have a lot in common. Some work at it full-time, others just on the weekends, and others have big budgets. But we are united in our desire to live in a just, peaceful, healthy society. At VolunteerMatch I noticed that many of the biggest ideas in volunteer engagement were coming from disciplines that were tangential to traditional volunteer management—digital communications, product development, social media measurement, branding, and management consulting all have much to offer us. Innovation, it turns out, often moves from the outside in. The VolunteerMatch .org web service, which evolved from a pro bono project sponsored by Sun Microsystems called NetDay 96, is just one example of this dynamic principle in action.[1]

I produced this book while living in a very old neighborhood in Kathmandu, Nepal. Working here was a strong reminder about the importance of leaning into the change that surrounds us. Here transformation is urgent and everywhere. But even though motorcycles and ringtones now dominate the ancient lanes, traditional ways of life grounded in family, prayer, and community are still the bedrock. Eventually those traditions will make room for more rights for Nepal's women, workers, and previously untouchable castes. Change can't be stopped—and why should it be? Indeed, Kathmandu Valley was itself once a vast lake—the basin its draining left behind became a "Shangri-La," a place where nature provided for all.

Recognizing the interconnectedness of things, I'd like to thank each of the 30 experts who gave generously of their time for this book despite their very busy schedules. I want to acknowledge Alison Hankey from John Wiley & Sons who has been an enthusiast for this book and appreciated its embrace of the unorthodox. Greg Baldwin, president of VolunteerMatch, got behind a 300-page print publishing project even though he knows more than most just how short our attention spans have become. Dr. Sarah Jane Rehnborg and Susan J. Ellis, true leaders of volunteer engagement both, pointed me in smart directions I would otherwise have missed. Darian Rodriguez Heyman and Ritu Sharmu, two social-change makers I've previously been fortunate to collaborate with, inspired me through their own devotion to nonprofit capacity building.

I am grateful to my friends in Kathmandu, especially Annie Seymour and Tim Stewart, who have been my cheerleaders and supporters while I completed the project. And, finally, I would like to acknowledge the enormous debt I owe my mother, Marilyn, who taught me the importance of giving back.

Robert J. Rosenthal (@socialgoodR)

Note

1. For more on NetDay, see http://en.wikipedia.org/wiki/NetDay.

Foreword

Holly Ross
Executive Director, Drupal Association

When my friends at VolunteerMatch asked me to write the foreword to this book, I was frankly a little bit uncertain.

For six years I served as executive director at the Nonprofit Technology Network (or NTEN), which is best known for our annual technology conference and our online education programs. Since 2013, I've been in a similar role at Drupal Association, the nonprofit that supports the development of Drupal, open source software that powers more than a million websites around the world.

Neither organization seems, at least to me, to exemplify the kinds of nonprofits that would likely be reading *Volunteer Engagement 2.0*.

When we think of the word *volunteer*, we tend to imagine individuals contributing their time to physical tasks, which are in short supply at nonprofits that are focused on technology. There are no playgrounds to clean or mailers to prepare when your mission is helping people use technology.

But as I began to reflect on my own experiences supporting and leading volunteer teams, I realized that all the questions I've ever had about volunteers are *essentially the same kinds of questions* faced by everyone I know who works in the nonprofit sector. The volunteer mix may be different from my organization to yours, but the lessons I've learned over the years should be relevant for anyone who is interested in transforming their programs to keep up with the frenetic pace of our changing world.

So what have I learned? Well, if I could bundle all my experience—successes and mistakes—into one lesson, it would be this: Respect and honor your volunteers. Everything else in volunteer engagement is commentary.

So many nonprofit professionals still think of volunteers as extra man-hours. But if that's your expectation going in, you're going to be very upset. When it comes to inspiring and harnessing the time and talent of volunteers, there's so much more involved—and more potential for greatness and meaning—than that. In fact, the real importance of a book like this is its potential to help more nonprofits understand how to better work with individuals to give meaning to their experience as volunteers. What an incredibly powerful responsibility!

Here are a few other things I've learned about respecting volunteers over the years:

Volunteer engagement is a process, not an outcome. Volunteers may not always bring efficiency, speed, or ease to the process, but they will bring ideas and experience that can create a better outcome if you are willing to listen. More importantly, because volunteering is an empowering act, volunteer engagement changes volunteers, organizations and the community every day and over the long haul.

Volunteers will bring their own ideas to the table and that's perfectly fine. Very often your job is to operationalize those ideas and build a structure around them that will provide a way forward for both your needs and the volunteer.

If you ask people for their opinions, you actually have to consider them. This may seem obvious, but your volunteers will know if you're asking and not really listening. And they won't like it.

Be prepared for disruption. Have an outline of what you want to accomplish but also the flexibility to allow the process to be derailed to accommodate volunteers and their ideas.

Never take a volunteer for granted. Just because they've done some task for the last decade doesn't mean they aren't dying to try something else. Instead, seek to provide paths for great volunteers to move around within the organization. Otherwise one day they'll move on.

Get to know your volunteers so you can reward them. Real respect means knowing your volunteers well enough to understand the human need that motivates them to be involved. Then you can give them the rewards and recognition that meet their needs.

Respect can only exist in relationships. With this in mind, sometimes it can be helpful to leave the boundaries of your institutional identity. Remember that a nonprofit organization, after all, is no more than a collection of people who are working together to solve some problem. Some do the work full time; some volunteer. But we are all connected through the cause we care about.

This, by the way, is why VolunteerMatch is the perfect organization to present a book like *Volunteer Engagement 2.0* to you. VolunteerMatch works at that magical place where engagement of volunteers first takes place. Through their network of hundreds of websites, the team at VolunteerMatch can actually see thousands of connections take place each day, and they have statistical evidence of what happens when a relationship flourishes and when it doesn't.

For VolunteerMatch, "respect" in volunteer engagement means being just as obsessed with helping nonprofits find a great volunteer as with helping volunteers find a great opportunity. Moreover, in always being willing to share and build bridges, VolunteerMatch is fundamentally an unselfish organization—which, to me, explains the willingness of so many of the field's great minds and experienced practitioners to take part in this book.

Ready to get started? Read on and engage.

Holly Ross

Holly Ross is the executive director at the Drupal Association. Holly has spent her career working with nonprofits and technology and comes to the Drupal Association after a 10-year tenure at NTEN: The Nonprofit Technology Network. She is thrilled to work with a community that shares her passion for using technology to make great things happen in the world.

Introduction

Greg Baldwin
President, VolunteerMatch

"Act as if what you do makes a difference. It does."

—William James

Democracies are made *possible* by the rights of free speech and assembly, but they are made *great* by those who use these freedoms as an opportunity to make a difference. If you are one of those people, or want to be one of those people, this book is for you.

Don't worry—this isn't going to be a book about the importance of volunteering, or a patronizing analysis of why people don't do it enough. It won't be a book about why volunteers are so often taken for granted or why the people who lead them don't always get the respect they deserve. This isn't a book about what volunteering has been—it's about what it can become.

Let's start with where we are. The most recent data from the Bureau of Labor Statistics estimates that about 25 percent of the U.S. population volunteers each year.[1] There are two ways to understand that number—the old way, and what is emerging as the new way.

In the old way this 25 percent is pictured as an idealized group of virtuous citizens who set aside their own selfish interests to address society's pressing social issues. Unlike everyone else, this 25 percent has managed to transcend—or perhaps not fully understand—the biological, social, and economic realities of self-interest.

Volunteers, after all, are often celebrated precisely because we see them acting contrary to the idea that we are hardwired to be self-interested.

Look around: As a result of this frame of reference you'll notice how much energy we spend as a society trying to figure out how in the name of reason, science, and progress we can convince more people to set aside their selfish ways to look after the common good. Or, as Richard Dawkins, author of *The Selfish Gene*, suggests, "Let us try to teach generosity and altruism, because we are born selfish."

And so the volunteer rate becomes a kind of scorecard for how well the effort to overcome human nature is going.

When we launched VolunteerMatch in 1998 we understood the logic of the old way, but saw a very different possibility emerging. What we saw to be true didn't square with this conventional wisdom.

Because our own experiences volunteering didn't seem to involve an effort to overcome an instinct for selfishness, we didn't see ourselves as heroes. In fact, volunteering at its best didn't even feel selfless at all—it was *fulfilling*, a word that indicated how much we were receiving from this supposedly selfless act.

We saw the fact only one in four Americans volunteer not as a measure of how hard it is to get people to volunteer, but as a reflection of the opportunities available to do it. We assumed that, like us, other people want to make a difference; our role wasn't to talk them out of being bad, it was to better organize the opportunities to do good.

We saw the possibility that maybe people are more complicated than science said. Technology would transform how people organize around things they care about. Businesses would take a more active role in social change. We saw that volunteering wasn't about the *importance of doing something for free*, it was about *the freedom to do something important*.

Since then, these emerging possibilities have become real:

- Science is discovering new evidence about the nature of altruism and generosity.
- Changing business models and new organizational imperatives are emphasizing the value of workplace giving and engagement.

- Technology is bringing scale, efficiency, and choice to the marketplace of engagement while reducing the barriers of place and time.
- Changing corporate strategies are realigning the relationship between profit and purpose. Workplace volunteer programs are bringing more specialized skills and pro bono resources into the volunteer candidate pool.
- Decades of trial and error and better measurement tools are informing new models of success and new methods of evaluation.
- Government, at least in the United States, has opened a path to enhance and extend the role it plays in supporting effective volunteering.
- And what was once an ad hoc field of practitioners has matured into a profession with research-based core competencies, a formalized code of ethics, and a well-regarded certification program.

At VolunteerMatch we still believe that people want to do good and that everyone should have an opportunity to make a difference. We've spent the last year putting together *Volunteer Engagement 2.0: Ideas and Insights Changing the World* because we know you are up to big things and people are more important than technology.

We've put this book together to update you on the state of volunteer engagement and hope that it will inspire you to leap beyond it. We've organized the ideas, insights, and inspiration you will need to transform your own ability to successfully engage the world today.

To keep up with and unpack the significance of all these changes we've invited the wisest people we know to share their perspective and advice. We organized their contributions into five sections that each explore a different aspect of the changing environment.

Part One: Changing Times puts volunteering into historical context. It explores the roots of giving time for social change, the myths that hold us back, the trends shaping the future, and the attitudes and expectations of volunteers young and old. In Part One, you will see how science is changing the way we think about altruism, why so few organizations invest in exceptional volunteer engagement, and what draws millennials and baby boomers to volunteer.

Part Two: Changing Relationships explores how to think differently about the connection between people and causes. It looks at the art of keeping supporters engaged, why to link volunteering and philanthropy, building a culture of engagement, and working effectively with supervolunteers. In Part Two, you will see how to build better relationships with your volunteers, why volunteering and giving multiply each other, and what it takes to transform a board of directors.

Part Three: Changing Technology tackles the digital tools and communications technologies that have accelerated the possibilities of volunteering. It covers the promise and pitfalls of social media, practical approaches to microvolunteering, the evolution of virtual volunteering, and settles once and for all the great debate over the value of hackathons. In Part Three, you will see how technology has changed the practice of volunteer engagement, why it is creating new forms of service, and what it takes to harness the possibilities and cut through the hyperbole.

Part Four: Changing Corporate Perspectives illuminates how businesses are rethinking their values, strategies, and relationships. It reveals changing attitudes among business stakeholders and the new opportunities this creates for communities and causes. It underscores the untapped potential of skilled and pro bono volunteering, the logic of volunteering as employee engagement, the growing alignment between purpose and profit, and the power of partnering to advance a cause. In Part Four, you will learn why so few organizations make use of skilled and pro bono volunteers, how smart companies approach cross-sector partnerships, and what prevents many causes from engaging the talent and marketing might of business.

Part Five: Changing Strategies takes a closer look at what makes good programs great. It demystifies measurement and assessment; takes a fresh look at the 3 Rs of recruiting, retention, and recognition; brings the power of national service for building capacity into full view; unlocks the engagement secrets of high-performing nonprofits; and offers a practical road map for career advancement. In Part Five, you will see how measurement and data improve performance, why effective volunteer engagement is so strongly correlated with overall organizational health, where national service fits in, and what it takes to earn a Certification in Volunteer Administration (CVA).

Thank you to everyone who has contributed to this effort. It has been a remarkable affirmation of the generosity of even the busiest people. Your work and the possibilities ahead have brought out the best in all of us.

We believe in you, so let's get started.

Greg Baldwin

Greg Baldwin is President of VolunteerMatch, the web's largest volunteer engagement network. Greg joined the founding team in 1998 as its Chief Imagination Officer to make it easier for good people and good causes to connect. As president, Greg oversees an organization that helps 100,000 nonprofits, 150-plus companies, and more than 12 million interested volunteers each year. Since 1998, VolunteerMatch has helped the nonprofit sector engage more than $5.4 billion worth of volunteer services. Greg completed his undergraduate studies at Brown University in 1990 with a degree in Public Policy. He is a lifelong volunteer and lives in Berkeley, California, with his wife, Kathryn, and kids, Ellie, and Matt.

Note

1. U.S. Bureau of Labor Statistics, "Volunteering in the United States, 2013," February 25, 2014, www.bls.gov/news.release/volun.nr0.htm.

PART ONE

Changing Times

Chapter 1

Big Shifts That Will Change Volunteerism for the Better

Tobi Johnson, MA, CVA
President, Tobi Johnson & Associates

"The future belongs to those who believe in the beauty of their dreams."[1]

Fifteen years ago, I was given the opportunity to build my first nonprofit program from scratch. At the time, I was short on experience but had enthusiasm and ideas to spare. Fortunately, the leadership team at Larkin Street Youth Center decided to take a chance. Founded in 1984, Larkin Street had already grown an impressive continuum of services and a solid reputation with San Francisco's street youth. The link between housing, support services, and lasting employment, however, was yet to be made. So, I set about developing a workforce-development program for homeless youth.

Larkin Street's team of dedicated social workers created a culture of youth empowerment through acceptance, encouragement, and a little bit of tough love. The youth responded in kind, some so committed they returned to job readiness class every morning even when they slept in Golden Gate Park the night before. It was truly inspiring, but we also needed to reach outside our walls for support. Our clients needed additional champions to believe in their potential.

When we asked, people helped. A team of volunteer attorneys from the San Francisco Bar Association became our first group of mentors. Employee volunteers from Bain & Company organized a job readiness fair. Employers like Macy's hosted informational interviews and hired youth for internships. Community volunteers helped as tutors in our GED and college-prep classrooms. Because of the first year of success—impossible without this level of volunteer and community involvement—our primary funder committed to multiyear support.

Fifteen years later, Hire Up continues to help homeless youth find a way off the streets. A lot has changed since then, but in some respects, much remains the same. The help that communities can offer remains critical to nonprofit success, and volunteers still willingly contribute their skills and talents to good causes. At the same time, the world has changed dramatically. Some might view the complexity of today's era as a liability. I see new advances as opportunities to forge even deeper connections with supporters who can offer so much value, helping lift programs, such as Hire Up, off the ground and keep them running.

Today, I help my consulting clients strengthen their own volunteer programs. Over the years, the social sector has experienced an evolution in the needs of volunteers, and our responses to those needs are transforming our practice.

Today's Consumer Is Tomorrow's Volunteer

We live in a complex era. Paradoxical themes of anxiety, self-help, rebellion, and collaboration are crosscurrents that embody today's experience. Futurists highlight many trends that may seem contradictory, such as:

- Superpersonalization versus "clanning" and tribes
- Indulgence and luxury versus environmentalism
- Focus on self- versus social awareness
- Escapism versus wellness and health consciousness
- Hyperconnectivity and multitasking versus simplification and mindfulness[2]

In spite of these tensions, or perhaps because of them, a "socially conscious consumer" has emerged. Ideas like fair trade, sustainable consumption, farm-to-table, and ethical fashion are gaining popularity, as the public strives to express their values and perhaps reconcile conflicting emotions. In turn, this trend has stimulated increased interest in corporate social responsibility and cause marketing, which offer even more choices to act on one's ideals.

We are in the midst of other big shifts in business, technology, psychology, and communities as well. Although consumers present a range of reactions to the speed and breadth of change—from joyous early adopters to anxious resisters—all have increasingly sophisticated expectations from the world around them. This extends to the nonprofits they choose to support. In this environment, volunteer programs are particularly vulnerable.

This chapter is intended to inspire deeper thinking about the current and future contexts of volunteer engagement and community involvement. By examining and capitalizing on new trends and recent discoveries across a wide range of disciplines, we can collectively revamp and refresh the field of volunteerism for the better. Each big trend that follows is accompanied by several ideas for action. Is your organization ready to harness the power of tomorrow's social citizens?

What Can Volunteerism Lose to Win?

Although there has been substantial growth in new nonprofits in the United States, expanding from 1.32 million to 1.44 million from 2002 to 2012 (an increase of 8.6 percent), volunteer involvement in organizations has decreased slightly and is at its lowest since 2002 (at 25.4 percent), and annual volunteer hours have been declining slightly.[3]

Altruism, on the other hand, appears to be on the rise. In 2011, over 65 percent of citizens said they helped their friends and neighbors (an increase of 9.5 percent over the previous year).[4] Although it is not entirely clear what is driving this trend, it may indicate that community participation is alive and well, but that current offers to volunteers by nonprofits lack appeal. It also suggests that informal, self-directed volunteering ("freelance philanthropy") and the flexibility and autonomy it allows may be preferred.

As society evolves, so, too, must volunteerism. Old habits die hard, but letting go helps make way for new ideas and unforeseen discoveries. Legacy mindsets may be obstacles to progress and bear examining, such as:

- Focus on individual volunteers versus team approaches
- Over-reliance on long-term volunteer placements over project-based work

- Increasing rigidity versus flexible, nimble management
- Reluctance to accept risks inherent in innovation
- Unequal power dynamics between organizations and citizens in planning and implementation of community solutions
- Assumption that answers to challenges must (or will) come from within our sector

The world will continue to revolutionize and renew itself, and we must heed the call for transformation. To break new ground, cross-disciplinary thinking is useful, along with a willingness to experiment and learn from failure.

Big Trend: New Insights from Brain Science

With the advent of imaging technology, scientists have made monumental leaps in what we understand about how our brains work. In the growing field of neuroscience, researchers have only scratched the surface, but several recent discoveries hold promise for volunteer organizations.

All human brains, not affected by trauma or illness, operate in the same way, regardless of culture, language, geography, or any other trait. Over 95 percent of our emotions, learning, and decision making occurs on the subconscious, rather than on the rational, level. Organizations are using these discoveries to their advantage, paying close attention to the "ecology of experience" that workers and customers encounter. Some have been deliberately designed for behavior change, working to create brain-friendly workplaces and using brain science to help guide marketing decisions and generate more persuasive ad copy.

The Compassionate Instinct[5]

Despite being characterized as selfish in nature, new findings show that humans actually have a "compassionate instinct." Compassion is an emotional response to suffering and involves an authentic desire to help. When we alleviate another's pain, or even watch someone else assist, the brain's reward center lights up.

The adage "giving is better than receiving" applies anywhere the world, regardless of country or socioeconomic status. Scientists argue that compassion is deeply imbedded in human nature and has helped us survive as a species. Compassion is also contagious. When we perform compassionate acts, our heart rate slows and hormones are released that promote bonding and a feeling of "elevation." The more one experiences or witnesses compassion, the more likely they are to act compassionately.

With the rise of the socially conscious consumer, our compassionate instinct now manifests itself in society. Volunteer programs can also inspire and channel our natural inclinations to help by making examples of their benefits to the community even more public.

Neuroleadership Models[6]

Neuroleadership is an emerging field that uses brain science to better understand how to motivate, influence, and lead others. Researchers argue that minimizing danger and maximizing reward is a key organizing principle of the brain. The urge to approach possible rewards and avoid potential threats is deeply ingrained.

The SCARF Model, developed by neuroleadership theorists, is based on addressing the threats and rewards that are most important. The model includes five domains that activate the brain's circuitry:

1. Status–our relative importance to others
2. Certainty–our ability to predict the future
3. Autonomy–our sense of control over events
4. Relatedness–our sense of safety with others
5. Fairness–our perception of fair exchanges between people

Neuroleadership has particular value in leading volunteers, and its remedy is simple. The more we perceive reward, the more we are able to collaborate and influence others. The more we feel threatened, the less likely we will be able to successfully team. Some volunteer management and training methods may unwittingly stymie the perception of reward for volunteers.

The Power of Peers

Peers as well as leaders influence behavior. Researchers now assert that group dynamics are even more powerful than we realized. No matter what our age, we are heavily influenced by what others think, and we have a fundamental need to maintain in good standing within our groups. Scientists argue that this desire to belong has evolved from a basic need for survival.

Although most of the time we maintain our standing, there is often a conflict between what we find enjoyable and what the group expects. Threat detection, as with the SCARF Model, becomes an important social skill. We scan our environment to determine whether there are signs of social acceptance and use these clues to monitor and adjust our actions accordingly.

The broadcast power of social media can magnify the effects of peer influence, both positively and negatively. Within volunteer programs, we can mitigate peer influence and reduce the stress of peer pressure by making organizational norms clear for new volunteers and fostering a culture of acceptance.

Ideas for Action

- Foster altruism by sharing stories (in videos and photographs) that exemplify compassion in action.
- Invite prospective volunteers to participate in a group volunteer project before they join to inspire compassion and commitment.
- Design volunteer onboarding so that it reduces threat and increases certainty and relatedness.
- Involve volunteers directly in strategic planning so they have increased certainty about the future.
- Review volunteer program policies to ensure that each is perceived as fair and equitable.
- Expand levels of autonomy to match a volunteer's knowledge and life experience.
- Use volunteer mentors to decode "unwritten rules" for newcomers.
- Train volunteer-led recruitment teams and speakers' bureaus.

Big Trend: Demographic and Generational Changes

Demographic shifts will undoubtedly affect society and volunteerism. By 2060, the United States will, for the first time, be comprised of more people of color than whites. Recent immigrants will make up more than a third of the population. Our population is also aging. By 2060, there will be as many age 85 as age 5, transforming the traditional age pyramid to an almost perfect square.[7]

The Myth of Generational Differences in the Workplace[8]

Although much has been made of the differences between generations in the workplace (Greatest Generation, baby boomers, Generation X, and millennials), research has been unable to support any fundamental and systemic differences between them and their attitudes toward work. This includes meaningful differences between job satisfaction, organizational commitment, or intent to leave based on generational membership. (See Chapters 5 and 6 for more on engaging millennial and boomer volunteers.)

Workers of all generations, moreover, were found to hold similar work values. The most critical drivers of organizational commitment, regardless of age, were personal characteristics (confidence), job characteristics (occupation and amount of challenge offered), and leadership qualities (communication and shared power). Likewise, job satisfaction was affected by employee expectations about continuing job stability, autonomy, and recognition for each age.

Scientists argue that a person's maturity, life stage, experience, education, socioeconomic background, and other factors are more likely to play a part in forging our unique personalities and preferences than a generational label. For this reason, they argue, interventions designed to support a specific generational group of employees won't be effective. This may prove true for volunteer workers, as well, suggesting that an analysis of generational traits may not be the best basis for management decisions or program design.

Differences as We Age

Demographics and economics do affect us as we age. Our youngest workers are the most racially diverse generation in America and have higher levels of student loan debt, poverty, and unemployment than their parents or grandparents. As digital natives, they are the most avid users of technology and, at the same time, are detached from institutions such as religious or political affiliations.

Younger workers have higher expectations of career advancement and work-family balance, and they are less likely to marry than their predecessors. There is generally higher job turnover in younger people than their elders. Many seniors have delayed retirement because of the depressed economy and are less likely than younger people to leave their jobs. Not surprisingly, they also lag in the adoption of new technology.

Other differences between the ages are evident. According to the experts, as people age, they prefer established relationships to forging new ones and are more drawn to positivity than younger people. Seniors, as opposed to younger counterparts, will volunteer more often based on belonging—a sense of being needed, helpful, and valued—versus a desire to build something new.[9] Perhaps because of this need to belong, psychological contracts (unspoken expectations about the relationship between the volunteer and organization) are vitally important to older volunteers. Conversely, the freedom to create and learn new skills is important to those younger.

Why Demographic Shifts Matter

Social, religious, and human capital—the networks, relationships skills, knowledge, experience, and belief that allow society to work together for the common good—are also important prerequisites for volunteerism to flourish. Some have decried the decline in social capital and civic engagement in recent years, and age and income may play their parts in that decline. There is new evidence of growing gaps in the social connectedness of youth, based on socioeconomic status, which may lead to decreasing civic participation and volunteerism.

Other realities, such as the economic burdens on the young to care for an aging society and a rise in community-generated civic engagement outside traditional institutions, may also present competition for attention and volunteer support, particularly for the young.

Ideas for Action

- Identify groups you need to engage and minimize their specific barriers to involvement.
- Resist the urge to prejudge the effects of a generational label; instead, take time to get to know each individual.
- Accommodate a variety of volunteer work styles, schedules, supervision preferences, leadership approaches, etc.

- Encourage intergenerational volunteer projects and use self-reflection to discourage generational stereotyping.
- List both the commitments the volunteer will make to the organization and those the organization will make to the volunteer in orientation materials.
- Develop an integrated recognition and retention plan that addresses work values and true drivers of satisfaction.
- Engage the emerging generation now by collaborating with schools and promoting family volunteering.
- Locate and partner with organizations that can help bridge cultural divides and design for greater inclusivity.

Big Trend: Technological Advances

As the digital revolution progresses, it touches virtually every part of our lives. The speed of innovation is notable, but perhaps more interesting is how easily new inventions are accepted and integrated. Consider the rapid adoption of smartphones. In 2013, 56 percent of Americans reported owning a smartphone.[10] Remarkable, given modern smartphones were mass marketed only seven years ago. What's more, nearly three-quarters keep their phones within five feet[11] nearly all of the time, making them a virtual appendage.

New digital functionality also boosts consumer expectations. Hyperpersonalization is now widely available, promoting an illusion of greater control and choice. Consequently, the volunteer of today has evolved into a "consumer" of opportunities to serve. Social change organizations risk becoming obsolete if they cannot meet emerging expectations. Nonprofits, often with limited resources and expertise, will be challenged to find a way, and new technology may provide answers.

Content Creation for All

Today, virtually everyone can be both content consumer and creator. Videos, blogs, infographics, and the ubiquitous "selfie" (Oxford Dictionaries' Word of the Year in 2013) are all created and shared. In 2013, more than 800 million Facebook status updates were published each day and over 100 million people took a social action on YouTube every week.[12] Online innovations and creativity are now admired and expected.

As social media gains popularity, fans now trump audiences as the most important people to cultivate. Although audiences simply watch a movie and head home, fans rate it, write reviews, and share their opinions online. These acts of content creation expand the film's initial reach to new audiences, as each fan influences their personal network. Companies and nonprofits have taken notice. The opportunity for authentic, compelling information about social causes, generated and disseminated by volunteers throughout their networks, has the potential to change public awareness and perception and build the case for increasing support.

Content that is created and curated collaboratively is particularly powerful. Digital "memes" (popular photos and videos with common characteristics that are imitated, transformed, and shared by users) are some of the most viral content. From time to time, they have been successfully leveraged for fundraising as we saw with the hunt for an African warlord in 2012 (KONY2012) and awareness of ALS research in 2014 (The Ice Bucket Challenge). Collaborative content and memes that champion volunteerism, however, have yet to be fully tapped, but could be effective recruitment tactics. (See Chapter 11 for more on volunteer engagement and social media.)

Integrated Ecosystems

Integrated approaches are boosting the potential of shared content. The combination of social, mobile, analytics, and the cloud (what's known as SMAC in tech circles) improve on what social media can do on its own. Imagine the fan-generated movie review—it might be written on a smartphone, shared on social media, and stored in the cloud. SMAC technologies take it a step further, adding the ability to track the discussion.

This ecosystem allows organizations to interpret, design, manage, predict, and personalize real-time consumer actions. This laser-like focus on "consumer experiences" represents a significant shift from the notion of audiences as passive consumers to fans as active creators and curators. In this context, SMAC becomes the interface and crystal ball, linking organizations and citizens in ways never thought possible. Imagine how SMAC could help us improve the volunteer experience through a deeper understanding of volunteers' digital behavior.

Data: Big and Smaller

Predictive data analysis has big potential. An estimated 2.8 zettabytes (that's 2.8 plus 21 zeros) of data were "saved" to hard drives by 2012. That number will double by 2015. These "digital breadcrumbs" we leave through our online behavior such as website registrations and log ins, social media posts, site visits, content downloads, keyword searches, and e-mail responses can be aggregated and analyzed to flag significant consumer trends. An analysis of data generated by volunteer behavior could result in a treasure trove of new information to improve volunteer program administration practices.

Aside from a handful of web services and software that specialize in analysis of big data (VolunteerMatch.org, Kiva.org, Change.org, etc.), its potential is yet to be fully marshaled. In the future, however, we can look forward to this level of inquiry as a required feature of volunteer management systems. Imagine if data across these systems were amassed and used to drive evidence-based decision making for future volunteer program design and management.

Small, individual data might also stimulate altruistic acts. With new technology, the status of consumers can now be tracked through geo-location and physiological responses (through EEG, MRI, and galvanic skin responses), and newer smartphones now include this functionality. Trend watchers have dubbed personal data collection and digital feedback the "Quantified Self." This capability makes possible greater self-awareness and perhaps greater well-being. The positive effects of volunteerism on health are well documented and early pioneers (like "The H(app)athon Project") have begun to integrate community involvement data into quantified self-initiatives.

Increased Screen Time

Americans spend over seven hours a day in front of screens (TV, computer, smartphone, and tablet). Will this trend be a boon or a bust for volunteer programs? There is evidence that a distracted public can still focus, when a cause's offer or invitation is compelling enough. Virtual, mobile, and microvolunteering may hold promise if volunteers can be persuaded to devote screen time to social good.

With less face-to-face interaction, "digital body language" becomes even more important for communication. Nonprofits may not have the resources or the inclination to track every click of their supporters; but the analysis of digital behavior can reveal valuable insights into what drives participation. Our ability to "read" volunteers' behavior and make our own explicit will be critical to increasing the quality and depth of communication.

Ideas for Action

- Find partners (like TechSoup and NTEN) who can help increase your capacity to nimbly navigate tech evolutions.
- Form a volunteer-led digital editorial board to create and share content about your program.
- Use smart technology, embedded into businesses processes, to seamlessly track volunteer activity and report it in real time.
- Track volunteers' "digital body language" to understand satisfaction and engagement levels.
- Collaborate with new social ventures (like those funded by the Points of Light Civic Accelerator) to co-pilot tech innovations that support your mission.
- Deliberately plan learning objectives and volunteer training to increase Web 2.0 competencies.
- Develop "reverse mentoring programs" in which digital natives help others learn to use technology.
- Try recruitment web services (like VolunteerMatch.org) that use data analysis to match needs and volunteers.

Big Trend: Workplace Shifts

We have a greater understanding of human motivation in organizational settings than ever before. Application of this knowledge can help us effectively engage and cultivate volunteer-based human resources. The challenge is to design volunteer training, team-building, and leadership models that are inspiring, personally fulfilling, and make the most of volunteer talents. New approaches to talent management, evidence-based training strategies, and research into workplace motivation offer fresh ideas.

Focus on Employee Engagement

Fifty-two percent of U.S. employees are disengaged, meaning they fail to work at their full potential. Another 18 percent actively undermine their organization's work. Collectively, this means that 70 percent of employees lack passion or energy for their work, triggering a staggering $450 to $550 billion in lost productivity each year.[13]

At the same time, today's employees are assuming a variety of new and entrepreneurial roles—contingency worker, contractor, teleworker—that require additional autonomy, challenge, and recognition. Likewise, companies have seen a rise in purpose-driven professionals who seek meaning beyond the paycheck. Efficiency is no longer more important than meaning in the changing workplace.

To regain employee attention and inspiration, some firms are looking to volunteerism as an employee engagement and team-building strategy. New expectations are emerging concerning corporate community involvement. Beyond traditional corporate social responsibility, thought leaders now argue for the development of "shared value" across corporate, government, and nonprofit sectors. Recognizing that what is good for society is good for business, the model focuses on local community needs, aligns business activities, and works to create more value so everyone benefits. Shared value requires the active participation of nonprofits and government to succeed. Each of these community engagement activities offers more opportunities for volunteer programs to engage new partners.[14] (See Chapters 15 through 19 for more on corporate volunteer engagement.)

Integrated Talent Management

New developments in human resources may also benefit volunteer programs. In the private sector, there is growing awareness that the HR function is critical to business success. Today's cutting-edge HR departments handle much more than compliance and administrative tasks. Integrated talent management is evolving as a new strategy to better manage human capital.

Talent management involves deliberate and integrated processes for recruiting, developing, and retaining people with the best skills to increase business performance. It is, above all, strategic in nature. Although older HR models focus on finding, hiring, and training capable employees, talent management uses outcome metrics, strategic alignment of HR activities, and targeted training and development to not only match the right people with the right jobs but to also meet organizational goals. Nonprofits that are concerned with how to realize the best return on their investment in volunteer talent may find talent management a helpful strategy to explore.

The Virtual Workforce

New technology has begun to support communications and team building across distances, but only when used effectively. Telecommuting increased 80 percent from 2005 to 2012.[15] As more people become skilled at offsite work, virtual, micro-, and mobile volunteerism will have even more opportunity to flourish. (See Chapter 12 and Chapter 13 for more on virtual volunteering and microvolunteering.)

Despite the available technology, virtual teams still experience a so-called "connectivity paradox"—the more connected people are, the more isolated they feel. "Virtual distance" is a new framework that describes and measures these psychological effects,[16] and researchers suggest specific steps to reduce virtual distance, such as:

- Proactively cultivating community and trust
- Clarifying team and individual goals
- Highlighting the skills of each team member
- Allowing time for interpersonal sharing
- Pointing out similarities in values and goals
- Relaying success stories
- Establishing standard communications paths

Ideas for Action

- Use team building and challenge as volunteer recognition strategies.
- Design a reengagement plan to reconnect with volunteers who have decreased involvement.
- Consider new "entrepreneurial" roles for volunteers that use their creativity to solve organizational problems.

- Develop relationships with corporate social responsibility programs that share your mission and will provide mutual benefit.
- Develop a business case for shared value that you can present to a variety of possible corporate partners in your community.
- Replace individual management methods with team-based volunteer models.
- Develop an integrated volunteer talent management model that strategically addresses your organization's goals.
- Increase effectiveness of virtual teams by integrating practices that reduce virtual distance.

Change for the Better

New trends in brain science, demographics, technology, and the workplace are disrupting business as usual and creating new opportunities to connect, collaborate, and mobilize for the greater good. Brain science helps us understand what inspires people to action and motivates continued participation. Emerging technologies enable us to automate and personalize experiences to better meet the needs of our supporters. New management and partnership models allow us to better develop and support volunteer talent, allowing their contributions to truly shine.

The more we rely on digital communication and technology to manage a fast-paced world, the more we will crave meaningful interactions, personal significance, and simple trust. Volunteerism is not just a way to collectively tackle community problems. It may also be what's needed to sustain cooperation in an increasingly dehumanized environment.

At its core, volunteerism is about connecting people. By embracing innovation, not hiding from it, organizations and individuals will be better equipped to build trust, form authentic human bonds, focus attention, and build the clarity of purpose needed to navigate the future and change volunteerism for the better. The future looks bright ahead.

Tobi Johnson is President of Tobi Johnson & Associates, a consulting firm whose mission is to help nonprofit organizations mobilize remarkable volunteers who share a common vision for a better world. Tobi has over 25 years direct experience in nonprofit management, volunteer administration, training delivery, and learning design, which she puts to use helping organizations transform their volunteer enterprise. She also shares strategies to attract, inspire, and activate top volunteer talent through *Tobi's Volunteer Management Blog*. Tobi is a native of the Pacific Northwest and now lives in East Tennessee with her husband and feline office assistant, Bailey.

Notes

1. Often attributed to Eleanor Roosevelt; however, this quote is not found in her writings.
2. Sources reviewed: Edelman Berland, Gallup, McKinsey, Trendwatching.com, Euromonitor, Kleiner Perkins Caufield & Byers, Institute for Global Futures, Berson by Deloitte, *Forbes*, *Harvard Business Review*, and *T+D Magazine*.
3. B. S. McKeever and S. L. Pettijohn, "The Public Sector in Brief 2014: Public Charities, Giving, and Volunteering," Urban Institute report, October 2014.
4. Corporation for National and Community Service (CNCS), "Volunteering and Civic Life in America 2012: Key Findings on the Volunteer Participation and Civic Health of the Nation," December 2012. Report is the most recent from CNCS.
5. For research and discussion on compassion, see The Greater Good Science Center website at http://greatergood.berkeley.edu/.
6. For an overview, see D. Rock, "SCARF: A Brain-Based Model for Collaborating with and Influencing Others," originally published in *Neuroleadership Journal* 1 (2008): 44–52, and D. Rock and C. Cox, "SCARF® in 2012: Updating the Social Neuroscience of Collaborating with Others," originally published in *Neuroleadership Journal* 4 (2012): 129–142.
7. P. Taylor, "The Next America," Pew Research Center, April 2010. Retrieved from www.pewresearch.org/next-america/. This website offers a visually engaging look at how demographics in the United States are changing over time.
8. For recent research on generational differences in the workplace, see D. P. Costanza et al., "Generational Differences in Work-Related Attitudes: A Meta-analysis," *Journal of Business Psychology* 27 (2012): 375–394 and T. Saba, "Understanding Generational Differences in the Workplace: Findings and Conclusions," Queens University Industrial Relations Center, 2013.
9. E. A. Welleford and E. Netting, "Taking a Broader Look at Preparing for Boomer Volunteers: Beyond Tips and Tricks," *International Journal of Volunteer Administration*, XXIX, no. 3 (June 2013): 23–30.
10. A. Smith, "Smartphone Ownership 2013—Update," Pew Research Center, June 5, 2013.

11. Jumio, "2013 Mobile Consumer Habits Study," report by Harris Interactive on behalf of Jumio, July 2013.
12. C. Zorzini, "The State of Social Sharing in 2013," *WIRED* magazine Innovation Insights blog post and infographic, April 15, 2014, www.wired.com/2013/04/the-state-of-social-sharing-in-2013-infographic/.
13. J. Clifton, "State of the American Workplace: Employee Engagement Insights for U.S. Business Leaders," Gallup report, 2013.
14. For more on the concept of shared value, see M. E. Porter and M. R. Kramer, "Creating Shared Value," *Harvard Business Review*, January 2011.
15. K. Lister and T. Harnish, "The State of Telework in the U.S.: How Individuals, Business, and Governments Benefit," Telework Research Network report, June 2011.
16. For more on managing virtual teams, see K. Sobel Lojeski, *Leading the Virtual Workforce: How Great Leaders Transform Organizations for the 21st Century* (Hoboken, NJ: John Wiley & Sons, 2010).

Chapter 2

A History of Change in Volunteer Engagement

Susan J. Ellis
President, Energize, Inc.

- *Who dumped the tea into Boston Harbor?*
- *Who ran the Underground Railroad?*
- *Who raised barns in America's rural communities?*
- *Who opened the first libraries on the western prairies?*
- *Who fought to achieve the vote for women?*
- *Who took part in the "sit-ins" at Southern lunch counters?*
- *Who writes the articles for Wikipedia, history's most comprehensive reference ever?*

Since you are reading this book, chances are you recognized the answer to each of these questions: volunteers! But would that have been your first response if I had put each question to you independently—and not in a book about volunteering? Probably not.

Citizen action—frequently not only unpaid but also quite risky—is at the heart of most social change. On a grand scale, we call the countless acts of individuals in support of a cause a "movement." Protest marches, lobbying legislators, civil disobedience, and fundraising are the common denominators of all civil rights and other movements. Volunteers organize themselves in similar ways on both sides of every issue: pro- and antigun control; pro-choice and anti-abortion; for and against a political candidate. Volunteers come in all political persuasions and are not always on the side of right and good. Volunteering is an effective yet neutral *methodology* for accomplishing a goal for all sides of an issue.

Volunteering is never in a vacuum, and what affects people affects volunteers: social change, world crises, advances in technology, communications, and more naturally influence volunteering. Even world wars; medical breakthroughs; the Great Depression and the Great Recession; trains, planes, and automobiles; the Internet; and smartphones. People volunteer *in response* to societal trends, often pioneering and experimenting with possible solutions when there is a vacuum of leadership or funds from other sources.

The Obstacle of Vocabulary

It is rare for activism, protest, and humanitarianism to be identified as *volunteering* in history books or contemporary social commentary.[1] That's because *volunteer* is a label with lots of baggage and many different definitions. Yet to appreciate the role that volunteers have had and still have in creating change, we need to get past vocabulary. There are too many unwarranted stereotypes and prejudices about who volunteers were/are and what they did/do. For example, the word *volunteer* was most often applied in the past to the work of women engaged in charitable human service work to aid the poor or sick. Some dismiss these women as upper class Lady Bountifuls, but we should never forget that—at the time in which they opened settlement houses, advocated for child labor laws, fought for family planning, and more—*no one else* saw and acted on the deplorable conditions requiring intervention. And the women battled parents and husbands at home none too happy about their efforts. Over time, as the role of women changed in terms of life outside the home, their ability to vote and own property, birth control, and more, women as volunteers evolved, too.

On the other side of the coin, perhaps my most-quoted sound bite is, "men have always volunteered, they just called themselves coaches, trustees, and firemen." That's still true. Today the male-preferred vocabulary includes terms such as pro bono work, donated professional services, and corporate social responsibility. But at the same time, military militias consistently prided themselves on being *volunteers* as opposed to unwilling draftees (even today the U.S. Army continues to say it is "all-volunteer").

The vocabulary of volunteering has continued to expand. We're in a period that seems to prefer the term *community service*, vague though it is. I tend to like *skill-anthropist* or *knowledge donor*, because those names elevate the giving of talent to match the respect that giving money brings.

What's important to remember is that you will rarely find the word *volunteer* in historical accounts, but you can be sure that the majority of cultural turning points and milestones we celebrate in history are the outcome of the collective, unpaid actions of individuals willing to roll up their sleeves and put themselves into action. Seen through this lens, it's clear that any history of change in volunteer engagement is, in part, a history of change in society overall.

The Stages of Creating Change

Volunteers play important roles at every point of founding and maintaining institutions, and individuals find their comfort zone at different stages of change. Although the historic examples in this chapter are mainly from the United States, it is important to understand that volunteering is *not* uniquely American. Humans help each other all over the planet and activists are at work even in the most restrictive countries. Although the settings, causes, and civic structures vary in different countries, the pattern of evolving change is similar everywhere.

One place one can always find volunteer activity is on the fringe. Whether in government, nonprofits, or businesses, volunteers are the *mavericks*, *protestors*, and *activists* who recognize the need for action before it's someone's job or there's profit to be made. We have had some great examples of this in recent history. The concept of hospice care was a protest movement started by a few angry relatives and radical nurses against the way doctors and hospitals treated the dying and their families; the legislation eventually creating reimbursement for hospice care uniquely *requires* continued involvement of volunteers alongside paid staff even today. When HIV/AIDS first surfaced, it was not understood as an epidemic; the dedication of local groups of gay men kept the pressure on until ever more diverse groups of people joined the cause. The entire country changed its attitude toward mixing alcohol and driving directly because of the awareness begun by Mothers Against Drunk Driving (MADD).

The Internet, or at least the World Wide Web, is volunteer intensive. From the start, open-source programmers have shared their code freely; discussion group moderators and bloggers most often post out of passion, not pay; activists are working on causes from protecting children online to keeping government control out of cyberspace. Virtual volunteering, the first truly new form of service in the last century or so, exists first because the technology exists but mostly because of those who are interested in putting its potential to connect like-minded people to great use. Social media, which makes many established agencies and businesses uneasy, is a fertile new ground for inspired activists, whether in natural disaster response such as the Student Volunteer Army[2] organized via Facebook after the earthquake in New Zealand or for viral fundraising campaigns like the ALS "Ice Bucket Challenge."

Volunteers are not always successful and they can support lost causes, too. There are still more than a million supporters of the international language Esperanto.[3] U.S. Prohibition, the result of an amazing temperance movement of volunteers, eventually was repealed due to the efforts of other volunteers (as well as liquor manufacturers, restaurants, and weary police officers). The highly publicized Equal Rights Amendment did not pass. There are volunteer organizations today that are seriously planning social structures for living on other planets, once we start exploring outer space, and on permanent residences at sea, once the "seasteading" movement[4] takes hold.

Once a cause surfaces and spreads, next come the *innovators* and *founders* who see a solution and work to set it in motion. These are the volunteers whose names appear on the incorporation papers of every nonprofit organization in the country (if you work for a nonprofit, ask who signed its paperwork and who they were).

Benjamin Franklin is the quintessential prototype of this type of volunteering. Beyond his enormous role in establishing our independent nation, he helped to start the first hospital in the United States (Pennsylvania Hospital in Philadelphia), the first organized fire company (still all volunteer), and the University of Pennsylvania. He founded the adult education effort called the Junto, organized the first subscription library, and was the first president of the American Philosophical Society—not to mention the many scientific inventions he created as a "citizen scientist." Toward the end of his life, he freed his own slaves and became an abolitionist. Franklin's energy and varied interests are in the historical record, but I have never heard him referred to as a "volunteer."

Although he did earn money from printing books and his diplomatic roles abroad, the majority of things he accomplished were far removed from a profit motive.

Few took activism to Franklin's level, but countless other people have been willing to tackle big projects and do the work necessary to form, fund, and initially govern or even staff the organizations we take for granted today in every community. Take a "history of volunteering" tour in your city and identify all the places you now will recognize as volunteer founded: agencies, museums, libraries, some schools, hospitals, and more. And don't forget the impact of faith communities, themselves voluntary associations, in aiding the poor, giving sanctuary to political dissidents, opening homeless shelters. Finally, remember that volunteers do not only work in nonprofit organizations. Government agencies at the local, state, and national level are supported by taxpayers willing to contribute time to public schools, parks and recreation, prisons, and more.

When we acknowledge how much has been done by visionary and hard-working volunteers, it becomes apparent that, almost by definition, volunteers are agents of change.

But not everyone has the interest, talent, or time to work on the cutting edge—after all, cutting edges can be sharp and have real consequences. This is a good thing for the long haul. After the activists and founders, we need the *sustainers*— volunteers willing to take the next steps to build, grow, and maintain the newly formed organizations. All three types of volunteers are critical, all can believe strongly in their cause, and all are necessary for community improvement.

In the beginning, volunteers provide the services, hiring a few staff for administrative and coordinating functions. Over time, as demand increases, staff are hired (by those first volunteers) to provide the most specialized services requiring continuity and eventually volunteers only assist in supplemental activities. This evolution is inevitable and generally necessary, but it has only fed the public image of volunteers as mainly nice helpers.

Somewhere between Benjamin Franklin and the person sorting cans in the food pantry lies the real story of volunteering. Volunteers sustain the core of many organizations, not simply add the icing to the cake. For one thing, the members of a nonprofit board of directors are mainly volunteers, although because of their key legal and fiduciary status they rarely apply that term to themselves. Although the emphasis and official reporting is all about the money, the truth is that fundraising for most organizations depends on an army of volunteers who organize and then attend galas, marathons, golf tournaments, and all manner of donation drives.

Most important, despite the current popularity of single days of service and smartphone "clicktivism," is the sustained, often intensive, volunteer role that is the difference between having a real impact and just making a splash. For example:

- Reading tutors in adult literacy programs.
- Mentors who spend time week after week with their young matches.
- Election workers of all parties, who canvass homes on foot and by phone, hand out leaflets, and watch the polls.
- Ham radio operators who relay calls for help, even now when more modern communication systems fail.
- Victim-assistance counselors who accompany traumatized persons through the stages of prosecuting their attackers.
- Coaches of a wide variety of youth sports leagues.
- The surgeons and nurses who give up their vacations to volunteer for overseas medical missions.
- Water pollution monitors who test streams and rivers.
- The firefighters and first responders whose volunteer units still protect more than 80 percent of American homes outside of large cities.
- Participants in community orchestras and community theater companies.

This is a short list of frontline volunteering that is essential to our communities every single day.

Much of the work is invisible or easily taken for granted. But, as in the parable of the man on the beach throwing starfish back into the ocean one by one, these volunteers matter to the people and projects they help.

The Emergence of a Profession

All groups of volunteers need to be led and, at the start of any new initiative, the first leader is generally the founding volunteer. As the effort grows, responsibility for guiding volunteers shifts to people in authority, mostly paid. A variety of careers require coordination of volunteers, though the people in those jobs do not consider volunteer management as their purpose: political campaign managers, clergy (even Jesus needed 12 disciples), alumni directors, many social workers, special event and parade organizers, and more.

What readers of this book would identify as a dedicated, paid position responsible for leading volunteer engagement in an organization only emerged in the last century. The same is true of volunteering infrastructure, such as volunteer centers. Paid jobs in the field led to the need for training, which in turn led to research, publications, credentialing, and other elements of professionalization.

A related development with far-reaching implications was adoption of the term *volunteer program*, which the person with the new paid staff position *managed* and in which volunteers worked side-by-side with—and increasingly *under*—a cadre of employees. Even if unintentional, the move toward professionalism in all areas of nonprofit organizations changed volunteers into an add-on group of helpers, rather than as an integral corps of supporters who offered a treasure trove of skills and talents.

Many, including quite a few of the experts in this book, currently prefer the term volunteer *engagement* over *management*; others prefer to speak of the field as volunteer *administration* or *involvement*. The word *engagement* has a buzz to it right now in a lot of fields—most especially in marketing, where it's used to signify meaningful interaction between a brand and its consumers. Practitioners in this field hold a wide range of job titles, but most are still variations of *director of volunteers*, *volunteer program coordinator*, and *volunteer resources manager*. Perhaps we should also be concerned about the *volunteer* part of our titles. Since so many other voluntary service terms are out there, we may be limiting the scope of our work. What would our positions look like if we were called *directors of community mobilization* or *friend raisers?*

Today we can find the full spectrum of volunteer leadership in any community. There are still volunteers leading other volunteers, especially in the vast all-volunteer association world from PTAs to service clubs to church guilds to fraternities. There are maverick volunteers galvanizing groups of people to march on city hall for some cause, preserve an historic landmark slated for demolition, or picket a movie with an unpopular theme. Employees in many settings still coordinate small groups of volunteers as a sideline to what they consider their real job.

Those who self-identify with the profession of volunteer engagement are only the tip of the iceberg in understanding volunteer leadership, yet we dominate the discussion of what our role should be and define the best practices others should follow. This requires us to be thoughtful and intentional about our interrelationship to the volunteers we have been hired to manage/engage, especially when it comes to change.

The Quest for the Next New Thing

We live in a modern culture that places a premium on what's "new" and, therefore, newsworthy. The Corporation for National and Community Service's Social Innovation Fund ("with the simple, but vital goal of finding solutions that work, and making them work for more people"[5]) and initiatives such as Reimagining Service are only two well-intentioned manifestations of the concentration of effort on what has not yet been invented. Numerous private funders also prefer the new and improved and are reluctant to support the continuation of ongoing services or basic overhead expenses to keep existing organizations running.

Consider that the title of this very book, *Volunteer Engagement 2.0*, is intended to convey the concept of the next generation of volunteering. Readers are urged to keep pace with what's new, and so they should. But *new* is not always *better*. Look at the list of significant volunteer roles discussed earlier, most of which would no longer be called innovative, yet they continue to be transformative. A volunteer role now considered traditional is not necessarily antiquated.

As leaders of volunteers, we need to identify who is pushing for innovation and why. In urging new ways of doing things, are these sources truly aware of what already exists that is on the path toward success? Given the intractable nature of the problems that many organizations are tackling, is it better to initiate new solutions or to apply more elbow grease to activities already underway until results occur? Do we have the *staying power* to take a new idea through the long-term effort needed to gain results?

Changing course or eliminating projects (especially to follow new money) directly affects those volunteers who are passionate about a cause. These are the dogged supporters whose main concern as volunteers is to provide the services they feel matter to clients. Paid staff may have to redirect their work to a new project because funding demands new activities, but devoted volunteers may not want to be diverted from something they believe continues to have value.

The pressure to innovate is an opportunity for leaders of volunteer involvement to pose some challenging questions as advocates for volunteers:

- How can volunteers, especially long-time volunteers, be included from the start of planning for new projects, not as an afterthought at the last minute before implementation?
- Upon the introduction of a new campaign deemed "innovative," can we make the case for maintaining activity that seems demonstrably useful to

clients and volunteers? Might willing volunteers keep that service going even if paid staff is refocused elsewhere?

- When faced with the potential cut of a valued service, can we engage committed volunteers as advocates for continued funding?
- Is there a mechanism for an excited volunteer to offer a suggestion for a new activity or approach to service? With all the talk about entrepreneurial volunteering, do we encourage such suggestions?
- Can we launch experimental pilot projects in which volunteers know that what they learn from the pilot may lead to full funding and staff jobs—with continued engagement of volunteers?

When Volunteers Resist Change

I don't want to fall into the trap of portraying all volunteers as visionaries or even as necessarily passionate about the mission of the organizations they help. They are people with all manner of reasons for joining our organizations from altruistic to selfish. They may act out of religious faith, anger, gratitude, court order, search for a mate, or to build a resume. Some may feel coerced into service, whether through legal mandates or because their child promised their participation. So we cannot assume commonality of motives. However, no one wants to waste precious time on useless activities.

All research shows that the most powerful motivator of volunteers is *to make a difference* by donating their time and skills. The quest for innovation ought to resonate with them, so they see it as making their efforts even more worthwhile. Yet in many organizations, it is volunteers themselves who show resistance to change.

It's important to diagnosis the cause of resistance in each situation. Change is uncomfortable even in best-case scenarios. People may like the status quo and not understand why things have to be adjusted, particularly if the outcome is uncertain. Volunteers now in leadership or coveted roles may worry about losing status or ownership. Opposition can mask uncertainty about how things will look and feel after the change, as well as fear of failure. Volunteers dislike having decisions made for them, not with them, and wonder whether the new course will actually give them a meaningful way to serve.

Do volunteers recognize and agree with the need for change or do they perceive it as change for change's sake? Perhaps the biggest factor in gaining their support is to make the case for taking a new direction in terms that matter to them.

The Leader of Volunteer Engagement as a Facilitator of Change

Most organizations do not have a vision for volunteer involvement and so do not approach it strategically. They hire "volunteer program managers" (VPMs) with job descriptions focused on finding and deploying unpaid helpers efficiently. Executives, who are rarely trained in the potential of volunteer engagement, have low expectations of their VPMs, mainly hoping we keep volunteers in line and happy. It's not that they prevent us from doing more, but that they cannot imagine what more can be done.

The great thing is that we can take initiative. What do we *want* our purpose to be? Is it our role to maintain a volunteer program or to identify unmet client and staff needs and find noncash resources in the community to meet those needs? Are we about *volunteers* or *solutions*? We create most of the roles volunteers fill. Are volunteers always assistants, or do we open opportunities for them to lead, be creative, experiment, and dream?

Satisfied volunteers are not the purpose of our work, *mission* is. By making sure volunteers do the things with the greatest meaning to the recipients of service, the lovely win-win is volunteer satisfaction, too!

This sort of approach to our work requires a certain tolerance of risk. Are we willing to rock the boat? Are we afraid of controversy, even conflict? Do fears about safety and liability limit our innovation? Are we worried about our own job security? Examine your reactions to these questions carefully and consider whether your personal discomfort might make you an unwitting obstacle to change by limiting volunteers.

Our role is to facilitate volunteer accomplishment. That raises more important questions:

- How do we react to new ideas posed by volunteers? Do we advocate for them to agency decision makers?
- How often do we go out and recruit new volunteers for their different backgrounds, skills, or opinions? Do we recruit to fill vacancies on a roster or do we invite people with creativity and drive to join the fight for our cause?
- Do we challenge and reeducate volunteers (and paid staff) who resist new ways of doing things?

- How often do we review volunteer position descriptions and ask: *Is this still the most important and effective thing volunteers could be doing?* And what do we do when the answer is no?

Looking into the Crystal Ball

History teaches that where there is change, there will be volunteers. Whether reactive to societal trends or proactive in urging solutions to problems, we can safely predict that volunteers will find whole new causes in the years to come. In what ways could a global pandemic force more people to become active in health issues in their local community? How will teleportation and holograms alter friendly visiting to those who are homebound (that is, if there will still be any homebound people)? Will there be an equal rights movement for the first extraterrestrials to settle on earth? What natural disasters caused by global warming will require emergency response?

Volunteering is a force of nature. It has always been at the vanguard of change because volunteers act out of determination to make things happen. If there is a human need or social problem not yet addressed by established institutions, volunteers will respond first. If the organizations that emerge from those initial volunteer efforts become unresponsive or unwilling to change, new volunteers will leave to start different initiatives—and the cycle repeats.

Not every volunteer is a leader or is willing to take the risk of challenging the status quo. Some people are joiners or dabblers, satisfied to support the work others lead. Not every volunteer is competent or inspired. But *collectively*, over time, the cumulative effect of donated efforts toward a cause can move mountains and change the course of history. And regardless of how much we are paid, what we choose to call ourselves, or how we are viewed by the general public, we who are leaders of volunteer engagement will be right in the middle of it all.

Susan J. Ellis is President of Energize, Inc., an international training, consulting, and publishing firm that specializes in volunteerism. Since founding Energize in 1977, Susan has assisted clients throughout the world to create or strengthen their volunteer corps. The Energize website (www.energizeinc.com) is widely recognized as a premier resource in the field.

(continued)

(Continued)

Susan is the author of 14 books, including *From the Top Down: The Executive Role in Successful Volunteer Involvement, By the People: A History of Americans as Volunteers,* and *The Last Virtual Volunteering Guidebook.* She has written for dozens of publications and writes the national column "On Volunteers" for *The NonProfit Times*. Since 2000, she has been publishing editor of e-Volunteerism: The Electronic Journal of the Volunteer Community (www.e-volunteerism.com).

Notes

1. When Katherine Noyes Campbell and I wrote the first edition of *By the People: A History of Americans as Volunteers* (1978), it took three years of digging through thousands of books, archives, and articles to glean and corroborate the volunteer roots of historical incidents. The book is now in its third edition, published in 2005 by Energize, Inc., and remains the only attempt to catalog the uncounted contributions of volunteers in every area of American life.
2. The story of the Student Volunteer Army is summarized in Wikipedia, http://en.wikipedia.org/wiki/Student_Volunteer_Army.
3. See Wikipedia's description of the Esperanto movement, http://en.wikipedia.org/wiki/Esperanto.
4. Learn more about seasteading at http://en.wikipedia.org/wiki/Seasteading.
5. Website of the Social Innovation Fund, www.nationalservice.gov/programs/social-innovation-fund.

Chapter 3

Debunking the Myths of Volunteer Engagement

Sarah Jane Rehnborg
CVA, *PhD*

We've all heard it: Volunteers are as revered as "motherhood and apple pie," regarded (incorrectly, I might add) as distinctly "American," and celebrated each April during National Volunteer Week. Yet, when it comes to organizational decision-making, managerial hierarchies, and funding priorities, volunteer programs and community engagement are rarely seen as "top-shelf" issues.

Staff tell us that they . . .

- Would consider engaging volunteers, but can't trust them to keep information confidential.
- Want it done right, so they have to do it themselves.

- Are tired of do-gooders that don't do much good.
- Can't trust volunteers to be there when needed.

The list goes on.
Meanwhile executive leadership and boards wonder . . .

- How to fund a leadership position for volunteers. After all, volunteers are free, and funders can't be expected to underwrite this position.
- If volunteer contributions are really worth the liability risk.
- If they let volunteers into the organization, will they ever be able to get them out if they don't perform to expectations?
- If days of service are worth the time and effort, especially now that these short-term episodic events have gained so much popularity.

All of which leaves volunteer leaders/managers asking:

- How will I ever get the support I need from this organization to effectively engage the community?
- Is there a career path for me within this organization?
- How can I make the case for community engagement and staff support when no one understands what I do?
- How do I develop a range of volunteer opportunities aligned with the needs of a changing society?
- How can I do my job when the structure of our organization seems to be stagnant?
- How do I intervene in a world saturated with newly minted professionals and needs-based thinking?

These aren't idle questions. Rather, they have vexed the field for as long as those who manage volunteers have reflected together on more effective strategies for engagement. These are also the questions that this chapter proposes to ultimately address by looking closely at the most pernicious assumptions in the field that keep organizations from greater achievement while clouding the role of volunteers and those who are responsible for volunteer engagement.

Revealing the Five Myths of Volunteer Engagement

As typically practiced, volunteer engagement efforts too often involve a self-reinforcing cycle of poor management, which are then seen as presenting a "catch-22," an unsolvable logic problem for which we then blame the volunteer. The process goes like this:

1. A nonprofit recognizes the need for assistance to achieve its mission.
2. It assesses its financial resources, finds them deficient, and reflexively turns to volunteers to fill the gap.
3. Leadership assumes that free volunteer labor requires little financial or strategic investment.
4. The organization engages volunteers who may or may not be qualified.
5. A staff person may or may not oversee the volunteer effort, and expectations, accountability, and communication remain unclear.
6. When the effort achieves little, volunteers are identified as the problem and are approached with skepticism, if at all, the next time a need is identified.

Does this sound familiar?

A variety of additional issues can make this skepticism worse. An organization facing cutbacks eliminates its volunteer manager position while increasing the expectation for volunteer involvement. Major organizational restructuring impacts the volunteer program, yet volunteers are never engaged in the process or informed of the outcome. A longstanding service tradition is discontinued without attention to the feelings or needs of those who will be affected or the foresight to create new roles or opportunities for volunteers.

In short, volunteers are frequently overlooked as stakeholders in the process, programs suffer, and the victim becomes the identified problem.

This cycle of dysfunction is widely accepted *even among those who champion volunteers*, leaving the underlying assumptions and perceptions that perpetuate it unexamined. This begs the question: To what extent are some of these assumptions and perceptions accurate? Are the perceptions of the volunteer managers accurate? Are they actually marginalized and misunderstood, or are their supervisors overworked? Do executive directors or board members really overlook community engagement as a component of organizational function or are they too busy to attend to these "details"? Do board members and executive directors actually spurn volunteers, even though trustees are themselves volunteers, or are they so focused on other responsibilities that their inattention is perceived as dismissal? Is it true that executive leadership doesn't regard volunteer management as a position that can be sold to a funder or to the board? Do executive directors believe that this work is "easy" and anyone can do the job (just as *anyone* can volunteer), or does the organization's leadership see the position as one that requires special training and expertise worthy of professional status within the organization? Do volunteers actually pose liability and confidentiality risks, or are these just smokescreens for other issues?

To look more deeply into these issues, the Volunteer Impact Fund project brought together a group of leaders in the field to try to figure out what executive directors really think about community engagement.[1] A purposeful sample of more than 35 executive directors of nonprofits participated in three focus groups held in Austin, Texas, and Denver, Colorado. Invitees were selected using the criterion of ignorance about the participants' perceptions about volunteers. In other words, if no one could readily identify what the executive director (ED) thought about volunteer engagement, they were added to the invitation list, and if someone knew that the ED was a "champion" of volunteer engagement, they were excluded from the sample. Each focus group session was recorded, and the discussions were transcribed.

Not only was turnout for these focus groups high, the rich discussion yielded considerable insight into the executive mindset about volunteer engagement. Wide ranging comments covered all aspects of the volunteerism "waterfront," so to speak, from the problematic . . .

> "*We do more work for volunteers than they do work for us.*"
>
> "*You tend to focus on what can go wrong.*"
>
> "*It's almost easier to not have volunteer-client contact.*"

to the more generous . . .

> "*We get a lot of people who want to volunteer . . . . It's folly for us not to find a way to engage those people, because it generates ill will if we can't utilize that energy.*"
>
> "*Today, our goals have to do with social capital building in the communities we serve . . . . Our thoughts about volunteer programs . . . have to change.*"

to basic management considerations . . .

"Each volunteer has an agenda, and we need to match that with our programs and mission."

"I can see that even though I was hesitant to hire a volunteer manager, 20 hours isn't enough . . . . I'm starting to see how this fits with branding and development—how it all goes together."

In analyzing the data from the focus groups, we found that the same five myths kept coming up:

- Volunteers are free.
- You can't "invest" in voluntary efforts.
- Volunteers want only what you want.
- Meeting volunteers halfway is a recipe for trouble.
- "Volunteer work" is best defined as that which staff wants no part of.

Our findings also helped us to hear more clearly the concerns of executive leadership about volunteer engagement, and find some clear ways to respond to the problems they encounter on the topic. In examining these myths and some of their root causes, we hope to provide a few guidelines to assist the leader of volunteers in targeting and addressing internal resistance to volunteerism.

Debunking the Myths

If you work to involve volunteers, you will undoubtedly run into many of the same attitudes again and again, and perhaps you've even felt these things yourself. Certainly, the myths that bubbled up in our focus groups aren't exclusive to executive directors. As you read the following section, I encourage you to first ask whether each assertion is familiar to you, and to explore the evidence that is used to reach the assertion. Then I invite you to consider the research findings and other materials that I present. There's ample information that these "truths" really aren't self-evident, but rather are easy responses to complex issues worthy of thoughtful analysis. How would letting go of them serve you, your organization, and the community interested in working with you to achieve important outcomes?

Are Volunteers Worth It?

- **Myth 1: Volunteers are free.**
- **Myth 2: You can't invest in volunteers.**

These myths, which are actually deeply intertwined, speak to perceptions of the "value" of volunteer engagement.

The language and vocabulary associated with volunteers may be responsible, at least in part, for some of these assumptions. The term *volunteer* generally connotes free choice, socially beneficial behavior, and the absence of market-rate financial compensation. In a society in which people are frequently judged by their salaries and their financial success, a service rendered at no charge is often construed as unskilled, menial, amateur, lacking in value, operating within the purview of thoughtless do-gooder-ism, or, in a sexist light, as "women's work." As Susan Ellis points out in Chapter 2 of this book: "Men have always volunteered; they just *call themselves* coaches, trustees, and firemen!"

Because volunteers are so often regarded as "free," the notion that they might require an investment seems paradoxical. As one executive director noted in our focus group, "*Volunteering sounds like it's free and not worth anything,*" thus, "*. . . it's tough to convince the board to use money for volunteers.*" Although it is true that volunteers operate without receiving market-value compensation for the work performed, serious organizational initiatives—of any type—require a strategic vision and an outlay of time, attention, and infrastructure.

Hagar and Brudney found just this in an analysis of 3,000 charities in 2004.[2] Based on extensive telephone interviews, the authors concluded that "organizations that invest in volunteer management capacity are likely to attain high net benefits." According to the study, key elements of an investment in volunteer management capacity would be having a volunteer coordinator, having "regular supervision and communication" with volunteers, buying "liability coverage or insurance protection" for volunteers, tracking hours, and having written policies and job descriptions for volunteers, among other things.

Hagar and Brudney expand their definition of investment to include volunteers themselves. This might mean, for example, giving them more responsibility for a greater array of tasks. As the authors found, "Investment in volunteers leads to higher net benefits, which in turn leads charities to make an even greater investment in their volunteers." Surprisingly, although this finding was true for nonprofits of all sizes, smaller organizations had slightly greater benefits when they invested in volunteering.

So, how, then, does one tackle the argument that it might be cheating to invest in volunteer, aka "free" labor? This is clearly tied into *the* complex issue that every service organization wrestles with—how to translate intangible services into tangible, quantifiable outcomes. What, for example, are the metrics that demonstrate the value of counseling services? How does a crowded hospital justify the costs associated with play space for children in an acute-care facility? How does an organization build the case for a marketing campaign or spend money on advertising? How does one argue the "value" of granting a final wish for a dying child or define the worth of the consistent support provided by a big brother or big sister? In the context of volunteer engagement, what is the value of a volunteer's service and how is this value identified, defined, and enumerated?

The answer, in part, is to acknowledge that most *products* require an underlying *process* in order to achieve a desired end goal. Yes, steel, plastic, nuts and bolts, wires, and computer systems go into the manufacturing of a car but so does human labor, and human labor is as vital an element of the nonprofit equation as it is in the for-profit sector. Moving closer to home, a great many nonprofits, and the foundations that fund them, require logic models, the linear planning tool that traces an organization's theory of change. Resources, or inputs, are part of the equation leading to outputs and outcomes. When included as a tangible input in the organization's logic model, the outcome of the community's effort can be more readily measured and quantified.

Just as solar panels capture the power of the sun's rays, we need systems that capture the power of the "free" labor of volunteers. We need to debunk the myth that volunteers are simply the result of the spontaneous combustion of "helping energy" and recognize that complex human issues require complex systems to address them. We need to focus the energy of those who want to make a difference, we need to prepare them for service, we need to account for their effort just as we account for the efforts of every other input, and we need to measure the return on that investment. It is a team sport, and we need staff, experienced volunteers, and board members who move our organizations to their finish lines. We invest in and measure what we care about, and we care about what we invest in and measure. (For more on this topic, see Chapter 20, "Measuring the Volunteer Program.")

What Do Volunteers Want?

- **Myth 3: Volunteers want only what you want.**
- **Myth 4: Meeting volunteers halfway is a recipe for trouble.**

In contrast to nearly every other relationship in the nonprofit sector, volunteers are often viewed as a homogenous group whose needs and motivations for volunteering are seen either as directly aligned with the organization's needs, or otherwise unimportant and distracting. Furthermore, if volunteers are seen as actually needing anything, they are considered a nuisance. As one focus group participant noted: "*Doing things to support volunteers . . . is that truly necessary? Do I have to do appreciation lunches? We want volunteers who are focused on the [client] and bringing them joy at no cost.*" Another executive director took this concern a step further: "*Volunteers are the biggest area that I struggle with in my job. They are time consuming. They contribute to mission drift.*"

Yes, the mission of a nonprofit organization, whether a charity or a public sector agency, is paramount. In practice, however, the needs and motivations of some stakeholders are deemed more important than others. Effective nonprofit relationships are characterized in win-win terms; foundations are selected based on sympathy with certain causes, grants are written to cultivate a positive response, and board members are solicited with an eye toward time, talent, and treasure. When our expectations are not met in these relationships, we don't dismiss the entire category of stakeholder as deficient. Rather, we work to analyze the problem and fix it.

In fact, effective exchange relationships are built on devotion to the mission, shared understanding, clarity of expectations, appropriate boundaries, and mutual respect. Nowhere is it stated that every applicant for a job must be hired, nor is it necessary to engage every volunteer that walks through your door. Carefully crafted job descriptions underpin both salaried and nonsalaried positions. What needs to be done and by when? What attitude and demeanor fit most appropriately within this workplace? Is training a pre-requisite for this position, or is training provided on the job? Do we need lots of people for a short time (distributing water at a marathon fundraiser), or are we seeking a person with specific skills (a bilingual translator)? The type of work, its nature, and duration all become factors in the development of the relationship as well as the latitude the manager affords the applicant, whether salaried or not. There is no "one size-fits-all" solution.

Yes, volunteers do "want something," but generally it's consistent with the needs and desires of the organization. Volunteers want to know their time is being well used. They want to know they can make a real difference. They may also want job experience or a new connection to the community. They may want to hone a new skill or make a donation.

To ascertain these needs and desires, the skills associated with effective human resources management apply. Targeted recruitment narrows the field; interviews illuminate motivation and temperament; and applications and background checks ascertain skill levels and hidden issues. These processes also provide the opportunity to set expectations and select the person who is most appropriate and exclude those who aren't.

Staff must also be prepared to work with volunteers to assure a win-win relationship. For example, staff members who have themselves volunteered somewhere are more likely to identify with the needs of the volunteer and design appropriate opportunities. Putting volunteer engagement into someone's job description further reduces resistance. Rewarding staff for creative teamwork with volunteers adds incentives, giving this part of the position credibility and excitement.

To bring the point home, it's helpful to think about *when* the "issue of volunteers" pops up within the organizational lifecycle. A developmental sketch of the history of most nonprofits finds a group of committed individuals gathered around a kitchen table sharing their dreams, concerns, and aspirations. These people—yesterday's organizational founders, today's social innovators—channel their energy and ideas to promote a shared common interest. Seldom are these early innovators salaried.

In other words, they came together as *volunteers*. Along the way, a board is formed, articles of incorporation filed, IRS designation sought, bylaws created, and funds solicited. As the history of the group evolves, these early *volunteers* seek funds to further their objectives and hire staff to hopefully reach new levels of success.

Generally, it is only after an organization is reasonably well established that a different and distinctly separate notion of *volunteer* emerges. Usually this is when an organization revisits its goals and realizes that its needs exceed its resources. Maybe volunteers can help! Of course, by this point in the evolution of the organization, barriers to engagement have already sprung up and the kind of robust volunteer energy, which helped launch the organization, is now considered extraneous and viewed as distracting the group from reaching its carefully constructed goals. Or, as one of our focus group participants observed, now the organization "*works on making sure that volunteers are giving what the organization needs, not just doing what they want to do.*" Maybe there would be fewer nonprofits if only we could keep engaging the energy and enthusiasm of those who want to make a difference in new and creative ways?

What Do Volunteers Do?

- **Myth 5: "Volunteer work" is best described as work that staff want no part of.**

"Should we save our volunteers for envelope stuffing and hire someone to work the front desk? Would this drive away our volunteers?"

Volunteer engagement, like any other critical aspect of organizational life, requires forethought and alignment with the group's mission, vision, and goals. The question is not "What can volunteers do?" but, rather, "What work needs to be done to achieve organizational success?".

There are no tasks that a volunteer with the requisite training and credentials can't do. Medical and dental clinics can be staffed by pro bono clinicians; attorneys and CPAs often donate their services; executives write business plans for startups without charging for it; speakers and trainers offer workshops to enhance skills; firefighters and first responders serve many of the nation's communities without compensation; cooks deliver gourmet meals; and U.S. postage special-issue stamps are selected by citizen advisory committees.

To not harness the skills and abilities of the community leaves a valuable asset on the cutting room table. Expanding your vision, it turns out, expands opportunities. Or, as one executive director in the study noted, "I wish I had known more about the literal 'dollar value added' . . . . I finally got that it impacts your bottom line and that having a healthy [volunteer] program benefits the organization."

Developing a vision for volunteers and broader community engagement begins with an open mind. To automatically assume that volunteers are somehow different from the rest of us is a myopic view of the potential of community engagement. When we add words like *pro bono, trustee, intern, student, corporate group*, and *friend* to the litany of words that describe our volunteers, this opens us up for skilled service opportunities, short-term as well as long-term experiences, and space for the generalist who wants to be associated with your cause.

Expanding our engagement circle also brings new life to the process. Most assuredly, the staff upon whom these plans rest need to be a part of the process, as do representatives of the community, clients, and other stakeholders whose outreach helps us harvest the necessary resources. Likewise, it is important to take stock of where you are with engagement efforts. Frequently, organizations have networks that may be invisible or underutilized. You may have friends who are waiting for the chance to be a part of your mission-critical work.

If you are new to the world of volunteerism and community engagement, think about employing pilot programs that allow some of these ideas to be tested and refined. Ask volunteers to help you try out ideas and establish guidelines before large problems emerge. Explore what other organizations are doing. Sometimes, the best ideas come from organizations unlike yours; at other times, you may want to benchmark your success based on the work of leaders in your organizational domain. And, finally, determine ways to measure success. How will you know if your efforts are a success? What baseline data should you collect? Are there new measures to establish, and if so, what are they?

The participants in the focus groups we introduced at the beginning of this chapter left with a number of observations. One person noted that he was "surprised that the issues are the same in a small organization as they are in a huge organization. You're thinking it's not going to be quite that complicated." Another commented, "If you can see that having a healthy [volunteer] program benefits the organization, and it's a sign of a healthy organization, it would be so much better. It's one of the 40 million things I wish I had known."

A point person, a vision, and the resources to spearhead the work of volunteer engagement are the critical ingredients of success. This isn't work that staff want "no part of"; rather, it's work that moves your mission one step closer to reality.

Conclusion

Nonprofit leaders operate in constrained economies with ambitious goals and even greater dreams. Meaningfully incorporating community into the equation of organizational success isn't just a nice idea; it is essential.

In *The Birth of the Chaordic Age*, Dee Hock's account of the founding of VISA International, which he led for 16 years before stepping away from business leadership, speaks eloquently about the nonmonetary exchange of value and essence of community. In going beyond the myths of volunteer engagement, his words might help to spur us forward:

> Without an abundance of nonmaterial values and equal abundance of nonmonetary exchange of material value, no true community ever existed or ever will. Community is not about profit. It is about benefit (p. 43) . . . . It is a mistake to confuse money with value. It is a mistake to believe that all value can be measured. And it is a colossal mistake to attempt to monetize all value (p. 44) . . . . The essence of community, its very heart and soul, is the nonmonetary exchange of value; things we do and share because we care for others, and for the good of the place (p. 42) . . . . Life is a gift, bearing a gift, which is the art of giving. And community is the place where we can give our gifts and receive the gifts of others. (p. 45)

Thoughtfully, meaningfully, and effectively engaging the community in the life of nonprofit and public service organizations is the gift of community, a gift that the volunteer brings to the organization and the organization provides to the volunteer.

Dr. Sarah Jane Rehnborg is Associate Director of The RGK Center of Philanthropy and Community Service and a lecturer in the LBJ School of Public Affairs at The University of Texas at Austin. Sarah is a member of the Reimagining Service Council and serves as a consultant, speaker, and trainer for numerous local and national organizations. She served as President of the Association for Volunteer Administration, developed the field's performance-based certification system, and served on the founding board of the Council for Certification in Volunteer Administration. Sarah earned a PhD from the University of Pittsburgh.

Notes

1. Sarah Jane Rehnborg et al., *Strategic Volunteer Engagement: A Guide for Nonprofit and Public Sector Leaders*, RGK Center for Philanthropy & Community Service, the LBJ School of Public Affairs, the University of Texas at Austin, 2009.
2. Mark A. Hagar and Jeff Brudney, *Balancing Act: The Challenges and Benefits of Volunteers* (Washington, DC: The Urban Institute, 2004).

Chapter 4

Rethinking the Status Quo

Evan Hochberg
Chief Strategy Officer, United Way Worldwide

Mei Cobb
Volunteer Engagement Director, United Way Worldwide

Volunteering has been part of United Way's culture since our founding in 1887. We have always invited volunteers—by serving on boards and in other capacities—to be part of our mission to create opportunity for all. Our model of social change works well, but just because we have been around awhile doesn't mean that we only rely on tried and true methods for achieving impact. The environment for all of us continues to change economically, socially, and certainly in the ways in which we view and engage our communities and each other. United Way needed to change, too. As a result, we're constantly innovating, updating, and refreshing how United Way goes about creating change.

It's meant challenging the status quo of United Way volunteer engagement in order to drive even greater impact. Beyond finding better ways to invest human capital, United Way must engage people directly in our work in order to increase understanding of—and public will to solve—the considerable challenges we face. This is one way our approach to volunteer engagement must evolve: raise the bar to where we help people truly understand and care about why people are struggling and how each of us can contribute to systemic change. So by rethinking how to educate, inspire, and mobilize volunteers to work with us on behalf of the greater good, we can overcome challenges and build stronger, healthier communities.

This chapter describes how United Way is leveraging its core strengths to align with principles set forth by the Reimagining Service coalition to rethink volunteer engagement. We're not talking about strategies to simply grow our volunteer numbers. We're talking about strategies that will fundamentally change the scope of volunteer leadership and the ways in which human need is owned and addressed for decades to come.

We hope these ideas and examples inspire you to rethink your approach to attracting and retaining volunteers, integrating volunteers as a core strategic function of mission, and positioning people within your organization to better leverage the experiences and strategic value of volunteers to advance the common good.

About United Way

United Way Worldwide is the leadership and support organization for a network of nearly 1,800 community-based United Ways in 41 countries and territories. We advance the common good by focusing on improving education, helping people achieve financial stability, and promoting healthy lives. Then we mobilize millions to give, advocate, and volunteer to improve the conditions in which they live.

More Than Just a Tagline

In May 2008, United Way issued a call to action to "Live United" and "Give. Advocate. Volunteer."[1] to achieve our 10-year goals in the United States in education, financial stability, and health:

- Cut America's high-school dropout rate in half.
- Cut in half the number of lower-income families who are financially unstable.

- Increase by one-third the number of youth and adults who are healthy and avoid risky behaviors.

You have most likely seen our ads since then prominently featuring these messages. Incorporating a call to action of "Give. Advocate. Volunteer." was a big deal for United Way. It signified that in becoming an organization focused on community impact we needed to explicitly call out the critical role of volunteers. United Way is uniquely positioned in that regard. Our corporate partners and their employees collectively contribute more than $2.4 billion through annual United Way campaigns. Prominently including "Volunteer" in our call to action was new. Not only did it demonstrate our belief that a donation of time is as precious and critical an asset as the donation of money, it also illustrates our intent to be even more strategic in terms of leveraging human capital to meet the shared goals we have for our communities.

Today, a guiding principle to achieving our goals through volunteering is: *build and deepen relationships for maximum shared impact, and inclusive and sustainable success*. In other words, just like the fundraising relationships United Way has built over time, we are now aiming to focus on outcomes and build loyalty among our volunteers.

Many employees of our partner companies have participated in annual United Way volunteer events created just for them. That's a good place for us to start leveraging human capital better, but it's not enough. Our challenge now is to deepen those relationships and create new ones through volunteering. Here is how we are doing it:

Staying laser-focused on what we want to achieve.

We start with our goals in education, income, and health and build volunteer opportunities to meet those goals. Many United Ways offer a menu of opportunities relating to these three issues to help ensure that volunteer engagement is focused on what we want to accomplish.

Making it matter.

More than anything, people want to know that their time and effort will make a difference. United Way provides meaningful volunteer experiences and helps volunteers understand the impact their volunteering will have in the community on the day they volunteer and over the long haul.

Emphasizing the personal benefits of volunteering.

Volunteering helps others and helps the volunteer as well. We let our volunteers know they can learn new skills, develop their networks, build self-esteem and confidence, and improve their health through volunteering.

Deepening Relationships.

United Ways are deepening relationships by offering not only episodic but also ongoing volunteer opportunities to the people we know best—employees of companies where we run our fundraising campaigns. ReadUP is one example that comes to mind—a program created by United Way of Central Indiana that brings employee volunteers to schools to help young children improve their reading skills. As the relationship with a company deepens, some United Ways are helping them develop mechanisms for formal corporate employee volunteer programs.

Playing the numbers.

And finally, there is power in large, visible volunteer events that are open to many people, to drive awareness and inspire year-round engagement. In our case, we are deepening relationships through "United Way Day of Action." On June 21 each year, United Ways around the world invite and inspire people throughout the community to join us in our work. In 2014, we celebrated our seventh annual United Way Day of Action, with more than 348 United Ways in all 50 states and 14 countries mobilizing volunteers in their communities.

But we're not stopping there. Rethinking the status quo means inviting volunteers to be part of a continuum of service, a variety of volunteer roles to help constituents understand, experience, and feel connected to our work. Welcoming volunteers to a movement—beyond annual days of service—builds trusting, deep relationships and creates passionate, informed people connected to their communities.

When we launched our call to action to "Give. Advocate. Volunteer." we weren't the only ones rethinking volunteer engagement. In 2009, President Obama launched United We Serve, a call to all Americans to join a volunteer effort and "be part of building a new foundation for America, one community at a time."[2]

About the same time, a national, multisector coalition called Reimagining Service came together to look for ways to increase the impact of volunteers. In the rest of this chapter we'll explore how United Way Worldwide and local United Ways are putting the coalition's "four principles" to good use.

Principles for Reimagining Volunteering and Service

Reimagining Service is "a national, multisector coalition dedicated to increasing social impact through effective volunteer engagement."[3] Founded by representatives of the nonprofit, government, and private sectors, the organization has conducted research and developed tools to help nonprofits and companies assess their volunteer engagement practices, a fellows program for graduate students, and other mechanisms to achieve its mission. Reimagining Service believes that one way to increase the impact of volunteering is to encourage the creation of more "service enterprises." A service enterprise is defined as "an organization that fundamentally leverages volunteers and their skills to successfully deliver on the social mission of the organization."[4]

Early on in its nearly five-year history, Reimagining Service identified four principles to guide its work. These four principles closely align with our new thinking at United Way and might be helpful as you rethink and improve your own volunteer engagement efforts.

Principle 1: The Volunteer Ecosystem Is More Effective When All Sectors Participate in Its Evolution

Realizing that we are interdependent is the first step in rethinking the status quo. Using that knowledge as a strength and unifier to improve volunteering across all sectors is the second. United Way embraces the idea that all sectors can give of their time and talent to advance the common good. With this mindset, we can strengthen the fabric of communities and achieve and sustain more positive social change.

So, how do we develop this mindset? It starts with getting diverse parties in the same room, exploring common interests, and committing to rethinking the status quo. *This is hard work.* Fortunately, bringing nonprofits, business, government, and others to the table is one of United Way's strengths and an important component of effective, positive community impact.

For instance, United Way of Dane County in Wisconsin has held several events that aim to ignite a community-wide conversation about service, volunteering, and what it means to the growth of Dane County. One was the "Reimagining Service Summit: Taking Good Intentions to Greater Impact," which brought together 125 representatives from county nonprofits, businesses, philanthropies, faith-based organizations, and government. Each of the participants were asked to rethink their existing volunteer engagement planning and form new action plans rooted in cross-sector collaboration and the other three Reimagining Service principles. The organizations also identified obstacles to implementing their plans, and United Way is looking for ways to help overcome them.

We applaud all those who form the coalitions, sponsor the meetings, and keep the conversation flowing. Starting the conversation is the first step to achieving "collective impact," defined as the "commitment of a group of important actors from different sectors to a common agenda for solving a specific social problem."[5] Collective impact is more than mere collaboration. At its best, collective action across sectors transforms each of the participants because the commitment to the cause becomes part of their identity. The key here is to agree on the challenge, and identify what every party can bring to the table, be it subject matter expertise, funding, or volunteers.

For example, as a follow-up to the Reimagining Service Summit, United Way of Dane County sponsored a workshop called "Sector Connector." The workshop focused on a skills-based volunteering partnership between CUNA Mutual Group and Porchlight, which provides housing and employment services to homeless and other people in need. CUNA Mutual Group employees produced a PSA and developed and trained Porchlight staff on using other marketing tools. They also developed new operations efficiencies. As a result, CUNA Mutual Group employees know a great deal more about Porchlight and the people it serves than if the partnership fell to traditional forms of volunteering like painting walls, landscaping, or serving meals.

We all have a role to play in the evolution of volunteering. Nonprofits can develop strong volunteer opportunities, business can create and support strong volunteer programs and policies, and government at all levels can play a more meaningful role in supporting and deploying volunteers. Integrating volunteer action into all sectors is what will lead to greater, sustainable outcomes and advance the common good.

Principle 2: Make Volunteering a Core Function—Not an Add-On

United Way and nearly all charitable organizations rely on volunteers to help achieve mission. They not only help advance the common good, they are also goodwill ambassadors for our organizations, and many also make financial contributions that sustain our work.

Since volunteers are central to the success of United Way (and, as we point out later, to businesses as well), it stands to reason that a good way for all of us to thrive is to elevate volunteering as a core function and recognize that experienced and knowledgeable volunteer managers are as important as the volunteers themselves. Outsourcing your organization's volunteer management—and viewing it as something "nice, but not essential"—won't cut it. Volunteer expertise needs to have a seat at the table and be part of setting and achieving organizational goals.

When United Way decided to issue the call to action to "Give. Advocate. Volunteer." we devoted resources to show our network how to do it strategically. We began by walking the walk and creating a volunteer engagement department at United Way Worldwide. Although originally housed in United Way Worldwide's Brand Department, our volunteer work has evolved and now resides within the department tasked with building the capacity of our network's Community Impact work, and is directly focused on what it will take to deliver on our goals in education, income, and health. Some of the 1,800 local United Ways were ahead of us on this with excellent volunteer engagement management strategies already in place. For most, however, we were and still are asking United Ways to do something new.

The new department defined what volunteer engagement means to United Way. To us, volunteer engagement is involving people in strategic volunteer roles to advance the common good and build their relationship with United Way. Following this, we put out a set of resources, tools, and new expertise to help all United Ways.

Resources for Success

Some of the major resources and tools that United Way now offers for volunteer engagement include:

- *United Way Guide to Strategic Volunteer Engagement* that explains our vision of volunteer engagement throughout the United Way network and provides tools for self-assessment and examples to consider.

- The United Way Day of Action as an international platform to invite members of the community—not just employees of our campaign companies—to engage with us on June 21.
- A series of *Volunteer Project Ideas* in education, income, and health help United Ways attract, nurture, and retain volunteers.
- The Strategic Volunteer Engagement Summit and ongoing trainings and webinars provide personal and tailored instruction, guidance, and feedback.

As a result, we've already increased volunteer engagement among United Ways by 17 percent.[6] However, making volunteering a strategic function throughout the United Way system will take time. The status quo is certainly more comfortable than change.

An even bigger hurdle to overcome, but as essential, is getting businesses to stop treating volunteering solely as an employee benefit. Too often employee volunteer programs are created where the dominant focus is the individual. A much more compelling and promising approach is to define a clear impact agenda that has volunteer needs as a critical part. Then it becomes more about engaging/recruiting volunteers into a proven strategy as opposed to just enabling lots of individual volunteer activities. (See Chapters 16 through 20 for more on engaging corporate volunteers and partnering with workplace programs.)

Although it is easy to point to the organizational and human resources required to make volunteering a core strategic function, it takes time to change the culture, even after the personnel and plans are in place.

Principle 3: Focus Volunteer Engagement on True Community Needs

Volunteer action should be more than just something that is nice to do for employees or that brings a family closer on a Sunday afternoon. Volunteer action can and should deliver social impact. That's why we need to be strategic and *focus first on what matters*. What matters to United Way is education, financial stability, and health—the building blocks for a good life. Nearly half of United Ways align their volunteers in some way around our work in these three areas.

Local needs may vary, but at every turn, we are consistent in our message: establish community goals and mobilize volunteers through a continuum of engagement to help achieve them. United Way has found that when we help volunteers really understand and focus on what's at stake, volunteers want to do even more. People are motivated to donate their time, expertise, and passion when they believe their actions really matter, when they can see that their efforts are connected to an end game. Here's what that kind of focus can look like.

To reach our goals around high-school dropout rates, in 2011 United Way launched an initiative called "Readers, Tutors, Mentors" with this simple call to action: pledge to become a volunteer reader, tutor, or mentor. Since then volunteer engagement has been substantial, with more than 300,000 individuals pledging.

Take Sean Hughes, for instance, a parent in Hartford, Connecticut. Getting involved as a volunteer reader through United Way of Central and Northeastern Connecticut helped him realize how much of an impact he could have. Just by showing up each week, he became a hero in the eyes of the girls he was reading to and mentoring. His community has dramatically improved education by focusing on school readiness, academic achievement, youth leadership skills, and parent education. As a result, 87 percent of 2,300 children in quality early-childhood education programs gained counting, literacy, and other skills; 80 percent of 5,000 youth improved study habits for long-term success; and 78 percent of 3,700 youth improved their performance from a range of after-school programs.[7]

United Way of San Diego County organized volunteers for a "speed mentoring" session with teens as part of Community Housing Work's after-school program. United Way volunteers from local employers coached youth in developing interview skills and soft skills such as direct eye contact and offered tips for the college application process. Melissa Watkins of San Diego County Credit Union interviewed Diego, one of six young people in her group, and was so impressed with him that she helped him get a real interview—and a job—with her employer.

These are real impacts, but the success of Readers, Tutors, Mentors goes even further. Each United Way is working independently to engage volunteers in ways that are efficient, effective, and relevant to their communities. As such, the initiative has become a breeding ground of knowledge and expertise, showing us what's working and what's not and offering a model that has relevance far beyond education.

Principle 4: To Get a Return, You Have to Invest

"Time is money," but when it comes to volunteering, both the business and nonprofit sectors need to make sure we value human capital as much as we value financial capital.

Companies tend to have relatively large numbers of staff focused on funds invested in the community compared to those devoted to managing and leveraging the investment of volunteer time. Measuring the value of employee volunteering needs to include not only the social impact, but also the personal and business return on investment. Volunteering increases the bottom line and employee satisfaction, strengthens work teams, boosts morale, and builds camaraderie among employees. It can enhance the brand when aligned with company values and goals. Employees can learn new skills, develop as leaders, expand their networks, and enjoy the health benefits that volunteering brings—all things that are good for them personally, and good for their employer as well.

Nonprofit organizations, too, need to recognize that time is money. Reimagining Service found that "charities that make volunteers central to their work and manage them well are able to generate as much as three to six times the community value from volunteers as the cost to manage them."[8] But volunteers aren't free. This is a case where you definitely get what you pay for.

We've been able to make the case to funders that supporting increased volunteer engagement is something worthwhile, and United Way Worldwide is investing in building the volunteer engagement capacity of local United Ways. Some local United Ways are also finding resources to invest in their own capacity and that of other nonprofits to attract, retain, manage, and recognize volunteers.

The people at nonprofits who create the vision for volunteer engagement and inspire and motivate volunteers have important jobs to do. Charitable organizations—and the government, business, and other sources of support—should not only position volunteer engagement at the core of their organization, but also should make an investment in their volunteer managers. A survey of area nonprofits by United Way of Central Indiana found that 56 percent of nonprofits had to turn away volunteers because they lacked the capacity to provide a quality volunteer experience.[9] Nonprofits simply cannot afford to lose volunteers, whether they are individuals, groups, or companies seeking volunteer opportunities for their employees. We all need to find the resources to support the team who oversees that effort as an integral part of the organization.

Creating a Multiplier Effect

Investing in human capital is simply good business. An investment of $1 in volunteer capacity building can deliver up to $6 in return. Here's one example how.

United Way of King County, Washington, has made strengthening volunteer engagement a priority for some time. Since 2009, United Way's Volunteer Impact Partnership (VIP), an intensive volunteer management training and consulting program, has helped 83 organizations more effectively deliver services and recruit, use, and retain high-value volunteers. Across the board, VIP participants have reported improvements in volunteer management and organization operations, including reduced production costs and inefficiencies. They've also experienced more effective recruiting and organization of volunteers; a boost in volunteer satisfaction; an increased number of volunteer hours; an extended reach of their services in the community; and a heightened ability to accomplish their mission.

For example, Rainier Valley Food Bank is using a variety of volunteers and their skills more efficiently. This has led to the food bank doubling its number of food drives and being able to hold new events to raise funds and awareness. Rainier Valley Food Bank has watched monthly volunteer hours increase from 800 to nearly 2,000, allowing the food bank to feed nearly 1,000 more people each month.

Research conducted by the TCC Group shows organizations that strategically leverage volunteers outperform peer organizations on all measures of organizational capacity and have greater impact. These "service enterprises" often deliver great results with fewer financial resources than peer organizations. (See Chapter 24 for more on service enterprises.)

Rethinking Your Own Status Quo

We hope these ideas, principles, and examples are useful to you as you rethink the status quo of volunteer engagement A few important points to remember:

- Money alone will not solve the problems we are trying to address. Strategic volunteer engagement—human capital—is needed to make lasting change.
- Be strategic. Begin with the end in mind. Focus on the problem you are trying to solve, the impact you are trying to achieve, and then determine how volunteers can be engaged to drive results.

- Volunteering is a key way to engage people not only to deliver critical services but to better understand the issues, to be connected, to be passionate, and to be part of a movement to create lasting change in our communities.

Even with the luxury of a large network of committed people throughout the United States and the world, change is hard. United Way is constantly seeking to strengthen and improve the way we attract, inspire, and deepen the passion and knowledge of volunteers. It is messy and it takes time, but it is the only way we can advance the common good in a lasting way.

Evan Hochberg is United Way Worldwide's first Chief Strategy Officer, where he leads development of overall strategy as well as innovation and alignment across major areas of the enterprise. Evan also leads United Way Worldwide's Impact, Strategy, and Innovation Team, engaging 1,800 United Ways and partners around the world to develop the organization's impact strategy. Previously, Evan was National Director of Corporate Citizenship for Deloitte LLP, where he was responsible for the company's philanthropic portfolio and engineered its groundbreaking pro bono program and award-winning efforts in education. Before joining Deloitte, Hochberg was the managing director of Community Wealth Partners, a leading social-innovation consulting firm.

Mei Cobb leads Volunteer Engagement at United Way Worldwide. Prior to her work at United Way, Mei was Senior Vice President for the Points of Light Foundation where her portfolio included volunteer center development, corporate volunteering, youth and family volunteering, national service, international volunteering, and disaster volunteering. Mei is also an international consultant and trainer who has consulted and conducted training in 26 countries and is a strong advocate for the leadership roles that volunteers play in creating and sustaining change around the world. Globally she helped develop Pro Vobis, the national volunteer center in Romania, and worked in the UAE to develop Takatof.

Notes

1. To learn more about our credo, "Live United," and find examples of how we are making it possible for more people to give, advocate, and volunteer, visit www.unitedway.org.
2. Barack H. Obama, "United We Serve Video," United We Serve, June 16, 2009.
3. Frequently Asked Questions, Reimagining Service, www.reimaginingservice.org/frequently-asked-questions.
4. Service Enterprise, Reimagining Service, www.reimaginingservice.org/service-enterprise.
5. J. Kania and M. Kramer, "Collective Impact," *Stanford Social Innovation Review* (Winter 2011): 36–41, www.ssireview.org/articles/entry/collective_impact.
6. United Way Worldwide Research, *Resource Development Overview: Database 2 Surveys, 2008–2013*.
7. United Way of Central and Northeastern Connecticut.
8. "Reimagining Service Principles," Reimagining Service, www.reimaginingservice.org/Principles.
9. United Way of Central Indiana, *2013 Nonprofit Volunteer Program Survey Results for Central Indiana*, March 2013.

Chapter 5

Engaging Millennial and Younger Volunteers

Aria Finger
Chief Operating Officer, DoSomething.org and President, TMI Agency

Lazy. Apathetic. Selfish. These are just some of the words that are thrown around to describe teenagers and millennials today. Much like the generations before it, whether it was the craze of Elvis Presley's music in the 1950s or the disdain for the peace and love movement that young people were harnessing in the 1960s and 1970s, this new generation of young people is, at times, getting a bad rap.

This bad rap isn't deserved. In 2013, a whopping 88 percent of millennials donated to charity.[1] In study after study, we see that millennials want more out of life than previous generations. Not more money, but more meaning. They want their work and their free time "spent" on making a positive impact. The good news is, they are fully capable of making that positive impact truly mean something.

I have the best job in the world. I have the good fortune of proving everyone wrong about teens and the Millennial Generation. Every day, I get to see and experience firsthand the amazing things that these young people are doing.

In 2008, DoSomething.org set out to run a campaign to help clothe homeless teenagers. We saw that homelessness was a huge issue in the United States—

especially among young people—with nearly one out of three homeless people in this country being under the age of 18. We wanted to do something about it. We called homeless shelters in several states and inquired as to what these homeless teens and children needed. Much to our surprise, it wasn't a shower or a cell phone (they needed those items, too!). Instead, the top item that homeless youth requested was a good pair of blue jeans. For a young person experiencing homelessness, jeans could be worn anywhere and anytime and still fit in.

DoSomething.org partnered with youth clothing retailer Aéropostale, who also cared about both young people and social change, to launch the first Teens for Jeans campaign in January 2008. We asked young people across the United States to collect and donate their gently used blue jeans at Aéropostale stores, which would then be distributed to local homeless shelters. Seven years later, the Teens for Jeans campaign has enabled these "apathetic" young people to donate over 4 million pairs of jeans, enough to clothe half of all homeless youth last year alone.

What is the moral of the story? Young people make excellent volunteers and are an exceedingly powerful generation. Nonprofits that don't engage young people are missing out on an incredibly smart, passionate, creative generation that can help you make an impact.

This chapter will focus on why it's useful to reach out to younger volunteers as well as how you can use new and different ways to attract them.

Going After Younger Volunteers Is a Smart Strategy

If your organization is not targeting youth volunteers, you may be missing out on a huge opportunity. This generation is massive. No matter how you define millennials—and people find a million different ways from saying those born in 1980 through 1995 or just anyone 18 to 34 years of age—this generation is a large one, about equal in size to the baby boomers with 77 million members.[2]

Attracting millennial volunteers may also help your bottom line by attracting corporate dollars. This can happen in two ways. First, many corporations are striving to find good volunteer opportunities for their employees. Not only do companies like Taco Bell, Best Buy, and H&M have a huge number of millennial employees at their retail locations, recent surveys have found that a full 87 percent of millennial employees enjoy company-side days of service.[3]

Secondly, many companies are also looking to attract the coveted 18-to-34 demographic as customers and future employees. By donating corporate dollars to nonprofit organizations that young people already care about, companies can "align" their public identity with the interests and passions of this audience. This is an opportunity for nonprofits: If you can show a company how their sponsorship of your volunteer event, program, or charity walk will reach 18- to 34-year-olds, you will make yourself seem more attractive to them.

As we learn in the chapter on the future of volunteering, millennials are particularly valuable because they could be with your organization for another 50 years (or more!) as volunteers and supporters (see Chapter 1). They also, as a generalization, have a greater facility with technology. This could be a huge asset in terms of helping you recruit additional volunteers or working with existing staff to amplify what you are already doing on social media.

Case Study

In the summer of 2014, DoSomething.org launched a seven-day campaign called Scavenger Hunt with Toyota where each day we highlighted a distinct cause area, including managing "back-to-school" stress. On August 2, we messaged our members and asked them to post a picture on Instagram to spread the word. Over 7,000 pictures with the hashtag #SuperStressFace were uploaded to Instagram that day. Assuming an average of 100 followers each on Instagram, 700,000 additional people saw the campaign through this one aspect of our social-media strategy. Toyota was thrilled with the success of the campaign and we are already planning for ways to motivate and activate even more young people for our summer 2015 campaign.

Younger Volunteers Respond to Different Outreach Methods

Now that we're on the same page about the fact that going after millennials is a smart strategy, we need to talk about *how* you're supposed to reach out to them. The same methods that have been used in the past, like direct mail or even e-mail marketing, may not still be effective.

One day I was sitting at my desk when I noticed excitement in the middle of the office.

Two co-workers had just sent a text to 500 "defunct" DoSomething.org members. These were members we had e-mailed every week for the past six months with no response. We assumed that they were uninterested and non-participatory and we were about to remove them from our e-mail list. At the last second, these two co-workers decided to send each person a text message asking them what they were up to.

More than 100 people replied within the first nine minutes.

That response rate is to die for. And these young people didn't just respond to our message with questions about unrelated activities. They told us how they were participating in DoSomething.org campaigns or asked questions about how to better run our campaigns in their own schools. These young people weren't disengaged; they were just uninterested in responding via their e-mail accounts. We've seen examples like this again and again. In follow-up tests, text messages were 10 to 40 times more effective than e-mail in getting young people to participate in our campaigns. That's not a typo.

Most people over age 30 don't use Snapchat, which is a messaging service for sharing, but not saving, photos and videos. Adults often tell us they don't understand it or that it's silly to have messages disappear; often they assume that young people are using the app for illicit activities like sending sexualized text messages. In reality, the majority of young people are not using Snapchat for anything untoward. They appreciate that Snapchat works like you're having a face-to-face conversation—no one is writing down the conversations that you have with your friends face-to-face and recording them for eternity. Snapchat is incredibly popular with the under-30 demographic with 50 percent of 18-year-olds saying they use it. Despite this popularity, very few marketers are using it to reach young people; so it can be a great place to get your message out there without too much competition.[4]

In February of 2014, DoSomething.org launched a "Love Letters" campaign with the AARP Foundation's Mentor Up program where we asked young people to create Valentine's Day cards for homebound seniors. To promote the campaign and reach young people, we created a Snapchat story telling our audience that our social media guy, Bryce, would deliver Valentine's Day cards dressed as cupid in quirky and fun ways. Members could vote via text about whether they wanted these cards delivered by bike or on ice skates (delivery would take place in Central Park).

A whopping 11 percent of the people who saw the story voted and, of those, more than half signed up to participate in the campaign to make Valentine's Day cards for senior citizens.

The Social Volunteer

DoSomething.org has found that, especially for younger millennials, the most important factor for where and when they volunteer is whether their friends are volunteering, too. This desire to volunteer with friends even trumps what causes the young person to decide to volunteer. DoSomething's research is echoed in the *2013 Millennial Impact Report* that says that peer influence is important in motivating millennials to volunteer. If you want to reach millennials, use social pressure and engage their friends.[5]

To give you a real-world example, a great way to engage a young person's friends is to "fame" the volunteer on social media. Your organization may already post pictures of your stellar volunteers on your Facebook page. Yet, what most organizations don't do is to e-mail/text/call/Facebook message the "famed" volunteer the day before the post goes live to *tell them* that they are about to be highlighted. Why alert them? We all like to see our name in lights. If a volunteer knows beforehand that she is about to become Facebook famous, not only will it make her feel good but she will become a one-woman PR machine and share that photo with all of her friends. It's a great way to say thank you to a millennial volunteer, it encourages sharing, and best of all, it's free.

Be Specific

People of all ages, but especially millennials, appreciate specificity. We are surrounded by choice in all aspects of our life, so sometimes we just want to be told what exactly we can do to help. Think about the last time you saw a cause-related documentary or were discussing a particularly intractable issue that you wanted to help solve. Did you want to—or have time to—sit around and brainstorm to come up with the best solution? Or would you have preferred for an expert to tell you exactly what you could do to help? For me, it's definitely the latter, and young people often agree.

In 2012, DoSomething.org launched a campaign about recycling aluminum cans. You can't get more boring than that. In the beginning, I was actually against running the campaign altogether. It was a good cause, but I couldn't help but think that it didn't live up to DoSomething's brand of "big, loud, and easy." Sure it was easy to collect cans, but where was the loudness and fun that DoSomething was known for?

Enter specificity. The brilliant DoSomething.org campaign team decided we would ask young people to collect cans in groups of 50 and they named the campaign "50 Cans." This specificity gave an easy way for people to jump onboard without feeling intimidated—most volunteers felt they could easily contribute at least 50 cans. And the specificity also let people's creativity shine through. For the "report back" pictures that we asked young people to submit proving that they had actually collected the cans, we received incredibly creative photos. Forget piles of 50 cans. We received amazing pieces of art—cans laid out in the shape of their home state of Alabama, cans in the shape of their favorite sports logo like the Chicago Bulls, and even cans tied together to create a 3D replica of General Washington crossing the Delaware! All told, these young people collected and recycling more than 1.3 million aluminum cans.

Being specific made 50 Cans accessible and freed up the minds of our volunteers to focus on creative and shareable report-back photos.

Use T-Shirts

You might be saying to yourself, "Ugh, that's the oldest trick in the book. T-shirts are expensive and an environmental nightmare because people only wear them once." Well, next time, make t-shirts that people actually want to wear! Wouldn't it be worth an extra dollar per t-shirt to make something in a soft fabric, with a beautiful design that your volunteers would proudly wear with their friends and on their college campuses and not just to bed or the gym (if you are lucky)?

Think about how you are going to use that t-shirt. Is it an incentive? A reward? A surprise and delight? Are people really happy to receive it? Why or why not? Have you not made it special enough?

At DoSomething.org, we go one step further and we give out two t-shirts, not just one, when we're rewarding our members. Remember that young people are social volunteers. Send your volunteers two t-shirts—one for themselves and one for a friend of theirs who they think will support your cause. These volunteers will know which of their friends will be most responsive to the message of your organization. It's the best kind of targeted marketing there is.

Effective College Internship Programs

DoSomething.org swears by our internship program. In an office of 51 full-time staff, we had 27 full-time, *paid* interns for the summer of 2014. Yes, it was a big expense but it was worth it in many ways. Each department got extra help for the summer, and DoSomething.org had an immediate focus group of our target market at our fingertips. But interns also paid off in two other important ways: as a hiring pipeline (our staff is fully 25 percent former interns and that number has stayed consistent over the past five years) and, counterintuitively, as a way to find our biggest fans and supporters by looking through the applications of people who *weren't* selected to be our interns.

Hiring bad people is one of the most expensive things that a nonprofit can do. An internship is a fabulous way to see if someone can cut it in your organization by essentially giving them a 10-week trial run. But if you don't give your interns real work, interaction with high-level people on the team, and an opportunity to shine, you will never know if they can cut it as full-time employees.

Our interns provide us real help—they don't just get coffee. And although our "Head of Fun" manages the internship program, each intern also has a direct supervisor who is a full-time employee at DoSomething.org. Their manager works with them to create summer-long goals—things they can own and be proud of, not just assisting full-time staff.

It is arguably harder to get a DoSomething.org summer internship than it is to get into Harvard. But nearly every nonprofit gets more applicants for its internships than there are spots available. So, the question is, what does one do with all the people who don't get in? These are your most passionate advocates—young people who love you enough that they want to spend weeks or months of their summer with you!

In the past, we did what most organizations do—we sent rejected applicants a nice note thanking them and encouraging them to apply again in the future. But then one of our staff members, Chris, had a fantastic idea: What if we tap our intern applicants to become our best volunteers?

Chris reached out to a pilot group of applicants and explained that they had been chosen for a special program. He created weekly social-change competitions based around the current campaigns we were running, complete with leaderboards, weekly "faming," and fun prizes. It worked. This small group of "rejects" accounted for nearly 20 percent of the impact in a recent campaign. Chris took a group of people who could have been the most disappointed and turned them into our biggest supporters. One young woman did such a great job in the competition that when we had an open internship position to fill, we hired her on the spot.

5 Steps for Creating an Awesome Millennial Internship Program

1. Give your interns real responsibility. This is what young people want most.
2. Have them report directly to a full-time staff person, instead of (or in addition to) an internship manager. They will learn more and you will be able to evaluate them better.
3. Pay them (even a small stipend). It's the right thing to do and you'll get a better, more diverse group.
4. Integrate them into your office. DoSomething has an "intern scavenger hunt" where the staff creates a list of work-related things for them to find around town. It's fun, it teaches the interns about the organization, and it's great bonding.
5. Provide them with diverse perspectives. We have a brown bag lunch series where someone on staff presents on their area of expertise, and every other Tuesday night we bring in external guest speakers from other organizations. Pizza is a great addition to this (and pretty much any) event.

Getting Millennials to Care About You

You may think what you're working on is the most important thing in the world, but your organization is competing with a lot of other amazing and worthy causes out there for the attention of young people. What to do? Use things that millennials care about—fame, fairness, creativity, or passion points—to relate your cause to existing millennial interests.

Use influencers

This is the new spin on the old celebrity public service announcement. With the explosion of YouTube stars and Instagram personalities, there are ever more influencers today and many of them hit very niche demographics. Find and partner with a celebrity or influencer who is genuinely passionate about your cause and who has a passionate millennial fan base. This person does not need to be the biggest star in the world—a strong niche tribe of followers and fans can often be much more beneficial than a super popular "mass-market" celebrity who doesn't resonate particular strongly with any one group. Plus, if they are generally less well known, they are probably going to be more accessible and willing to help.

Make your cause about fairness.

Millennials are passionate about fairness and justice. If your issue is school lunches, don't talk about how nutritious fruits and vegetables are good for them—talk about how unfair it is that young people in certain low-income neighborhoods live in food deserts and don't have access to the nutrition they need.

Make it creative.

We saw with the 50 Cans campaigns that millennials want to unleash their creativity. Let them. DoSomething.org did the same thing with our Love Letters campaign when we asked young people to create Valentines for homebound seniors. The idea of making unbelievably creative cards brought in craft mavens from all over the country who were excited to join. In the beginning, they may not have known anything about the specific cause of senior isolation, but we used their passion point—crafting—to loop them in and give them exposure to the issue.

Make yourself relatable by asking about their passions.

Survey the millennials that you already have onboard and see what passion unites them. Are you a music organization? Perhaps your young supporters are all aspiring musicians. Are you a running organization? Find out if all of your young volunteers also love baseball. Figure out what already motivates passionate people toward your cause and use that to involve even more.

Key Takeaways

For those in need of a cheat sheet, here is a summary of the whys and hows of reaching millennial and younger volunteers.

- *They're altruistic*. Millennials truly care about the world, and if you engage them you have a great opportunity for smart, passionate volunteers who might also become lifelong donors.

- *They're a huge generation*. Depending on how you look at it, the Millennial Generation is as big as the Boomer Generation.
- *They can be used effectively as interns*. Whether it's a pipeline to future donors, volunteers, or full-time employees, or just an impromptu focus group, having full-time, paid college interns can be valuable.
- *Treat them with respect and cater to their needs*. They're not aliens but they do behave differently than previous generations.
- *Use the technology that they respond to*. Whether it's Instagram, Snapchat, or SMS, figure out the platforms where your biggest brand advocates hang out.
- *Use their passion points*. Figure out how to relate your cause to something they love.
- *Don't assume they're all alike*. This is a diverse generation (in every way). Reach out to them as individuals whenever possible.
- *Don't treat them like children*. Or like morons who just text on their phones all day and don't have anything else to offer.
- *Enlist them as your best free marketers*. By giving them two (high-quality, well-made, fun) t-shirts . . . one for them and one for a passionate friend.
- *Be specific*. We all need help figuring out how best to engage with a nonprofit, and millennials are no different.
- *The Social Volunteer*. Give them opportunities to volunteer with their friends.

Conclusion

If you're not tapping the power of millennial volunteers and reaching them how they prefer to be reached, you're missing out. Just to reinforce this point, let me share the story of the Dance Marathon at Washington University in St. Louis (my alma mater), which was led by my awesome co-worker, Greg Perlstein, during his senior year.

Dance Marathons at colleges across the country raise millions of dollars for children's health causes—predominantly Children's Miracle Network and its affiliated hospitals. Although some Dance Marathons are fundraising juggernauts that have been around forever, that doesn't mean your organization can't learn from the tactics they use and apply them to your own millennial outreach.

When Greg was a freshman, he saw a flyer for the WashU Dance Marathon asking if he wanted to dance for 12 hours to support children's hospitals. Greg was already passionate about children's health and wellness, so he decided to attend the first meeting. He loved it. Why? He enjoyed the idea of being able to help a good cause while also participating in this totally ridiculous, silly, fun, and crazy event. It was a win-win.

The first year Greg was a participant and the Dance Marathon raised somewhere in the ballpark of $40,000 for two local St. Louis children's hospitals—a great donation to be sure, but there was more to be done. Over the next few years, Greg and the Dance Marathon team made some changes and worked hard to make that $40,000 donation quadruple. In Greg's senior year, they raised the most money in WashU history.

How did they make this happen? Well, first, they were empowered. They had great advisors from WashU faculty and from Children's Miracle Network, but these people were just that—advisors. The students led the show. The students could make changes to the structure of the on-campus organization to make it more effective. They put in place their 22-person-strong executive board and 80 morale captains and used these morale captains to recruit. Captains could offer up their own wacky and crazy ideas. They worked hard because they felt ownership.

Greg's senior year was 2007, before there was Twitter and before school organizations were allowed to have their own pages on Facebook. So the Dance Marathon team had to get creative. They did everything that social college students do—they tabled like crazy, they handed out flyers, they were a force at student activities, and they used bullhorns to call out and ask random students to get involved. They hosted dance-ins where they set up on campus for 48 hours and wouldn't stop dancing until they hit their volunteer sign-up goals. Each morale captain was responsible for getting 10 dancers to raise $150 each and sign up to dance for 12 hours on the day of the event.

The event in Fall 2007 was a smash. Think themed dance hours, inflatable bouncy castles, costume changes, spirit competitions, and performances from WashU student groups and the St. Louis Rams cheerleaders. Over 1,000 student volunteers helped out plus WashU faculty. Best of all, kids who had been beneficiaries of Children's Miracle Network came to the event, too. All of the volunteers could see firsthand the amazing and brave children that they were helping.

Children's Miracle Network raised $176,000 and engaged 1,000-plus awesome volunteers as a result of Dance Marathon WashU that year. And what did the college volunteers get in return? A fun and amazing experience where they knew they were making a difference. Oh, and Greg met his future wife on the Dance Marathon host committee. It doesn't get any better than that!

Aria Finger oversees business development, finance, and campaigns as Chief Operating Office for DoSomething.org, the largest organization for young people and social change in the U.S. with 3 million members and counting. Finger is also the founder and President of TMI, a strategy agency that advises Fortune 500 brands and top NGOs on how to reach young people. She was one of the first 10 World Economic Forum Global Shapers, is an adjunct professor at NYU, and was the youngest person named to the 2012 *Crain's NY Business* "40 Under Forty" list. She's also ridiculously passionate about prison reform.

Notes

1. "2014 Millennial Impact Report," Achieve, 2014, www.themillennialimpact.com.
2. "The Millennium Count," Pew Research, 2014, www.pewresearch.org/daily-number/the-millennial-count.
3. "2014 Millennial Impact Report," 2014.
4. Jeff Beer, "How 12 Brands Used Snapchat," Fast Company Co.Create, August 12, 2014, www.fastcocreate.com/3033793/how-12-brands-used-snapchat.
5. "2013 Millennial Impact Report," Achieve, 2013, http://www.themillennialimpact.com/research.

Chapter 6

The Great Boomer Volunteer Revolution: Boom or Bust?

Beth Steinhorn
President, JFFixler Group

Introduction: Two Boomers Ride the Bus

Meet Tom. Born in 1950, Tom graduated high school and joined the Air Force. After four years of service, he attended college, met his future wife, and was hired by the human resources office of the Air Force Academy in Colorado. His government role brought him to positions throughout the United States and abroad. His wife and he traveled and raised two sons while creating homes throughout the United States and Europe.

Always enthusiastic about work, Tom nonetheless looked forward to retirement—though actual retirement came a few years later than planned. "With the recession," reflects Tom, "it was better to continue working and contributing to the 401k." For Tom, retirement meant seeing more of his sons and grandchildren, having more time for reading, exercise, motorcycles, guitar, travel, and "giving back." With this vision in mind, when retirement came, Tom and his wife left Germany and headed back to Colorado where they bought a house to remodel and be near family. Between the hardware store visits, he also sought out ways to serve the community, surfing the Internet for volunteer opportunities, but none spoke to his interests.

Meet Judy. Unlike Tom, whose journey started in Colorado and carried him around the world, Judy's journey began in Germany and eventually brought her to Colorado. Judy's parents, Holocaust survivors from Poland who fled to Siberia, made their way to a displaced persons camp in Germany, where Judy was born in 1946. Eventually, the family settled in Colorado. There, Judy grew up and became a teacher. She led a busy life—working hard and raising a son. As a single parent, she planned to retire after her son had completed his education in order to ensure she was in a better financial position. Yet that didn't stop her from fantasizing about how great it would be to have extra time when retired.

When Judy did step down after four decades of teaching and being so active, the much anticipated extra time proved challenging. She realized that she needed something to fill her days.

This past summer, their journeys intersected on—of all places—a yellow school bus. Judy and Tom were volunteers for an innovative program called Lunchbox Express, which operates as a sponsor of the USDA's Summer Food Service Program, a federal program that makes nutritious lunches available during the summer at approved sites with high concentrations of low-income children. As Lunchbox Express volunteers, they rode the bus to city neighborhoods, feeding hungry children whose access to free or reduced-fee lunches in their schools had ended with the school year.

Just as their individual paths to retirement varied, so did the way that they found this volunteer opportunity. Tom, who always knew he would volunteer during retirement, couldn't find what he was looking for online. Yet, the hardware store he frequented was within sight of a food pantry operated by Jewish Family Service of Colorado (JFS), the agency that operates Lunchbox Express. After checking out the JFS website, he reached out, interviewed with the Director of Volunteer Services, and has been volunteering there for more than a year. Joining the Lunchbox Express team was part of a series of positions he has held with JFS that included visiting homebound seniors and helping in accounting.

Meanwhile, with only a few weeks before Judy was set to retire, a newspaper article about Lunchbox Express caught her eye. She immediately saw a connection to her experience as a teacher. The fact that the program began distributing books in addition to the lunches only reinforced the connection to Judy's passion for literacy.

As the summer ended, both Judy and Tom felt valued for their work. As Judy later reported, JFS staff went out of their way to make it a good experience, all the way from the in-depth interview to the volunteer welcome and appreciation events. Most important for Judy and Tom, the experience was satisfying because the children and their families were palpably excited when the buses pulled up with lunches and books each day.

Though Lunchbox Express is on hold until the buses rev up again next summer, Judy's and Tom's roles are not over. Both are exploring other positions with JFS. Tom will continue his work by putting his decades of human resources experience to good use, helping with filing and documentation in the agency's HR department. He looks forward to next summer when his wife will also be joining him on the Lunchbox Express program. Judy, meanwhile, has accepted a part-time job a few afternoons each week to keep herself busy, but still plans to volunteer. She is talking with JFS staff about helping in their immigrant services program or in their mentoring program. After all, given her personal path to the United States, the opportunity to help immigrants study for their citizenship test would be extra meaningful to her.

"Here Come the Boomers"—The Anticipated Volunteer Revolution

Tom and Judy's stories are not unique. These two represent millions of baby boomers who are seeking to find meaningful work—paid or volunteer—in the so-called "second act" of their adult life. On New Year's Day 2006, as the world celebrated the first boomers turning 60, nonprofit trend watchers had anticipated with a mix of excitement and fear an impending wave of more than 78 million boomers retiring over the subsequent 5 to 10 years. Would this cohort turn out to be the volunteers and donors that the nonprofit sector had been waiting for?

Although predictions of the outcome varied, everyone had agreed that the eventual impact of boomers would be huge. Although *The Chronicle of Philanthropy* trumpeted such headlines as "Make Room for Boomers: Charities Look to Engage a Generation about to Turn 60,"[1] many leaders in the sector acknowledged publicly and privately that nonprofits were not ready to engage boomers in the ways boomers actually wanted. To address this need, new organizations dedicated to closing this gap like Experience Corps, Civic Ventures, and RespectAbility began popping up to help both the sides of the divide.

With the benefit of time and hindsight, how have Tom's and Judy's experiences as volunteers stacked up against the predictions? Most importantly, what can organizational leaders learn from the lessons of the last few years and from volunteers like Tom and Judy in order to tap into this generation's time and talent on behalf of their mission—before the opportunity has passed?

Back in 2007, many economists and sociologists feared the aging Baby Boomer Generation would drain society's coffers of Social Security, Medicare, and other resources. They even immortalized their fears with gloom-and-doom nicknames like "The Silver Tsunami" and "Gray2K." Yet, at the same time, others painted a picture of a different possibility. Marc Freedman, founding president of Civic Ventures and co-founder of The Experience Corps, described a far more optimistic scenario in which "longevity, demography, human development, generational experience, fiscal imperatives, labor market dictates, and the particular historical moment [would combine] to lead boomers to contribute longer and to use their education and experience in areas with jobs to offer, deeper meaning to confer, and broader social purposes to fulfill."[2] He foresaw a world with new rites of passage for boomers, such as gap years, new industries to support boomers on their paths to new careers driven by impact rather than income, longer life expectancy, and the prospect of boomers eventually retiring in their mid-seventies after meaningful "encore careers."[3]

Freedman was not alone in his more optimistic view of the future. His and others' predictions were based on emerging data about boomers' attitudes and interests toward work, health, retirement, and service. Boomer-focused reports such as those conducted by Civic Ventures (2005), AARP (2007), and VolunteerMatch (2007) all shed light on what boomers expected and hoped for the years ahead:

- Baby boomers were optimistic about retirement and defined it as a chance to spend more time with family, enjoying hobbies, and having leisure.[4]
- Most boomers (79 percent) planned to work in retirement, whether for fun or out of necessity.[5]
- Between 1998 and 2007, boomers' expectations around retirement were relatively consistent, though their expectations around finances had become much more conservative, likely due to the recession that began in early 2001 and was aggravated by the 9/11 attacks and subsequent war on terror.[6]

Volunteering and service were tightly woven into boomers' vision of retirement. More than half planned to devote more time to volunteering[7] and many desired to start while still in their fifties so that they would have time to learn any necessary skills and have a measurable impact.[8] According to VolunteerMatch's *Great Expectations: Boomers and the Future of Volunteering* report from 2007,[9] not only did more than half of boomers plan to volunteer, but among those already active in volunteering, three in four viewed volunteering as one of the most important things in their lives.

Boomers were also very clear on what would make the volunteer experience attractive to them: skills. For boomer men, the opportunity to use their professional skills was very important, whereas for women, the chance to learn new skills was key. Already, boomers were changing the volunteer landscape by bringing a consumer mentality to the arena: If they did not find an opportunity that fit their schedule and desires, they would look elsewhere. *Great Expectations* showed that many boomers were not volunteering because they had not found the right opportunity; boomers were twice as likely as younger generations to pass on an opportunity if it wasn't a good fit.

Facing such a discerning volunteer pool was new to nonprofit organizations. It turned out that even many organizations that were already engaging boomers as volunteers were either underutilizing their skills or having difficulty finding all the volunteers they needed.[10]

It was clear to all that boomers would be redefining retirement. To most, it was also clear that, in doing so, boomers would be redefining volunteering in some way. However, it was not yet clear to all nonprofit leaders that the volunteer structures that had worked so well for so long to engage Greatest and Silent Generation volunteers (those born before and during World War II) would not work for boomers. But the disconnect between what boomers wanted and what organizations were offering in terms of volunteer opportunities was obvious to anyone who cared to look.

> *To prosper and leverage this [Boomer] resource, nonprofits must reengineer volunteering to align boomers' skills with organizational vision, mission, and goals in a purposeful way. Gone forever are the gray-haired men and women who, after spending forty years at the same job, became reliable volunteer office assistants and crossing guards. Boomers want to be challenged.*
>
> —Jill Friedman Fixler, *Boomer Volunteer Engagement* (2010)

From articles and tool kits to webinars and workshops, the topic of boomer engagement headlined conferences and bookshelves across the sector. Motivated either by a desire to tap into this tremendous resource or by the fear of a volunteer corps that was aging in place with no cadre of volunteers lining up to take their place, nonprofit staff were eager to learn more about the Baby Boom Generation and the strategies that would harness their time and talent.

The Great Recession Rewrites Retirement Plans—and More?

And then, just as this flurry of boomer-focused attention was gearing up, the Great Recession hit. From December 2007 until June 2009, the 18-month recession was the longest in U.S. history since World War II and the eventual recovery was slow and prolonged. Near-record unemployment rates ballooned to 10 percent before slowly, painfully declining. Indeed, seven years later, unemployment rates are still above the prerecession rate of 4.7 percent in November 2007. Many organizations faced drops in philanthropic dollars, decreased program revenue, and staff layoffs, all amidst sharp increases in demand for services.

And what of the boomers? How did this unexpected economic challenge impact their optimistic plans for rewriting retirement? Did the anticipated boom in volunteering come to pass? Or, did the recession result in busted dreams? Certainly, the stock market slump combined with fears around major financial institutions failing significantly ate into many boomers' retirement funds—affecting their plans at best, or dashing them entirely at worst. A 2013 study by the Brookings Institution[11] explored the significant ways that the Great Recession affected boomers in terms of their work patterns. The report shows that the initial effect of the recession was to accelerate the retirement of some Baby Boom and Silent Generation workers who were laid off and did not seek—or were unable to find—equivalent jobs. But by 2010–2011, when the layoff rate declined, the trend of boomers working longer—already indicated long before the recession began—resumed in force. As one author wrote in relation to this study, "The financial crisis not only dented many [boomer] nest eggs, it also reshaped our labor market. . . ."[12]

In other words, although some boomers chose or were forced to take an early retirement, many have fulfilled the prerecession vision of continuing work either full- or part-time late in their fifties and into their sixties. Although their original vision may have been to work because they wanted to, many are now working because they need to.

Boomer Terms of Engagement

Yet, volunteering has remained an important avenue for self-fulfillment, giving back, and staying active and healthy. Both statistics and the experience of many volunteer engagement professionals in the field support this.

Statistically speaking, although the percentage of baby boomers who volunteer has declined slightly since 2007 (from about 30 percent to 28.2 percent), this generation remains the only one to consistently outpace the national average. And, for nearly all of that decade, boomers led the nation in volunteering.

Out in the field, both boomers and the organizations hoping to engage them share similar stories—most of which bear out the predictions from 2007 and before. Boomers are seeking ways to volunteer and serve, they want to make a tangible impact on their communities and the world, and, yet, demand to so do on their "terms of engagement":

Time—Boomers want flexible schedules that allow them to balance their volunteering with travel, caring for grandchildren and aging parents, or their part-time jobs.

Impact—Boomers remain achievement-oriented and demand that their time and effort have a meaningful impact.

Skills—Boomers seek to use their skills or gain new ones through their volunteer endeavors. (But if they do not find one that meets them on their terms, they take their time and talents elsewhere.)

In light of that reality, organizations are challenged to meet boomers on their own terms while also staying true to the organization's mission and strategic priorities. The situation has demanded new strategies to achieve this balance. New best practices have emerged—yet there remains a long way to go before the sector fully embraces these practices and leaves behind the traditional ways of engaging volunteers that worked for earlier generations, but not for boomers (much less the generations that follow them).

Seeing the Challenge as an Opportunity: One Organization's Success Story

One of the best ways to explore these strategies for boomer engagement is to learn from an organization that has successfully put them into practice. One such organization, PIH Health, approached the challenge of boomer engagement in two distinct phases.

Located primarily in the California cities of Whittier and Downey, PIH Health is a regional healthcare network with two hospitals, outpatient medical offices, a medical group, and home healthcare and hospice services. In 2009, the leaders at PIH faced a common challenge: Despite a long history of volunteer engagement and a large volunteer force, most of those who served were over 75 years old or younger than 25. They had a gap of 50 years in their corps. PIH's Director of Volunteers, Nancy Whyte, recognized that the hospital was changing and that it needed volunteers who could meet new challenges, serve patients and staff in new ways, and utilize new technologies. The hospital needed to fill that 50-year gap.

After hearing speakers on the topic of boomers, gathering resources, and making the case to her colleagues, Nancy garnered support to launch a strategic initiative to engage boomer volunteers. She knew it would not be easy and that they would need to overcome initial resistance in order to change the structure of the department and the way the hospital views volunteers. It took a few months to get ready, during which PIH hired my team at JFFixler Group to provide expertise, resources, and coaching. But once they began the first phase of their work, the momentum—and results—really grew.

PIH's Boomer engagement initiative had four steps:

1. Forming a team
2. Learning and assessing needs
3. Developing new positions
4. Evaluating

Nancy and her colleagues convened a group of four staff and four volunteers. The team included such skilled professionals as a recently retired COO of another hospital. Some team members were boomers and all were selected because they brought a lot to the table. Most importantly, team members could envision a different culture of volunteer engagement that utilized volunteers in new ways.

The initiative launched with a full day of training to help the team understand new strategies for volunteer engagement. The workshop was designed to help team members identify critical issues for change (pressing needs of the hospital). From the start, the team also identified areas where the volunteer department itself would need to change policy. For example, they had always required volunteers to make a rigid commitment of 100 hours of service, four hours per week. The team quickly realized they would need to release that requirement in order to recruit skilled boomers who might be traveling or working.

With the list of critical needs in hand, the team developed volunteer assignments that would intrigue and engage boomers. Each of the positions also relieved staff of duties so that they could focus on other work or filled gaps that staff lacked the capacity to achieve. A closer look at some of the new roles reveals how impactful the work was.

Patient Biographers

Before the initiative, patients who were in the hospital for an extended stay interacted with clinical staff in a very formal way without ever getting to know them. The new volunteer role of patient biographer significantly changed and improved those patients' experience. Drawing on interviewing and writing skills, the biographer role attracts journalists, social workers, and educators. Biographers interview patients, learn about their lives and family, and then write a brief patient biography. After vetting the biography with the patient, the story is framed and hung in the room. Once posted, hospital staff members learn about individuals and have new ways of connecting with them.

Healthy Living Educators

The Community Education Department was a small group with a big mission: to empower older adults with chronic conditions to self-manage their care. With 13 cities to support, the small staff could not possibly be everywhere. So, the team developed a new volunteer corps of Healthy Living Educators. These are volunteers with teaching skills who spread out among neighboring communities, delivering the curriculum, and teaching classes on chronic disease management, food, and nutrition. Through this effort, the department increased its reach into the community without hiring any new staff.

Interview Committee

Prior to the initiative, volunteer department staff used to spend a great deal of time interviewing potential volunteers. Through this effort, the hospital sought out boomers to create an interview committee. The role attracts teachers, human resources directors, and managers to conduct interviews of volunteer candidates. Staff is now free to do other things that they had little time to do before.

Volunteers Orienting Volunteers

Department staff also used to spend a lot of time delivering the four-hour orientation required of all new volunteers. Building on the idea of the healthy living educators, they cultivated a small group of volunteers with teaching or management experience to deliver the volunteer orientation. By creating this role, staff was freed up to do other work. More importantly: the hospital sends a very clear message to potential and new volunteers about how much the hospital trusts and values its volunteers.

Leveraging Success and Scaling Up

PIH's initiative dramatically shifted the way the hospital does business. Very quickly, staff in all departments began to view volunteers as invaluable assets, without whom they could not do their job. Staff began to request volunteers to take on more highly technical roles, from clerical assistance with databases and records to a research team to conduct patient surveys. Hospital leadership, sensing that the boomer initiative had only scratched the surface, green-lighted the second phase of PIH's boomer engagement initiative, the Team100 project, three years later, with a goal of recruiting 100 new skilled boomer volunteers within one year.

Through Team100, existing boomer volunteers were invited to get more involved, use online recruitment, talk to people in the community, attend community events, distribute brochures, and talk to their friends. The strategy celebrates the fact that the most effective way to recruit boomers is to engage their current volunteers as ambassadors and talent scouts. And it worked. One hundred new skilled boomers joined the hospital's volunteer corps within 12 months.

Today PIH Health has a thriving cadre of skilled volunteers who comprise the Interview Committee and a new Patient Advisor Committee, teach healthy living classes, conduct patient surveys, develop and write a newsletter, provide pet therapy, and serve as ambassadors for the hospital throughout a vast region. Marianne Cota, who took the reins as the Manager of Volunteer Services after Nancy retired, says the need is still growing: "We are about to launch another recruitment initiative for next year because we cannot do this alone. We need the skilled volunteer-force. Our staff loves the boomer volunteers. We can't fill the spots quickly enough."

The Combination to Unlock Success

The secret to PIH's success and similar initiatives that we've researched or consulted on is that there is no secret combination to unlocking the treasure trove of boomer skills and talents. Other organizations have met similar levels of success by going through some of the same steps—including Colorado's Jewish Family Service where Tom and Judy volunteer. JFS also committed to an intentional effort to engage new volunteers as part of its strategic planning process that occurred at about the same time as PIH's boomer initiative. For JFS, the goals included "creating a fertile environment for volunteer engagement" throughout the whole agency. Both JFS and PIH incorporated these crucial steps to their efforts:

- *Learning*—They invest time and money in receiving training on boomers and volunteer engagement trends and strategies.
- *Adjusting Expectations*—They use what they learned about boomers to develop realistic goals that align with those trends.
- *Assessing Needs and Identifying Strategic Roles*—They systematically and continually assess the needs of the organization and only then do they design roles for volunteers; all roles emerge from the place of overlap between what volunteers want and what the organization needs.
- *Engaging Champions*—Both organizations intentionally engaged both staff and volunteers who could envision a different future and were excited about the possibilities that strategic boomer engagement could offer; the enthusiasm and entrepreneurial spirit of those individuals helped to create momentum and allay fears or concerns from others.
- *Learning Through Pilots*—They started small, with a discrete number of pilot roles and evaluated them continuously, learning and tweaking along the way.

- *Going to Scale*—Following the pilot phase, they learned which elements of the initiative could be replicated or expanded; they gained competencies in engagement, built buy-in, and then were able to successfully bring the effort to scale.

Boom or Bust?

So, was the anticipated great boomer revolution a boom or a bust? The Baby Boomer Generation remains a valuable resource—with skills and talents to share and a desire to give back in this new phase in their lives. Since boomers had long expected to work beyond traditional retirement age, the fact that some of them are now working longer because they *need to* rather than simply *want to* does not mitigate their interest in or commitment to volunteering. It merely underscores their original plan, which was to volunteer on their terms of time, impact, and skills. If boomers can find an opportunity that offers flexible hours, has a measurable and meaningful impact, and taps into their abundant professional or personal skills, they will show up and invest their time and talents.

The answer to the question of whether the great revolution is a boom or bust is one for each organization to write for itself. Organizations such as PIH Health and Jewish Family Service have made the decision to embrace volunteer engagement as a key business strategy by reinventing their volunteer model and reengineering their organizational structure to include volunteers at every level. By doing so, they have shifted to a new culture that is appealing to boomers and refreshing to their staff. They have chosen to answer the question with a resounding "boom!" What will your answer be?

Beth Steinhorn is a nationally recognized leader, writer, and innovator in organizational engagement and management. As President of JFFixler Group, Beth helps organizations achieve mission through strategic volunteer and member engagement. JFFixler Group's proven model for piloting engagement innovations has led countless organizations to embrace a culture of strategic engagement to increase impact. Beth has worked with museums, education agencies, faith-based and human-services organizations, among

(*continued*)

(Continued)

others. She regularly presents at conferences and has published many articles and books, including the two-book series *Boomer Volunteer Engagement*. She lives in Denver and enjoys cooking, running, and traveling.

Notes

1. S. Perry, "Make Room for Boomers," *The Chronicle of Philanthropy* (November 24, 2005), philanthropy.com/article/Make-Room-for-Boomers/58187.
2. M. Freedman, *Encore: Finding Work that Matters in the Second Half of Life* (New York: PublicAffairs, 2007), 3.
3. Ibid., 4–6.
4. Roper ASW, *Baby Boomers Envision Retirement II* (Washington, DC: AARP, 2004), 16–17.
5. M. Freedman, *Encore: Finding Work that Matters in the Second Half of Life* (New York: PublicAffairs, 2007), 9.
6. Roper ASW, *Baby Boomers Envision Retirement II*, 5–6.
7. VolunteerMatch, *Great Expectations: Boomers and the Future of Volunteering*, 2007 (San Francisco, CA: MetLife Foundation), 11, www.volunteermatch.org/nonprofits/resources/greatexpectations.
8. MetLife Foundation/Civic Ventures, *New Face of Work Survey* (2005).
9. VolunteerMatch, *Great Expectations: Boomers and the Future of Volunteering*, 2007 (San Francisco, CA: MetLife Foundation), 10, www.volunteermatch.org/nonprofits/resources/greatexpectations.
10. Ibid., 12.
11. G. Burtless and B. Bosworth, *Impact of the Great Recession on Retirement Trends in Industrialized Countries* (Washington, DC: The Brookings Institution, 2013).
12. C. Dowd, "Boomers' Retirement Security Still Hurting from Great Recession," *The Boomer* (February 13, 2014), www.foxbusiness.com/personal-finance/2014/02/13/boomers-retirement-security-still-hurting-from-great-recession.

PART TWO

Changing Relationships

Chapter 7

Keeping the Volunteers You Have

John L. Lipp
Associate VP, Volunteer Engagement, JDRF

Retention has long been one of the holy grails in the field of volunteer engagement. Along with recruitment and recognition, it's one of the original 3 Rs of volunteer management. Talk to any of your colleagues about the concept of retention as a key metric for measuring the success of your volunteer program, and I guarantee you most people will nod in agreement without really understanding what you even mean by the word.

For the most part, they're right. Retention is usually a good thing. (Except when it's not! More on that later.) We know that volunteers are not free. There is a cost associated with recruiting, screening, placing, training, and supporting our volunteers. Just like employees, that cost is usually front-loaded—meaning we invest a lot of resources up front with the anticipation that the return on investment (ROI) will pay off down the road. If people don't stay long enough to justify the initial investment—a revolving door of volunteers—you never fully realize the potential of your program. Thus, from a strictly bottom-line business sense (and our donors expect us to manage our resources efficiently), retaining our current volunteers is a lot more cost-effective than constantly recruiting and onboarding new ones.

Of course, most volunteers—myself included—don't like being thought of as a commodity, a bottom-line investment that needs to be fully realized on a balance sheet. To that end, retaining volunteers should not just be a metric, but a *shared value* that puts people first in any organization. Ask yourself: Are my organization's volunteers just a means to an end, or is involving volunteers a core part of our mission?

But what exactly does good retention look like? How long does a volunteer need to stay to ensure you have a good retention rate? How long is too long? What happens when the bad volunteers stay—yes, even though they are rare, there are bad volunteers!—and the good volunteers leave?

As National Director of Volunteer Engagement at JDRF, the leading global organization funding type 1 diabetes research, I deal with these questions on a daily basis. Our department works to maximize the impact of people's time and talents by ensuring volunteers are well placed, trained, recognized, and supported at every level of the organization. To achieve our department's mission, we work hard to keep our current volunteers engaged and coming back, while making sure new volunteers are welcomed with open arms and set up for success.

In this chapter we'll look at the various things to think about as you define what "good retention" means to your organization and how to ensure everyone is working toward the same goal of keeping your volunteers fully engaged and committed to achieving your mission.

Retention by the Numbers

Most studies on volunteer retention tend to focus on a variety of factors that predict an individual's likelihood to stay volunteering. The Corporation for National and Community Service, in a 2007 brief[1] that analyzed data from several studies, concluded the following:

1. Volunteer retention rates, similar to volunteer rates, increase with age.
2. The higher a volunteer's level of education, the more likely the volunteer is to continue volunteering.

3. Volunteers who devote more time to volunteering have the highest volunteer retention rates.
4. Volunteer retention is related to the type of organization in which a person volunteers. Volunteering through a religious organization tops the list.
5. More challenging volunteer activities tend to lead to higher retention rates.

A traditional way to measure retention is to view how many of your active volunteers are still active a year later. Past analysis from the Corporation for National and Community Service suggests that about one-third of volunteers don't continue volunteering from one year to the next.[2] I find that this snapshot approach, although it gives us some interesting benchmark data, isn't really helpful when trying to determine what's really important for most organizations. That's because a successful retention rate is not about one size fits all, but more about individual roles. A volunteer serving in a leadership capacity will, by the nature of that role, have an optimal retention rate higher that a volunteer who signs on to help stage a fundraising event.

I prefer to use the following approach, broken out by individual volunteer positions, to determine an optimal retention rate for any given position. The first thing is to determine your current retention rate. (See Table 7.1.)

Table 7.1 Volunteer Retention Rate Worksheet

1.	Volunteer role	
2.	Minimum term of service	
3.	Number of volunteers currently in this role	
4.	Number of volunteers who left in the past year before completing their full term	
5.	Subtract Line 4 from Line 3 and enter total here	
6.	Divide line 5 by line 3 and multiple by 100 to determine a baseline retention percentage	

Once you have a baseline retention rate, ask your colleagues—retention of volunteers should be everyone's responsibility—to answer the following questions:

1. Given that there are a variety of reasons out of our control that impact volunteer retention, are we happy with our current rate?
2. If not, what can we do in our recruiting practices to ensure we're reaching the right volunteers, an important predictor of a successful retention rate?
3. What can we do to ensure we're getting our volunteers onboarded effectively so that they feel welcomed and are set up to succeed from the very beginning?
4. What can we do to recognize and acknowledge our volunteers so they feel valued for their service?
5. How can we better communicate with our volunteers to ensure they feel valued as "insiders" and have the right information at the right time?

When determining your optimal retention rate, keep in mind that different age groups have very different expectations of retention. Not surprisingly, just as volunteer rates tend to increase as people age, so do retention rates. I've noticed that today's volunteers—across all generations—tend to view volunteering much more selectively than in the past. Rather than jumping in with both feet, volunteers today tend to start "dating" before they enter into a "long-term" relationship with an organization. This is a positive trend, allowing both the organization and the volunteer an opportunity to take it slow and make sure it's a good fit. Volunteering needs to be a win-win relationship if we want our volunteers to stay.

The Volunteer Experience

I was fascinated by the UPS Foundation study, *Managing Volunteers* (1998), and its finding that "People are more likely to volunteer when they feel an organization is well-managed and will make good use of their time."[3] Although this has implications for recruitment strategies and job design, it's also an important factor in volunteer retention. In the ensuing years, everything I've experienced in the field has validated this research. With the explosion of online tools to research the effectiveness of charitable organizations, a renewed commitment to transparency from the field, and a social media climate that allows people to easily share individual experiences and perceptions, an organization's reputation is now more important than ever to both recruiting and keeping volunteers.

That same study also found that "two out of five volunteers have stopped volunteering for an organization at some time because of one or more poor volunteer management practices."[4]

A 2004 report from the Urban Institute underscored the importance of focusing on the volunteer experience and included an analysis of the UPS Foundation study, concluding: "Charities interested in increasing retention of volunteers should invest in recognizing volunteers, providing training and professional development for them, and screening volunteers and matching them to organizational tasks."[5]

Recognizing that good volunteer management practices are only part of the equation, the Urban Institute also stated, "In addition to adopting certain management practices, charities can provide a culture that is welcoming to volunteers, allocate sufficient resources to support them, and enlist volunteers in recruiting other volunteers. All of these practices help charities to achieve higher rates of retention."

The professionalism of volunteer engagement has been an ongoing theme over the past three decades. Instituting best practices, many with their roots in the field of Human Resources, has led to a much more formalized approach to how organizations manage their volunteer workforce. I predict we'll see a slight pendulum shift in the future back to more informal practices that accommodate volunteers seeking flexible opportunities to create their own service opportunities. For example, at JDRF, our online Team JDRF portal allows people to create their own community and personal volunteer campaigns to raise money and awareness for type-1 diabetes research. These are all 100 percent volunteer-driven campaigns by people serving outside the formal organizational structure; but nonetheless, still valuable contributors to our mission.

Even with a shift to less formalized programs, there are four best practices that should not be lost. These practices help ensure volunteers have a meaningful experience and, in the process, increase volunteer retention.

Job Design

Having carefully crafted volunteer position descriptions in place is a central tenet of successful volunteer engagement programs. The process of drafting the position descriptions, with clearly outlined duties, helps ensure the work being assigned to volunteers is specific, meaningful, and impactful. Completed position descriptions help clarify expectations for both staff and volunteers and, with a screening and interview process in place, greatly increase the odds of getting the right volunteers to the right positions—a key predictor for successful retention.

Onboarding

First impressions matter and help set the stage for long-term retention. Onboarding that includes a detailed orientation to your organization and the roles of volunteers, an opportunity for new volunteers to "meet and greet" other volunteers and staff, and, depending on the nature of the role, an assigned volunteer mentor, will help ensure that new volunteers feel welcomed and get the information they need.

Learning and Development

Ongoing training and professional development opportunities can be a huge benefit for volunteers and send a strong message about how much your organization values its unpaid workforce. A training program that supports professional development and advancement opportunities, part of a strategic volunteer career path, helps ensure people stay motivated to continue serving.

A Culture of Appreciation

Sure, study after study ranks recognition as one of the least effective ways to impact volunteer retention. But do we really expect our volunteers—most of whom serve selflessly—to say they want to be thanked in order to continue serving? The reality is, ongoing recognition is a critical component of volunteer retention. By combining both formal and informal methods of recognition, an organization can create a "culture of appreciation" in which both volunteers and paid staff feel respected and valued for their contributions and feel a deeper sense of connection to the organization and its mission. This results in increased retention, improved quality of work and, ultimately, a more pleasant work environment for both volunteers and employees.

Retention versus "New Blood"

When given a choice in life, most people pick the path of least resistance. Working with volunteers is no different. It's so much easier to go back to the same people over and over again; volunteers who we know will say yes, have a track record for success, and are easy to work with—however you define easy!

Given all the benefits of retention, it's hard to disagree with this strategy. But if you only focus on the same volunteers, you run the risk of burning these people out and, more important, lose the opportunity to cultivate new volunteer leadership. Although the institutional history that longtime volunteers offer can be a huge asset, it can also easily stifle creativity and innovation. "But we've always done it this way" is the most detrimental phrase a volunteer can say!

New volunteers bring a lot to an organization, including a different point of view, experiences, skills, energy, and both personal and professional connections—all vital resources for a thriving and successful organization. There is often a tension between longtime volunteers and new volunteers who are eager to make an impact and share their talents. Involving longtime volunteers in the onboar-ding and mentoring of new volunteers is one of the most effective ways to help ease this transition.

It's important to note that focusing on retention shouldn't mean you ignore bad behavior or volunteers who simply need to move on. Transition is a natural part of life and volunteering is no exception. One of my favorite volunteers—yes, we all have favorites!—informed me of her intention to leave an organization she had been a part of for many years and, indeed, had truly helped transform. "My 'sell-by' date has already passed," she told me. And with her gracious, self-deprecating humor fully intact, she reached a conclusion that I knew was the right thing for both the organization and her.

Technology—The Good and the Bad

Social media plays a vital role in keeping people connected and informed. Technology is opening whole new ways to engage people as volunteers. Taken together, these are powerful tools for increasing retention. They make it easier for people to volunteer and offer platforms to help reinforce a sense of community—shared values, a focus on mission, and opportunities to celebrate the people who make it happen.

There's also a downside to technology and the chance of overwhelming people with constant communications that lead to information overload. Just because you can send an e-mail with a push of a button or tweet in a second doesn't mean you have to. The goal of these technology platforms is not about bombarding people with reams of data, but making sure your information is easy to access and reinforces a sense of community.

Depending on a single technology platform to communicate can also have disadvantages. Intranets work great as a centralized repository, a single platform to post general information. If volunteers have access to an intranet and know that is the "go to" place—like a physical bulletin board in a centralized location—it can be a powerful resource for posting communications and helping to ensure volunteers feel like insiders. The problem is, intranets are passive and users have to proactively access them to benefit from their content.

Social media platforms like Facebook and, to some extent Twitter, are also passive—people have to proactively access them or set their mobile devices to receive push notifications. E-mails are definitely a more pro-active approach but, in this day and age when inboxes are flooded with a variety of communications, it's easy for important e-mails and messages to get lost. Texting is more immediate and ensures a written record and, with the wide adoption of smartphones, is an effective way to share short and time-sensitive information with your volunteers. (See Chapter 11 for more on communicating with volunteers via social media.)

But if it's truly important, I find there is one piece of technology, circa 1876, that still can't be beat—the telephone!

An organization that I worked with found itself in a situation of having to change the location of its board meeting with only a few hours' notice. The staff contact, focusing on her preferred method of communication and not on what was most effective for her volunteers, opted to send an e-mail that she tagged as "urgent." Most of the board members got the message, but one very important member—the board chairman—did not. As you can imagine, it unintentionally sent the wrong message and undermined past work to keep the volunteers engaged and supported. In a situation like this, the staff person should have used a blended approach—e-mails, texts, and phone calls—to ensure everyone got the message and verified it back.

Using technology as a communication and retention tool has tremendous benefits for an organization, but none of it replaces personal relationships that develop when people talk and interact in real time.

Retention—A Process to Maximize Volunteer Talent

Even though our good friends at Merriam-Webster define *retention* as a noun, the truth is that retention should really be thought of in its action-oriented form as a verb—*to retain*. It's less about a single act, and much more about all the things we do to keep volunteers feeling engaged, connected, and appreciated.

One of the best development directors I ever worked with summed up the secret to raising money from other people in a single word—"listen." I think that same advice applies to working with and keeping our volunteers engaged. We need to truly listen to our volunteers to understand what they want, what's working for them, what isn't, and what they need to be successful.

At the end of the day, people who volunteer want to make an impact and those who stay do so because they feel their volunteering is making a difference.

Conclusion

I've been fortunate to work with thousands of volunteers over the years in a variety of settings. When I think back on some of the best of the best, those volunteers who truly made a difference, I don't remember how long they served. What I do remember is what they accomplished. Ironically, although so many of our recognition programs and measurements are all about length of service—pins for years of service?—what's most important is the impact people make on our mission. Retention is often part of that impact—after all, it often takes sustained, long-term commitment to solve serious social problems—but it's only part of the picture.

In researching this topic, I came across an article I had published back in 1992 for *Voluntary Action Leadership*, a former magazine from the then-named Points of Light Foundation. The article listed ideas on how to retain volunteers. Although the world of volunteerism and service may have changed a whole lot over the past 23 years, much of what was on that list still makes sense today. People are still people, and the things that keep us connected to an organization remain remarkably constant over time and, I suspect, into the future as well. It turns out that treating people with respect, making them feel welcomed, giving them clear guidance, training, and ongoing support, and taking the time to acknowledge their impact will never go out of style.

With that in mind, here is my list of the top 12 ways to retain volunteers—ready to share with all your peers who partner with volunteers to fulfill your organization's mission:

12. *Be prepared.*

    The worst thing an organization can do is waste a volunteer's time. If volunteers show up prepared to work—whether for a committee meeting or to staff a silent auction or to mail invitations—you should be prepared to welcome them and support their work.

11. *Manage conflict, don't avoid it.*

    We usually think of conflict in the negative sense, but there is something to be said for a "healthy tension" when passionate people work together to achieve the best results, each bringing their unique point of view and talents to the table. Of course "good conflict" can easily escalate into a no-win situation in which people become entrenched in their opinions and things turn personal. This usually happens when small disagreements or differences of opinion are ignored and a triggering event, usually something minor, escalates the conflict. When working with volunteers, it's important to always have open and honest discussions, be direct yet respectful, and keep the discussion always focused on what's best for your organization's mission.

10. *Say "thank you" often.*

    I've never heard of a volunteer quitting because they felt over appreciated.

9. *Practice active listening.*

    Active listening is not just about hearing what people say, it's about understanding what they mean. It means actively reaching out to your volunteers to ask them how they're feeling about their experience, what's working, what's not, and what they need to be successful. It's also about looking for danger signs ahead of time—the defensive driving of working with people—and picking up on signs that people may be discouraged, overwhelmed, or are becoming disengaged. It's also about making sure you're present when talking with your volunteers—not multitasking with smartphones, papers, or other distractions.

8. *Understand that your organization is not your volunteer's number one priority in life.*

    Guilt may be a powerful motivator for some people, but it's not a good strategy to keep volunteers motivated and coming back.

7. *Pick up the phone.*

    Every now and then, skip the e-mail and pick up the phone to communicate with your volunteers. And it's okay to call just to say "hello" and "thank you."

6. *Ask for feedback.*

    On an annual basis, ask your volunteers to give an anonymous evaluation of the volunteer program and their experiences with your organization.

5. *Implement the best of it.*

    Listen to what your volunteers say in the anonymous evaluation (see #6 above) and, if they offer good advice, execute on it!

4. *Learn what makes each volunteer tick.*

    Get to know your volunteers as individuals and find out what they want to get out of their volunteer experience.

3. *Be flexible.*

   The ability to compromise, negotiate, rethink, problem solve, put yourself in another person's shoes, and find a win-win solution is key to not only successfully partnering with volunteers, but also to working with all people.

2. *Provide ongoing support.*

   Like all of us, volunteers need continuous feedback and support to stay connected and ensure everything is on track. Even the best and most committed volunteers can get sidetracked or find themselves on overload, and it's important to check in at appropriate intervals to offer support, check progress, and of course, just say "thank you."

   And the number-1 tip . . .

1. *Practice the Platinum Rule.*

   Treat others as *they* would want to be treated.

   Our sector provides an incredible opportunity to work in partnership with caring, passionate, and giving people. At the end of the day, 99.9 percent of our volunteers want to roll up their sleeves, make an impact, and feel valued for their contributions. Working with these people—all unique and wonderful—is a great gift. Putting ourselves in their shoes and understanding what they want to achieve helps us not only make a connection, but make a difference, too.

John L. Lipp is a writer and consultant on volunteerism and nonprofit management who has worked with a variety of organizations over the past 27 years and has served as a trainer and keynote speaker for national and international audiences. In 2002, he presented at the first Asia-Pacific Regional Conference on Volunteer Administration in Busan, Korea, and in 2005, he presented on volunteerism for the U.S. State Department in Argentina. John has published extensively and is a contributor to the online journal *e-Volunteerism* and Energize's Everyone Ready® series. John is the author of *The Complete Idiot's Guide to Recruiting and Managing Volunteers* and currently serves as National Director, Volunteer Engagement for JDRF, the leading global organization funding type-1 diabetes research.

Notes

1. Corporation for National and Community Service, *Volunteer Retention* (Washington, DC, 2007), 1–4, www.nationalservice.gov/issue-brief-volunteer-retention.
2. Corporation for National and Community Service, *Capitalizing on Volunteers' Skills: Volunteering by Occupation in America* (Washington, DC, 2008), 6, www.nationalservice.gov/pdf/08_0908_rpd_volunteer_occupation.pdf.
3. UPS Foundation, *Managing Volunteers* (St. Louis, MO, 1998), 12–14, academic.regis.edu/volunteer/specialcollection/SpecFiles/1998UPSsurvey.pdf.
4. Ibid., 14.
5. Mark A. Hagar, *Balancing Act: The Challenges and Benefits of Volunteers* (Washington, DC: The Urban Institute, 2004).

Chapter 8

Wholly Engaged: Integrating Volunteer and Donor Programs

Kelly Moran
Associate VP of Community Development, National MS Society

Taylor Mallia
Executive VP of Development, National MS Society

We are fortunate to work for the National Multiple Sclerosis Society where thousands of volunteers each year are engaged in all facets of our work. Volunteers participate in everything the organization does, from building the strategic plan to executing events and programs. Inherently, everyone knows that volunteers are critical to our organization, but is it right to stop at asking for their time?

In addition to our thousands of volunteers, National MS Society also has tens of thousands of donors who generously contribute each year. Similar to how the organization engages volunteers, National MS Society also has staff members who cultivate, solicit, and steward these financial gifts.

As colleagues, not long ago we began to notice how our work overlapped. By re-organizing some of our stewardship and cultivation procedures, and by thinking differently about the assumed relationship between giving time and giving money, we were able to inspire a greater number of volunteers to become donors, and we realized we were on to something big.

The verdict is in that volunteers give more than individuals who don't volunteer. Important recent research from both VolunteerMatch/Fidelity[1] and Blackbaud[2] shows that donors give more money if they also volunteer—7 to 10 times as much. But why? And how can organizations best take advantage of this?

Defining the "Holistic" in Cause Engagement

Merriam-Webster defines *holistic* as "concerned with wholes or with complete systems rather than with the analysis or treatment of the parts" of a system.[3] The *holistic in cause engagement* might be said to deal with all aspects of an individual's entire relationship with an organization or cause—including the time, money, or skills he or she might give at various points in time or simultaneously.

Because it views each aspect of this relationship as irrevocably connected with every other aspect—by positing, for example, that a declining jobs market might have a measurable impact on long-time volunteers—holistic engagement is likelier to produce sustainable outcomes than traditional cause engagement.

The obvious way to capitalize on this is to ask all volunteers to give—for example, by including them in the year-end appeal. But while that might make for a successful single fundraising campaign, it will not create long-term, holistic engagement. For a sustainable answer, consider examples in your organization that indicate that individuals successfully donate and volunteer. This is whole engagement. What is different about these relationships? Do these people naturally come to the table with everything they have? Or did they happen to be engaged differently by the organization in a way their time and money could work together to create a larger impact?

Volunteers are motivated to give because they are personally invested in the organization. We would wager that every reader of this book views time as their most precious commodity. When people volunteer with an organization they see their impact, feel a part of it through their participation, and understand the value their resources bring to the organization. Volunteers feel proud about this investment of their time and are motivated to return.

Organizations can take advantage of this type of engagement by treating volunteering and financial contributions as equal opportunities to engage, weighted and suited to meet each individual's needs. This will lead to a relationship-focused strategy that encourages each person to bring their whole self to the organization. Interested in learning more? Read on!

Same Mission, Similar Work

Volunteers are frequently invited to take part in delivering the mission of the organization. They are asked to plant gardens, design websites, deliver food, produce fundraising events, and even provide services to clients. The work they do bonds them to each other and to your staff.

Donors, on the other hand, are often cultivated with ideas. We educate them about our organizations and the problems we exist to solve. They are invited to luncheons, tours, shopping nights, and informational meetings. We share how their donation makes an impact and tell stories to help them see their generosity at work in the mission of the organization.

It's not hard to see how a volunteer's involvement taps more deeply into the emotional connection they might have for your cause. Volunteers often know from direct experience that their work made a difference in a person's life—they don't need to read about it in an annual report. Participation leads to empowerment. Empowerment leads to whole engagement. By directly delivering on the mission of the organization, people feel empowered. Opportunities that are both challenging and meaningful, and also connect people to other key staff and volunteers, are critical in accomplishing this.

Staff members are often the first offenders in perpetuating the notion that volunteers and donors are distinct groups. Certainly, this isn't something that your supporters probably ever consider! For reasons of history and tradition and "what makes business sense," specialization is the order of the day for more nonprofits that have reasonably large operations. Typically, one department leads volunteer engagement and another leads fundraising or donor engagement. And because only one of these departments is bringing in the cash, guess which one gets more resources?

We challenge this. Our experience—as well as much of the research available on why people give—has shown that individuals *simply want to be involved.* And involvement means consideration of all resources at their disposal—both time and money. By not labeling a person as a volunteer or a donor, you free them to contribute in all the ways they see potential. And they can engage more quickly in all parts of the organization of interest to them.

Whole engagement is much simpler than it seems. Engage supporters more deeply, and raise more money in the process.

Stewarding the Relationship

When you stop thinking about donors and volunteers, you start to notice that supporter engagement is a two-way street. Yes, we want to encourage our volunteers to give. But it's equally important to encourage our donors to volunteer. The idea is to encourage people to invest themselves wholeheartedly in the organization.

Volunteer engagement builds organizational capacity. We spend considerable time establishing strong volunteer engagement programs that connect volunteers with meaningful opportunities to create stronger results for the organization through greater impact. We publicly recognize how important their support is, and we shower them with gratitude via thank you notes, gifts, and recognition events.

But, once the project is complete and their great work has been acknowledged, what happens? Those volunteers often are put back into a database where they'll remain until the next project or organizational need arises.

What if we used the time between volunteer hours to steward their good work and to identify if they have the capacity and interest to make a financial contribution? Organizations often focus on how to steward gifts from donors, but do they spend time developing strategies to steward volunteers? If they did, what would happen?

Through consistent, meaningful communication, the organization would develop a stronger relationship with the volunteer, resulting in greater organizational capacity, stronger community connections, and increased donations. Stewarding volunteers is not unlike stewarding donors. The same basic principles apply.

Stewardship begins with the first volunteer activity or the first donation, and it continues until the volunteer or donor no longer has a relationship with the organization. So how can we be good stewards of time and money?

- *Acknowledge the good work.* Thank early, thank often.
- *Carve out time and resources.* Plan your work, work your plan.
- *Learn your volunteers.* Understand their motivations for volunteering and help identify their potential for giving.
- *Think before you ask.* Stewardship is not about preparing for the next ask. It's about engaging the volunteer more fully in the organization.

Effective stewardship ensures volunteers know they are valued, their efforts are acknowledged, and that they connect more fully with the organization—resulting in increased involvement.

Case Study: What Stewardship Looks Like

An individual had been a volunteer fundraiser for the National MS Society for two years. At an event, he struck up conversations with leadership staff and key volunteers and learned new insights into the work of the organization, The next day he called and said he wanted to make a small gift from his family foundation. The volunteer fundraiser told us about his family's history of entrepreneurship and his desire to give in a way that would strengthen the organization. We shared a new program the staff wanted to start that would offer funds and support for entrepreneurial volunteer leaders. We told him what it would take for this to be successful.

In the end, he not only funded the program, he also joined a leadership committee tasked with launching it. Six years later he remains a key volunteer and funder to the program. His support has helped us attract other donors and volunteers to the program. Additionally, he and his family have become involved in other programs, giving both their time and money as leaders in the organization.

This experience was successful because we enabled an individual to bring his whole self to the organization; we provided the opportunity to use both his financial resources and personal expertise to create change. Not forcing him to fit a mold yielded deeper levels of satisfaction for him and stronger results for National MS Society.

Movin' On Up

Although they may not know what it's called, donor development teams commonly apply moves-management methodologies to drive financial relationships forward. Moves management, popularized by David Dunlop at Cornell University, is the process of strengthening donor relationships over a period of time—commonly 12 to 18 months—using a series of initiatives to reach a desired goal. Dunlop, who led Cornell's major gifts program in the 1970s, described the process as "changing people's attitudes so they want to give."[4]

Moves should be viewed as cultivation opportunities within the defined plan that resonate with the donor and help staff learn more about their prospects. Simply put, they move the relationship with the donor forward toward the desired end goal. Examples of moves include a tour of your facility, invitations to special events, a meeting with the board chairman, or the opportunity to provide input into the organization's strategic direction. Internal processes will vary from organization to organization, and there isn't a one-size-fits-all approach that will work for every nonprofit. Instead, successful implementation of a moves-management plan depends on the ability of staff to both own the plan and be flexible in its execution.

Applying moves-management planning to your work builds the foundation for a proactive, strategic approach to volunteer and donor development. It serves as the road map for each relationship, and can drive collaboration and clear communication between departments as they are further developed.

So, how do we use moves management to ensure whole engagement? Plan, organize, and track moves designed to:

- Bring in prospective donors or volunteers.
- Establish a connection between them and your organization.

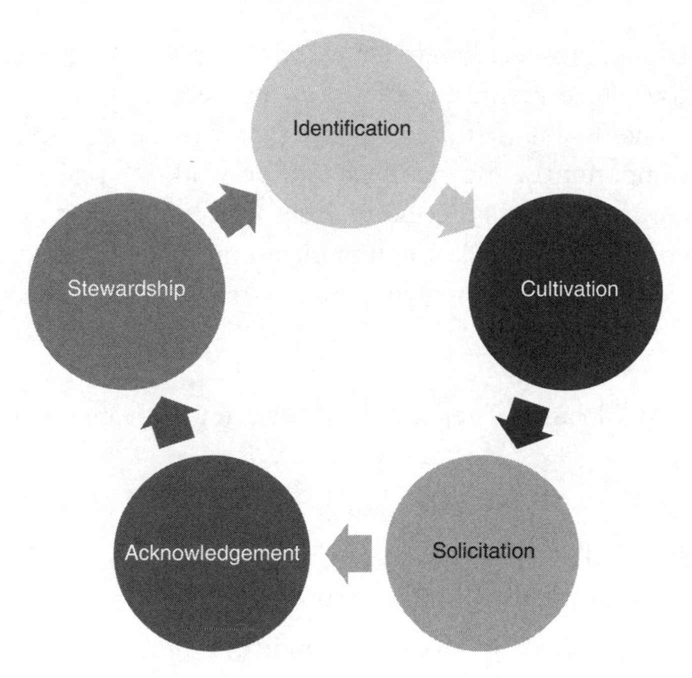

Figure 8.1 The Engagement Cycle
Source: National MS Society.

- Engage in lasting relationships that will increase both volunteer engagement and donations.

The strategy for each prospect should move them through the engagement cycle. (See Figure 8.1.)

At the end of the day, successful donor development and volunteer engagement are built on the same foundation: the ability to form deep, lifelong relationships between the individual and the organization. This is a critical skill that development and volunteer engagement leaders have mastered.

Too often, we focus on connecting with the individual personally. This is a natural tendency and is a comfortable way to get to know someone. But it does not establish a connection with the organization. The relationship becomes singular in focus and lacks depth. Often, if that staff member leaves the organization, the relationship goes with them.

To realize success in relationship building through moves management, it is critical that all departments are working together to develop and realize the plans. This can be the trickiest part of the work. We first have to identify our top volunteer and donor prospects, and then we have to pull a comprehensive team of staff from various departments and possibly volunteers to discuss each prospect, and then we have to build strategic plans that will move these relationships forward. Most importantly, the team has to then work the plan, discuss progress regularly, and course correct as necessary. It seems so simple, but working this way requires proactive planning, clear communication, and diligence.

Here are a few tips for applying moves management to create holistic engagement:

- Recognize and document relationships between your organization and its supporters.
- Build broad, organization-wide strategies that further relationships and subsequent support.
- Engage people in the planning process.
- Establish best practices and tools to support the process.
- Be nimble in order to respond to the changing needs of your organization and its supporters.
- Track progress to ensure success and communicate the results with all involved.

Buckets and Silos

Often, organizations put people in buckets. Supporters are managed by staff in different departments. Staff becomes focused on achieving their individual fiscal year goals without regard to collective, organizational goals. Communication breaks down. These buckets create natural silos.

Has silo become a four-letter word in your organization? It should be! Silos and siloed thinking are abstract concepts that don't reflect how the outside world views an organization. Volunteers who are willing to put the resources at their disposal to work for your mission don't see the walls we create internally. They see us as one unit. Each time you force volunteers to enter an organization through more than one door, you risk diluting their motivation or, worse, having them give up and walk away. Your organization has to operate in a way that supports the entire relationship, symbiotically.

Someone may begin supporting your organization by volunteering for an event, and then move to a program committee before eventually being invited to and accepting a board position. If we are intentional in this path, we grow the relationship through small steps, applying moves management. By weaving in opportunities to donate, you can identify those volunteers that may become donors. The key is not to make assumptions about how people want to engage with the organization, financially or otherwise.

A family who regularly donated to our organization moved from one part of the country to another. During this transition, staff from the two chapters connected to ensure a smooth transition for the donors when they arrived in their new city. Traditionally they had been donors and fundraisers, and were highly valued constituents.

Upon the family's arrival in their new hometown, they met with the local staff, and with that had the opportunity to redefine their relationship. As their goals and interests were discussed, it became apparent that they were interested in connecting with other couples who were involved like them. To accomplish this, we began inviting them to volunteer opportunities, in addition to the donor opportunities, to see where their interests would be strongest. The result of all of these connections was that the husband and wife each accepted separate leadership volunteer roles with different parts of the organization. Through these roles their giving and fundraising increased, exceeding what they initially contributed when we cultivated them only as donors.

An important thing to note is that not every volunteer will be a donor just as every donor will not volunteer. Strong moves-management plans that incorporate both volunteer and giving opportunities will allow the prospect to self-identify the most meaningful opportunities for them. Think of it as a real-life Choose Your Own Adventure book (remember those?)!

Getting Started: Moves Management

If you have a supporter you would like to engage further, reach out to your peers. Hold a discovery meeting at which each person who works with the individual can share what they know. Then use this information to tailor opportunities to their interests.

Listen and Learn

A cornerstone of relationship building is listening. In fact, it could be that listening is powerful because we so rarely do it! Most of us are uncomfortable with too much space in a conversation or a sales pitch, so we often feel it necessary to provide too much information, confident that the extra information will hit home. It's ironic then that people will usually spell out what they want the relationship to look like from the very first meeting, if we just let them do it. Learning to ask the right questions and actually hearing the answers will take you farther than any agenda developed before the meeting.

Some of our favorite questions include:

- What was your first gift to philanthropy and why?
- What inspired you to support this organization?
- What are your top three charities? If we aren't number 1, what do we have to do to get there? If we're not on the list, why?
- If you had a few minutes alone with our CEO, what would you say?

Along the lines of stewardship, volunteering is a strategic way to connect donors to your organization between contributions. Especially for stop-and-think gifts, donors may enjoy the opportunity to see their dollars at work, or even better, participate in moving the project forward that they are already supporting financially. This provides organic, two-way communication that connects the donor to the project and the exciting milestones along the way. This also changes the perception that organizations only call when they want money.

Frequently, nonprofits are reluctant to ask volunteers to give because they are "already doing so much." Nonprofits need to get over that one! Volunteering is an opportunity to build trust in an organization, which we believe is one key reason volunteers more often give than those who are not volunteering.

Getting Started: Listening

Practice makes progress. Set up a role-play scenario and try out a few questions of your own. With practice, you'll identify questions with which you are most comfortable to get people talking!

Bringing It All Together

Creating ways for volunteers and donors to interact is a critical step in helping supporters develop strong relationships with each other and create natural crossover. Peers can naturally encourage each other in a way that is different from paid staff members. Having a facilities tour for donors? Invite some of your key volunteers to attend who you know are interested in this work. Recognizing volunteers for their work? Invite the donors who funded the project and they can join you in sharing thanks.

Although peer-to-peer interactions are vital, staff members facilitate these opportunities. Talented staff are critical for any nonprofit to thrive. Individuals who specialize in volunteer engagement help organizations effectively engage leaders, equip volunteers, and encourage staff to work differently. It is at this last point that the capacity of organizations can be expanded, and it is there that volunteer and donor engagement can be integrated.

Volunteer engagement and donor development professionals can best work together in a partnership when the needs of the individual engaging with us are placed at the center. By looking at them as a whole person, we remove the labels of volunteer or donor that potentially limit us as an organization. Additionally, the work of each team can be improved.

As an example of this work, we point to our partnership, which led us to writing this article. We lead the donor development and volunteer engagement teams at National MS Society, South Central, but we understand each other's roles, goals, and the work we do. Individually we engage donors and volunteers in our portfolios, even though our focus is specialized. And we use the same core skills to achieve our objectives: relationship building, strong communication, and empowering supporters to impact the mission. By removing competition and focusing on results, a natural, easy partnership can be established that ensures the elimination of silos and allows our prospects the space to determine their most meaningful path.

We realize it's a bit pie-in-the-sky to expect departments to naturally want to consistently partner with each other. This brings us back to volunteer engagement being a part of everyone's job. In addition to making this part of the organizational conversation, each staff member should have performance goals that relate to volunteer engagement. Although this may sound rigid, there is a great deal of flexibility available. The goal could be to engage volunteers, or volunteers could be involved in the tactics for meeting the goal. For example, a person could have a goal to engage a committee to develop a new fundraising stream. Alternatively, in a goal to increase fundraising percentage, volunteers could be engaged to identify leads and solicit funds.

Beyond performance metrics, integrated tools are a key component for this to work. A database that shows the full picture of a person's involvement, in terms of both time and money, is essential. Beyond software, collaborative goals that keep the individual at the center will meet the objectives of both departments.

As you embark on this work, it is important to not try it out with everyone at first, but to select a few individuals who are ripe to be cultivated and then track their progress through the organization. Measure your success, learn from your work, and then see how your organization can blur the lines between volunteer and donor development. You will find that talented volunteer leaders are developed more efficiently and effectively when you encourage people to bring their whole selves to the organization.

Kelly Moran has worked to engage volunteers in creating a world free of MS for more than 10 years and today leads volunteer engagement for the South Central Region of the National Multiple Sclerosis Society. Kelly believes that fully engaging volunteers is the responsibility of every person at a nonprofit organization, and works to equip staff to utilize volunteers to accomplish meaningful, strategic work. She earned her Certified Volunteer Administrator credential in 2012 and currently serves on the test development committee to certify other experts in the field.

Taylor Mallia has worked in development and marketing for 15 years as a fundraiser, leader, and mentor. She now serves as Executive Vice President of Development for the National MS Society, South Central, leading the region's $30 million-plus fundraising efforts. Taylor's distinct knowledge of relationships with donors and fundraisers has been instrumental in the formation of the organization's current development model. Additionally, she has done extensive volunteer work with the American Lung Association, Make-A-Wish Foundation, SIRE, and Vita-Living. Taylor earned a BA in English and a minor in Public Relations at Texas A&M University.

Notes

1. VolunteerMatch/Fidelity Charitable Gift Fund, "Fidelity Charitable Gift Fund Volunteerism and Charitable Giving in 2009" (San Francisco, CA, 2009), 2, www.fidelitycharitable.org/docs/Volunteerism-Charitable-Giving-2009-Executive-Summary.pdf.
2. Blackbaud, "Connecting Online Advocacy and Fundraising" (Charleston, SC, 2011), 2, https://www.blackbaud.com/files/resources/downloads/WhitePaper_ConnectingOnlineAdvocacyAndFundraising.pdf.
3. For the complete definition of "holistic," visit www.merriam-webster.com/dictionary/holistic.
4. http://en.wikipedia.org/wiki/Moves_management.

Chapter 9

A New Engagement Model for the Internet Era

Mark Surman
Executive Director, Mozilla Foundation

Eleven years ago, thousands of volunteers rallied behind a small but scrappy Mozilla team to launch the campaign that eventually broke up the greatest monopoly the Internet had ever known.

At the time, if you had a computer, the chances were good that it came with Microsoft's Internet Explorer installed on it. This meant that your gatekeeper to the web, an open global network whose founders intended that it would be a public resource shared by all, was Microsoft, a single private company. Microsoft did not have a superior product. In fact, Internet Explorer 6 (IE6), released in 2001, was so universally disliked that it would later show up on many lists of the worst technology products of all time.[1]

Microsoft didn't have to try harder. They held such a big share of browser market worldwide—more than 95 percent—that they could afford to sit on their laurels. IE6 broke a lot of websites and left out many of the most innovative web technologies. Viruses and pop up ads plagued the browser. And—as Microsoft attempted to fuse the web into its integrated vision of Windows, Office, and

MSN—critics warned that Microsoft products might eventually be required in order to communicate, collaborate, and conduct global commerce on the web at all. Microsoft had become an empire seeking to set the rules for how people accessed and shaped the web.

Mozilla Foundation was created to change this. Building our first product, Firefox, from the bones of an early browser called Netscape, Mozilla launched into the limelight with an audacious and memorable ad campaign. On the right panel of the ad was the new Firefox logo hovering above a message announcing the new Firefox 1.0, "the free, open sourced browser from the Mozilla Foundation." On the left, the logo was set against a backdrop of printed names of more than 10,000 campaign supporters and the simple question: "Are you fed up with your web browser?"[2]

The December 2004 ad was the death knell for Microsoft's dominance of the web. Firefox struck a nerve with web users who cared about innovation and freedom. Soon independent and very engaged Firefox supporters were speaking out everywhere about the need for openness in new technology. Teens were installing Firefox on their parents' computers and teaching them how to use it. And although IE6 would remain in active circulation for another three years, its successor would eventually include so many of Firefox's features that a joke went around: What was the best version of Firefox ever? Answer: Internet Explorer 7.

The Power of the New Engagement

No single mastermind can claim credit for this achievement. Instead, it was a wildly diverse, global community brought together through their shared commitment to a singular goal: to protect and build the open web. But the notable thing wasn't the ad's size or reach, but that Mozilla didn't pay for it or place it. It was a grassroots effort, dreamed up and funded by 10,000 engaged Firefox users. Mozilla had a marketing person who jumped in to help make sure the ad actually made it into the *Times* on time, but the concept, design, money, and grassroots push were all led by an inspired movement of independent supporters with a vision for a different kind of Internet and a belief that the Mozilla Foundation offered the most effective means for getting there.

In their book *The Networked Nonprofit* (2010), Beth Kanter and Alison Fine argue that, in the future, organizations would act more as conduits for social change—absorbing, directing, and amplifying supporter passions to create more resilient communities.[3] They use the phrase *free agent* to describe these volunteers, but *ambassador*, *agent*, *champion*, and *affiliate* could all refer to the independent volunteer with a passion to make a difference, a commitment to a specific nonprofit's approach, and the freedom to innovate to support the cause.

Can volunteers help your nonprofit be successful? Turn the question upside down: Can your nonprofit help supporters create the world they want to live in? In this chapter I'll explore what motivates volunteers like Mozilla's to want to do more for the organization they care about. I'll suggest ideas for how you might think about developing a new engagement model that fits for your organization. And, I'll open up about the big challenges ahead that keep my team awake at night and how we plan to mobilize volunteers for global impact—even if we don't yet know all the details.

Today the browser wars are over and Mozilla Foundation is a nonprofit social enterprise generating north of $300 million a year. At the same time, the free and open web is facing vast challenges similar to those it faced when we first started out. In fact, the issues are more complex and the empires who seek to control the web are stronger. To win these battles, Mozilla's supporters will again be the most critical piece.

Don't Be the Change, Be the Solution

Attracting truly committed supporters starts with being good at what you do. It means being visionary and pragmatic. It means being real. The fact that most nonprofits can't demonstrate their impact well makes it relatively easy to stand out.

The new engagement that will drive social change in the future makes demonstrating impact paramount. In the Internet era, people who really care about an issue will simply start up their own organization if there isn't already a great one to get behind. Existing organizations need to not only be working on a cause that people want to support, they need to convince potential supporters that getting involved with them is *one of the best ways in the world* to live their values. This requires something more than giving supporters just a way to pitch in and volunteer; it requires giving them a platform to build the world they want to see.

Although the truly engaged supporter is *motivated* by a fierce passion to fight for the cause with you, his or her work must be *empowered and amplified* by organizational programs and strategies that provide the ability to get involved at more than a passing level. To put it another way—for your volunteers to be the change, your organization needs to be the solution.

Have a Clear Enemy or Goal

Getting involved with a cause is essentially an act of imagination: *Can we create the change we want to see?*

One thing that gave Mozilla a clear leg up was that it was easy to name the bad guy. For a lot of people, Microsoft was sort of like the Borg from Star Trek: powerful, amoral, everywhere. Resistance was futile. The face of Microsoft was CEO Bill Gates, the richest man in the world. (This was before he became synonymous with philanthropy.) Huge numbers of people thought Microsoft needed to be stopped.

Can you put a name or a face on your enemy? For a lot of organizations today, the enemies are abstractions like illiteracy, hunger, sickness, and death. But it helps to be more specific. A certain piece of legislation that will defund after-school programs. Big banks that force families to take on subprime loans. The Ebola virus. Volunteers are the hero of their stories, and every hero needs a villain so their own role is clearly defined and can easily be communicated to others.

Have a Compelling Call to Action

Mozilla's first volunteers weren't necessarily regular activists. We couldn't rent a list of names of people we thought would support us. And because they were from all over the globe, we didn't know them personally. They were drawn to us because they saw in Mozilla a group of people that shared their values, their fight, and were positioned to make a difference.

The initial question that motivated Mozilla was big: Will the values of freedom and openness from the first 20 years of the web continue for the next 200? And essentially the message that we were trying to convey to the world was our answer to this question: *By supporting Mozilla, installing Firefox, and spreading the word about it, you'll help take back the Internet and keep the web open forever*. This was a message that resonated with a lot of people who could see how technology was changing the world.

Figures 9.1 through 9.4 show a few other resonant messages from organizations you've probably heard of before. They're all kick-ass, if you ask me, and millions of engaged supporters over the years have agreed.

Good messages have a way of sliding past all the barricades we put up to reduce the static of modern life. As you consider a new engagement strategy, ask whether your core message is strong enough to entice and ultimately inspire someone you've never met before to take action.

WIKIMEDIA
FOUNDATION

You can help bring the sum of all human knowledge to the world.

Loans that change lives

For as little as $25 you can create opportunity around the world.

Help students by giving great teachers what they need to succeed.

TEACHFORAMERICA

Help fill all classrooms with passionate, high achieving teachers.

Figures 9.1, 9.2, 9.3, and 9.4

Sources: Wikimedia Foundation 2014/CCBY-SA 3.0; Kiva.org 2014; DonorsChoose.org 2014; Teach for America 2014

Let People Run with Your Message—and Your Brand

The world is both shrinking and also getting more diverse as social technology enables people to organize into groups defined by shared interests. Today there are niche communities built around geography, social backgrounds, politics, and every lifestyle. If scaling up your mission to make a big impact depends on reaching a lot of people with your message, you need help doing the talking.

Until very recently, brands of all kinds (including for-profits) struggled with the idea of giving up control of who represents them and how. Back then, conversations about using social media to advance a cause were often dominated by "what-if" scenarios and urged to have social media policies and to invest in training and messaging platforms to help keep supporters and staff in line.

Today organizations that get the new engagement know that it's not about control—it's about empowerment. If the "SpreadFirefox" campaign were to take place today, there's no doubt it would have taken place in social rather than mainstream media—and controlling the message would be impossible. Fortunately social media also makes it easier than ever for organizations to educate and inform supporters in real time about issues, equip them with consistent, coherent, and sharable media, and provide spaces in the real world and online where peer-to-peer activities can take place. (For more about social media and volunteer engagement, see Chapter 11.)

Theory of Change: Use Supporters + Product to Shape the Market

The founders of Mozilla wanted to create something popular enough to push the entire market where we wanted it to go. That was key to our theory of change: build our values into products that people want to use—which will ultimately build our values into the web. Think of environmental groups trying to create demand for recycled paper. If consumers want recycled paper, it's not just the small eco-businesses that are making doing the right thing popular, it's also the big paper companies. It's this type of systemic change that we were trying to do by building the values of openness and freedom into Firefox.

Getting into the marketplace also had one huge advantage for us as a nonprofit: it made it a lot easier for potential supporters to find us and take action. They simply needed to install Firefox to get started. This powerful fusion of people and product has been key to Mozilla's impact thus far—and we know it will power our future as well because engaging volunteers is a key part of our theory of change.

What's a *theory of change*? A good way to look at it would be to imagine what the world will look like when your organization reaches its goals, and then map backward to fill in all things that will be required in order for it to happen.[4] The more embedded or fundamental supporters are to exacting your theory of change, the more likely you are to get the resources to keep them moving. In our case, as an organization that wants to stay meaningful and powerful for as long as it takes to solve the root issues we are working on, it's essential for us to sustain and draw in new supporters. Knowing that Mozilla is built from the ground up for this makes it easier to plan programs and products that are people-powered.

Lessons Learned

1. Have a clear enemy or goal.
2. Have a compelling call to action.
3. Let people run with your message—and your brand.
4. Use supporters + product to shape the market.

Expanding Our Engagement Model

When Mozilla Foundation started out, we had little more than a base of code donated by Netscape, 10 employees, some donations, and a bit of seed money. Today we have 1,000 employees and millions of "Mozillian" supporters and donors around the world. Not surprisingly, while the organization grew and evolved, the model for how we worked with our supporters has had to expand, too.

Our first supporters helped out in much the same way you see in the open-source movement. People with coding and design skills contributed to make a better product. (See Figure 9.5.) This group of "Core Contributors" led to the release of Firefox 1.0.

In our second phase, nontechnical folks got involved as brand advocates, marketers, and campaigners to spread the word and grow the Mozilla brand. During this time, our group of core tech contributors kept growing and churning

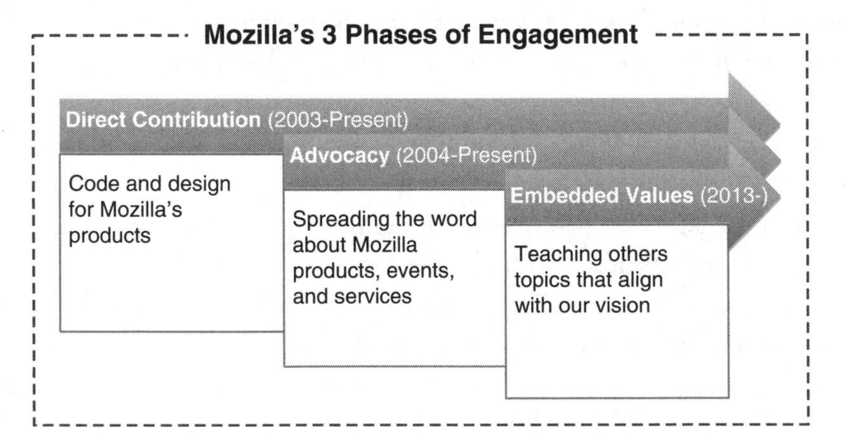

Figure 9.5 Mozilla's Three Phases of Engagement
Source: Mozilla Foundation, 2014.

out new versions of Firefox and other Mozilla products. You really saw this in the SpreadFirefox campaign.

Today, supporter engagement at Mozilla continues to involve people who contribute code and people who produce Firefox—but it's also expanding in important ways as the landscape has changed. Although the web has made our lives better for the most part, it both faces and offers new threats. People who care about choice and independence on the web are looking to Mozilla for solutions to create, teach, and share in non-commercial ways, to be good citizens of the web and the world, and of course to use the open Internet safely and securely on any device. Figuring out how to do all of this will take time—but it's possible that the next phase of supporter engagement will center on a global community that may be more interested in the cause of an open and independent web than in using any specific Mozilla product.

Each of these phases required a different way of thinking about how we leverage our most engaged volunteers. Each required different tools and resources, and each phase necessitated new ways of measuring and assessing success.

With the explosion of Internet-connected gadgets, our work is getting a lot more complicated. Today our objectives have expanded to encompass the much bigger challenges. One of these challenges is educating a growing world of technology users and developers about a free and open web. But even among Mozilla's 1,000-plus current staff, we have nowhere near the local knowledge that we need to effectively engage communities in far-flung places like Bangladesh or Nepal. With Firefox we were able to achieve both depth and scale. To do the same with digital literacy means Mozilla must reach into local communities around the world.

Fortunately Mozilla has a theory of change that balances product potential with people power to give us a competitive edge. As Figure 9.5 shows, the new engagement means going beyond developing products like Firefox that people can believe in and instead seeing Mozilla itself as the platform for engagement—becoming a tool to help potentially millions of people who care about the open web inspire and engage others. This is a big conceptual shift for Mozilla, frankly, and we are actively testing several programs in this area because we aren't yet sure what will be most effective. But if things work, by 2017:

- We'll have demonstrated that investing in volunteer activity has a significant return on investment for our products and our volunteers.
- We'll have built these activities into programs that have impact at scale.

- Mozilla activities will occur around the world without centralized decision-making.
- There will be more "Mozilla" activities than employees can keep track of, let alone control.

Case Study: Mozilla's Webmaker Program

Mozilla Webmaker is a pilot program launched in 2012. The idea was to test a promising approach to engaging individuals around the world as teachers and advocates for web literacy and what's possible with an open web. The program was inspired by the Maker Movement, a global subculture based on using existing technologies in new ways. The fundamental challenge for Webmaker is how to get both *depth* and *scale*. By 2024, there will be more than 5 billion people using the web; to be global *and* local also means having native understanding of languages, customs, and habits.

Mozilla set up a site (www.webmaker.org) with tools, event calendars, and teaching guides to allow "Webmakers" to create content and learn how the web works. The program encourages motivated groups of mentors in local communities to teach and train others in the culture of "making as learning."

Mozilla has developed curricula, but it's also inviting people to write their own plans, conduct their own trainings, plan their own events, and organize their own clubs. Importantly, the program design reflects the same values of independence and freedom that Mozilla is trying to teach.

In its second full year, Webmaker has already gone well beyond expectations. More than 5,000 teachers, librarians, parents, designers, engineers, and marketers have helped to organize 2,513 learning events for more than 127,000 learners in 86 countries. Mozillians in India organized 250 events in two months. Iran, New Zealand, and Sweden all saw their first-ever Webmaker parties, adding to the evidence that this effort is truly global.[5]

Because of Webmaker and our other new-generation pilot programs, in just a few years Mozilla has already seen great value in peer-to-peer contact and that it's possible to develop a mix of high-, low-, and no-touch activities that can be sustained at scale moving forward.

These things may seem self-evident, but they aren't; they come from years of work in the world and a great deal of internal reflection. We don't have all the answers about what we need to do next, but we can see where we want to go. And we can see the key ingredients in keeping supporters engaged as we go there.

No matter where your organization is on the subject of change, here are some ways to think about finding an engagement model that fits your organization.

Openness and Transparency

Many of us say we value working in an open, transparent fashion, but openness can also make us uncomfortable. That's why we tend not to know what our coworkers are earning.

Openness and transparency are vital for nonprofits that want to achieve lasting participation and breakthroughs from independent volunteers. Volunteers may want a say in your day-to-day decisions, to know their true social impact, or be able to see what's going on so they can collaborate together better. These are just a few scenarios in which openness and transparency are a functional requirement for working with volunteers at a high level.

What level of openness are you comfortable with? For us, these values are central to the "Mozilla effect" of getting people to galvanize around our products and programs. Today, even as large as we are, anyone can still get the phone number to call into our weekly development meetings. We practice what we preach—operating Mozilla in the same "open" fashion we demand of the web.

Clear Roles and Identities That Supporters Can Grab Onto

Although many of our original volunteers understood what was at stake in the browser war, many others connected with Mozilla because they identified as rebels in their own lives. Fighting Microsoft was a way to express this identity, just as volunteering anywhere is a powerful way to let others know who we are and what we stand for—and, more, a way to act on it.

It could be because our engagement model continues to evolve, but a decade later, identity is still a challenging thing at Mozilla. For example, I tend to use the word *Mozillians* interchangeably with *supporters* or *volunteers* in this chapter, but not everyone agrees with me. In fact, beyond the core contributors who work on our products, it's not always clear which volunteers get which labels—and this is a topic that comes up surprisingly often during Mozilla's many online and in-person gatherings.

Volunteers can't easily travel or come into the office, and often they'll never get to meet the staff of your organization in person. So markers of identity become critically important "badges" of their involvement in your cause. Take care when considering how to brand these volunteers so they can stand out and communicate their values to others. You can also organize online groups, events, and gatherings to help cement supporter identity and a sense of belonging.

A Way for Supporters to Innovate and Find Breakthroughs

In the traditional nonprofit lens, volunteering is about individuals pitching in. The language we use tends to be about mobilizing advocates and generating donations. One problem with this is that it may not do enough to create opportunities for skilled volunteers to achieve breakthroughs.

Breakthroughs are the giant leaps that really move things forward, and they require more than creativity. Organizations need to have process built up around innovation so that breakthroughs, when they come, can be transformed into supported programs that achieve real gains. In the early days, we did this by letting people submit new ideas through code or putting their own spin on our marketing campaigns. Today we're looking for new ways for this to happen by inviting people to teach the web in new ways and then share their curriculum with others. We're constantly trying to get better at this.

Whatever the specific approach, creating opportunities for breakthroughs from volunteers is one of the most difficult—and most important—challenges that modern nonprofits face. That's because here the question of leadership is also the question of innovation. In fact, deep in the heart of the challenge of creating opportunities for breakthroughs is the challenge of modeling an organization that is open from the inside out at the very top all the way to the very bottom.

The formula for volunteer involvement should be straightforward, right? Just find the right people, get more of them, and get them all aligned around your challenges. But what about when you are relying on supporters for innovation?

For some organizations, big ideas are handed down from the top. At others, like Mozilla, big innovations often come from the edges of our network via supporters with ideas we might not have been able to see on our own. Have an idea to make a crop circle? If it aligns with our mission, just do it. Remember: In the new engagement model, volunteers have their own personal agency and anything they can do that moves in the direction of the mission is welcome. If they don't need to ask first, all the better. Eliminate a permission culture.

This question of distributed leadership versus core leadership is one of those big, meaty business school topics that can be hard to wrap your brain around. But if volunteers are critical to the success of your organization, it's worth considering. At Mozilla, we design for edge innovation as a core value.

Tools and Training That Let People Get Involved

When planning to engage highly independent supporters, it's easy to get sidetracked with the details of creating ambassador marketing kits, developing free-agent trainings, launching do-it-yourself learning management systems, and signing people up for peer-based listservs. But the bigger questions are about organizational culture, innovation, and leadership. Those need to be in place first.

I don't want you to think that having the right tools and systems in place can be avoided. Very often the best contributions we've had from our supporters have been aided and shaped by the systems we've deployed. It's just that quite often Mozilla's core supporters have also done amazing things regardless of the tools we've given them!

In Mozilla's case, we have tended to develop new tools for organizing and supporting the efforts of our volunteers either well before they were needed, or well after the great work was already happening. Along the way, we've also learned that there are times when you need to budget to spend money on logos, marketing pieces, and distribution systems.

Key Ingredients for the Future

- Openness and transparency
- Clear roles and identities that supporters can grab onto
- A way for supporters to innovate and find breakthroughs
- Tools and training that let people get involved

Conclusion: Beyond the Next Million Mozillians

When I became executive director at Mozilla I wrote a blog post summarizing the challenges I thought we faced titled "The Next Million Mozillians." The goal was exciting but seemed really enormous at the time. Six years later our impact is profoundly greater but so too are the stakes. One thing that hasn't changed is how we demonstrate what Mozilla can be when it is at its best—thousands of people assuming leadership and helping to inspire and empower others around them to do amazing things.

There's no doubt that pivoting to new engagement models built on empowering supporters to create their own change will help any organization accomplish more. But that's true of all deep involvement in a nonprofit mission by volunteers. The greater opportunity represented by the new engagement is that your community will grow more resilient to these changing times. You will never know what the future will be, but having a network of truly engaged volunteers will help you be open and ready for what comes.

Mark Surman is the Executive Director of the Mozilla Foundation, the makers of Firefox and one of the largest social enterprises in the world. Prior to joining Mozilla, Mark worked as a consultant and social entrepreneur designing and implementing community-driven technology projects for organizations including the Government of Canada, Amnesty International, and Greenpeace. He has raised more than $30 million, authored two books, presented at more than 100 conferences, written dozens of papers, and traveled to more than 40 countries. Mark was awarded a Shuttleworth Foundation Fellowship and holds a BA in the History of Community Media from the University of Toronto.

Notes

1. http://en.wikipedia.org/wiki/Internet_Explorer_6.
2. Download the ad at blog.mozilla.org/press/files/2013/11/nytimes-firefox-final.pdf.
3. Beth Kanter and Allison Fine, *The Networked Nonprofit* (Hoboken, NJ: Jossey-Bass, 2010), 204.
4. http://en.wikipedia.org/wiki/Theory_of_change.
5. For a full report on Mozilla's Webmaker events, see https://party.webmaker.org.

Chapter 10

Meet Your New Board

Linda Davis
CEO, Center of Volunteer and Nonprofit Leadership

David Styers
Manager of Program & Business Development, Presidio Institute

Although it may seem self-evident, a nonprofit's board members are volunteers, too. In fact, there may be those nonprofits that do not use direct-service volunteers, but every nonprofit has to have a board of directors. These governance volunteers may come from a nonprofit's pool of direct-service volunteers, but often nonprofits do not treat their boards like the valuable volunteer resource that they can be. And this negative perception about boards can lead to nonprofits having a hard time attracting board members.

The new board needs to be one that is sure of its purpose and value to the organization, besides being just a legal requirement. As in any volunteering, engagement is the key to maximizing volunteering involvement and helping board members feel they are making the most impact. With board service, nonprofits need to think about not only what new energy and perspectives they need on the board but also what new types of board members they require that may be very different from ones in the past.

Anticipating tomorrow—constituent and stakeholder needs, shifts in funding streams, board composition, and on and on—is critical for leadership today. The nonprofit sector has been undergoing tremendous change in recent years from the downturn in the economy to the beginning generational shift of organizational leadership. Nonprofits, their boards, and volunteers are all having to learn to live in the new normal that has resulted in society, communities, and daily lives, and adapt accordingly. If your board has not changed much in the past decade or so, then the time to meet your new board is now.

Engaging Your New Board Members

Do your board meetings feel like a replay of the last one, or those of the past decade? Are your board members feeling burned out, or does your board struggle to reach a quorum? Do board members feel trapped and guilty about rotating off, or do you have board members who don't realize they have overstayed their welcome? These signs can be symptoms of a disengaging board.

Serving as a board member is one of the most challenging and rewarding volunteer assignments in any nonprofit. Not only will volunteer board members get to make a difference in people's lives, but they will also have new leadership opportunities negotiating decisions and building relationships with peers in the boardroom. A great benefit for board members is gaining a fresh perspective of their community and earning recognition both within the community and at work.

The nonprofit sector in the United States includes more than 1.6 million tax-exempt organizations registered with the IRS.[1] And the average size of a nonprofit board as reported by BoardSource is 15 members.[2] Accordingly, there is a collective need of nearly a quarter of a million volunteers each year to serve as board members. And although everyone should engage as a volunteer, not everyone is right for a board.

Nonprofits need to start with whom they have. Look at your current board members. Are there any auditors—meaning anyone who acts more like they are "auditing" the board like a college class as opposed to being engaged for a grade? Hopefully, most board members are there for a grade, and a high one at that! Board members who are not up to performing need to either move on or step up their level of performance.

Conducting a board self-assessment every two to three years is a great way for a board to understand where its strengths lie and where improvements are necessary. These improvement areas identify what new skills and talents are needed in new board members. Finding new board members will be discussed at the end of the chapter, though, as in fundraising, developing current board members who are ready to up their game is easier than finding a replacement board member.

Tips for evolving a board member include making sure:

- There are clear roles and responsibilities.
- Board members are held accountable for these expectations.
- Training is provided on effective board governance.
- Exceptional board members are recognized as models for others.

Direct-Service versus Governance Volunteering

Every person has something to give to nonprofits, whether time, talent, or treasure. Nonprofits should focus on finding the best volunteer fit for each individual. Particularly for boards, nonprofits need to make sure all board members have a passion for the mission and understand the difference between being a direct-service volunteer as opposed to a volunteer board member. Each is needed, valuable, and in demand, and many individuals may serve one or the other or both at a nonprofit at any given time.

Consider board service from the perspective of volunteers. As direct-service volunteers, they:

- Are active on a regular basis, often setting their own schedules with the organization.
- Can be involved in hands-on activities, either where their skills are the strongest or where they are doing something totally different from what they are used to doing.
- Can feel good about saving money for the organization they want to help, because it does not have to pay someone to do it.
- Do not have any legal responsibilities for the organization.

But as a board member, they:

- Influence the present and future of the organization as they help determine its priorities.

- Use their strategic skills and have a chance to brainstorm about the key issues affecting the organization.
- Serve as a thought partner to the chief executive and staff and as an official ambassador for the organization.
- Can rely on their people skills as they function as a member of a (usually) small team of different people with different perspectives.
- Are not committed to daily work or a "regular" schedule—but the more time they are willing to devote to board responsibilities, the more appreciated and valued they will likely be.

As individuals toggle back and forth simultaneously as board members and volunteers, it is always important to solicit feedback during their tenure and especially after (i.e., an exit interview) to get their perspectives and thoughts on how better to improve the organization and most importantly advance its mission. Ask questions such as:

- What has been your proudest moment or a highlight experience?
- What has been your biggest disappointment?
- What are the organization's greatest strengths and opportunities?
- What are the organization's severest weaknesses and threats?
- What are your wishes for the organization's future?
- Would you recommend someone else serve on this board—why or why not?

Passion versus Competency

There may be a lot of pressure to find new board members (or coerce current board members) to be bigger givers and fundraisers for the organization. This attitude is a self-defeating battle. A disengaged, dispassionate board will never be successful in ensuring the necessary resources for an organization.

Many people volunteer for nonprofit boards because they strongly wish to support a cause that is personally meaningful to them. Others may feel that after achieving success in the world, they have the skills or means to contribute back to the communities in which they live or which have been generous to them in the past. Sometimes nonprofits may feel that they have to pick between a potential board member who is passionate about their mission versus another who has strong competencies in management, nonprofit governance, or some other relevant skill set.

Passion is the most important criteria any nonprofit should use in selecting board members, and those with needed competencies can still be engaged as pro bono, skill-based volunteers. Without passion to help, there is no hope for success, and from this seed, passion for the organization will continue to grow if nurtured. Crises of some sort or another, such as financial or leadership, inevitably can hit any nonprofit. Board members who are not passionate about the mission are more likely to bail when the going gets tough. It takes a great passion for the mission to motivate board members to take on the hard, even yeoman, task to help a nonprofit weather a storm. Without these passionate individuals, the organization will likely sink.

In addition to passion, these individuals must also have a desire to truly engage and be engaged in governance. No one comes to board service with a major in nonprofit governance, so much of the expertise needed is learned on the job or through educational offerings by nonprofit management and governance support organizations. Also, it is important to learn about the prior board experiences of board members. Some may clearly understand what it means to be an effective board member today ("Board 2.0"), whereas others may be stuck in old models of board service ("Board 1.0") or have no board experience at all. All board members have to serve on their first board, and it is up to every nonprofit to make sure that they have a meaningful experience and will want to serve on subsequent boards in the future.

Building a constructive partnership between the board and staff, particularly the chief executive, is critically important. Staff members are connected daily with the mission of the organization and need to learn how to share their passion and experience with the board. Board members need to be engaged but not be disruptive by interfering with staff operations (micromanaging) and getting lost in the weeds. Giving board members meaty governance issues to chew on will keep them involved at the right level looking at the right things.

Thus, nonprofits need to deliver in appropriate and intentional ways. Even the most passionate board members will lose heart if he or she does not feel appreciated or that he or she adds value to the governance of the organization. And the competent ones will be so frustrated that they jump ship if they feel like they can't make positive change or if they believe their time is being wasted. Exceptional boards see their members as a value add and are committed to engaging them. By providing board members with opportunities to develop their governance competency and increase their passion for the mission, boards will capitalize on their talents and skills to have generative conversations to make the best decisions for the organizations.

The Mind of Today's Board Member

Usually, nonprofits talk about what their needs are and recruit volunteers to meet those needs. Particularly with board service, individuals may be overwhelmed with expectations and responsibilities. Understanding board obligations is important, but agencies should also sell the benefits of being board members. Regardless of the reason someone volunteers, committed board members, like any volunteer, stand to gain both personally and professionally from participation on nonprofit boards in the following ways:

Experience—Peers on the board are likely to come from a wide range of backgrounds, experiences, and social groups. As part of the board team, board members are required to plan and make decisions for the good of the organization. They have opportunities to practice new ways of working in groups, influencing decisions, and negotiating toward a common goal and opportunities to network and to interact with other business professionals and community members.

Board experience helps volunteers cultivate valuable human relationships while developing important leadership skills, such as decision-making; consensus building, and influencing peers; in addition to practical skills, such as financial planning, strategic planning, fundraising, and so forth. Nonprofits benefit from the experience of a diverse group of passionate ambassadors to outreach to the community and lead the organization into the future.

In thinking about the new board, a changing aspect of volunteering that applies to boards is the transition from a motivation centered on "How can I help the agency?" to one based on the proverbial WIIFM—"What's in it for me?" Too many boards during recruitment focus on what they need from potential new board members, and most (too often) just focus on money. Board members are looked at for their transactional interaction with the organization (sometimes as nothing more than ATM machines) as opposed to what type of relationship the organization should build with the board members. As mentioned, there are many benefits from serving on boards, and organizations should make it clear what those benefits are for service on their board.

The nonprofit sector is entering a period of generational transition and opportunity. (For more on these trends, see Chapter 1.) Generations X and Y represent more than 100 million potential volunteers, yet only 17 percent of current board members are under the age of 40.[3] With more than 78 million individuals, baby boomers make up a huge chunk of today's board membership, but with a dramatically smaller Generation X population of around 46 million soon to follow, it's clear there will be fewer people to lead and fill board positions for some time.

So the new board will inevitably have to be younger and more open to change. Although the nonprofit sector has made some progress on increasing diversity among board members,[4] organizations need to realize that to successfully recruit and retain the best staff and volunteer leaders, they have to show that they value unique talents and invite multiple voices. Boards that reflect the diverse nature of society are in a better position to remain relevant, effective, and grounded in the needs of the community. Also, grant makers are increasingly focused on diversity, and diverse organizations are more likely to attract diverse donors—people give where they feel welcomed or valued.

To engage younger board members, boards need to look at their current practices and see if they are potentially creating barriers for participation. The time and/or location of board meetings potentially will need to be adjusted. Even the method of meeting, including more virtual meetings, may be required.

Retaining Your New Board Members

Retaining is easier than recruiting. And although there should always be regular turnover and refreshing of the board by bringing on new members, nonprofits need to make board service a rewarding way to make a contribution to society. Like any volunteer experience, board service should be a positive one, or these individuals will not come back or will swear off board service altogether, which hurts the entire nonprofit sector. Yet, any board member who does not look forward to fulfilling his or her board responsibilities should not be on the board.

To ensure that board service at your organization is fun, satisfying, and rewarding, most of the same principles that guide effective volunteer engagement can be applied to board development, too:

- *Create a Plan*
  - Conduct regular assessments of gaps and future needs of the board.
  - Ensure diversity of board composition.
  - Determine the best number of board members and their terms.
  - Stay current on board governance trends.

  - Assess board positions on a regular basis.
  - Write position descriptions for board members, officers, and committees.
  - Build a team of staff and board members.
  - Review and revise your bylaws and structure as appropriate.
- *Recruit*
  - Plan a board recruitment strategy.
  - Organize a recruitment team, which is often the governance committee.
  - Implement the recruitment plan.
  - Create a screening process.
- *Orient and Train*
  - Organize board-orientation training for the new and current members.
  - Organize general education about the organization and its cause.
  - Involve new board members in committees.
- *Supervise and Recognize*
  - Hold board members accountable for their involvement and commitments.
  - Understand the internal and external motivators of your board members.
  - Develop and implement a board recognition plan.
  - Have a beginning, middle, and end for board projects and the work of committee task teams, and recognize member accomplishments.
- *Evaluate*
  - Develop a plan to evaluate board meetings as well as the board as a whole.
  - Use the results of the evaluation in future planning.

For more on retaining volunteers and board members, see Chapter 7.

Finding Your New Board Members

Have you ever found yourself in this tricky situation? A cherished local nonprofit had been serving the community for decades and never needed to scramble for donations or board members. The beloved chief executive of the organization retired after years of service, and the board chair worked swiftly and with little guidance to bring on a new leader.

Two years later, the organization stagnated under the inconsistent, disappointing leadership of this new chief executive. One by one, the chair saw fellow board members resign, frustrated and disillusioned. The chair, too, was beginning to feel hopeless, especially now that her comrades—and their critical connections—were leaving the organization.

A couple of weeks before the annual meeting at which new board members are elected, the nominating committee gets together to figure out how many seats are now vacant and which of their friends they can con into filling them, as they all worry about the organization collapsing on their watch. Does this board recruitment scenario sound familiar to you?

As with direct-service volunteering, one of the biggest challenges facing nonprofits is recruiting new board members. Board responsibilities and the commitment needed to fulfill them should never be underestimated. Candidates should understand the nature of the job and be selected, not because they deserve to receive special recognition, but, rather, for their dedication to uphold the mission of the organization. For the board to be effective, board members need to take their appointment seriously.

Use of Technology and Third-Party Recruitment

Boards need to be reflective and representative of a wide range of individuals in the community from both the public and private sectors. A good board is made up of individuals who can contribute critically needed skills, experience, perspective, wisdom, time, money, connections, and other resources to the organization. Because no one person can provide all these qualities, and because the needs of an organization continually change, a board should have a well-conceived plan to identify and recruit the most appropriate people to serve on the board.

Imagine a future in which you have a waitlist of people wanting to serve on your board, in which you are turning down potential board members or at least saying "not now." Ideally, every board would have a growing pipeline of prospective board members. These individuals would typically have some involvement or association with the organization, whether as direct-service volunteers or, at least, participants in programs or special events, and, ideally, as donors. "Cold calling" potential board members is usually just as ineffective as cold calling potential donors. In nearly every case, your organization should start with the circle of people closest to you to recruit board members—for example, volunteers, funders, and constituents.

Many organizations, however, find themselves at a loss to identify new board members. And recruiting board members the same way a board has always done may cause it to fall into the trap of bringing on more of the same. Here are some tips on reaching out to recruit board members from your own network and beyond:

Use the 'net to fish a deeper sea.

Technology has certainly changed the way all aspects of society and organizations function, including volunteer and board recruitment. Although board members usually come from "within the family," posting board member positions, just like any volunteer position, on various volunteer matching websites such as VolunteerMatch.org or Idealist.org allows the organization to cast a wider net, and attract potential new interest into the fold from a bigger, untapped, and unknown candidate pool.

Consider an executive-search process.

Given the leadership potential that new board members bring, some organizations invest in hiring outside consultants or executive search firms to proactively recruit potential board members. This process, which can also be led by a skilled volunteer with relevant professional experience, is similar to recruiting for a new chief executive. Board recruitment experts can craft position descriptions, develop processes, turn over new stones, and employ the best practices of human resource management to find new board talent.

Create a governance committee.

Instead of having a nominating committee that functions on occasion, the board should appoint a governance committee that focuses on board composition, education, and evaluation on a year-round basis. The governance committee functions like a "board search committee" identifying needs for the board in the future, cultivating potential individuals to help meet those needs, and recruiting the right board members for the organization.

Get tips from your team.

For boards to be diverse and inclusive, they need to be networking with a diverse group of people who can connect them with new board members. The search committee should ask current board members, senior staff, advisory committee members, stakeholders, and others to suggest potential candidates with needed characteristics.

Move outside your typical spheres of influence.

To expand its pool of potential candidates, boards need to find ways to connect with potential diverse candidates by visiting outside its usual suspects, such as reaching out to new civic and neighborhood associations, and making one-on-one introductions with the organization and leaders to get others interested in their organization. Inviting them to attend events and volunteer for the organization and keeping them informed of your progress helps with the cultivation process.

Partnering with Other Organizations to Help Find Board Members

Many communities have volunteer centers or other nonprofit management support organizations that can help local nonprofits find new board members. For example, in Marin County, California, the Center for Volunteer and Nonprofit Leadership offers BoardMatch Marin, a free, personalized matching program that seeks to connect service-minded individuals from the community with nonprofits that are in need of board members. Based on a candidate's background and personal interests, BoardMatch Marin provides recruitment and placement of qualified board members as well as expert training and consultation, with services available to board candidates, current board members, and executive staff.

Potential board candidates complete an online application describing their board service interests, and likewise, nonprofit agencies complete an online application describing their board needs. Master Volunteers, also known as "MVPs," offer free, personalized consultation sessions to prospective board members. The MVP suggests board member opportunities that meet a prospect's interests, skills, and schedule and offers ongoing support until he or she is successfully matched.

Agency staff, current board members, and prospective board candidates should look for organizations in their community that offer governance training and support services. On a national level, BoardSource offers an online board recruitment center with tips and tools to help find board members.[5]

Linda Davis has served as the Chief Executive Officer of the Center for Volunteer and Nonprofit Leadership since 2002. Linda has over 30 years' experience in nonprofit management, working with both local and national organizations on a diversity of issues. Linda is the immediate past board president of the California Association of Nonprofits and a board member for the Marin Economic Forum and Marin County School to Career Partnership. She is past president of the Marin National Organization for Women, and a former member of the Marin Independent Journal editorial board and the Marin Red Cross Leadership Council.

David Styers brings more than 22 years of consulting and training experience in leadership development and board governance. Since 2012, David has served as senior board governance consultant for the Center for Volunteer and Nonprofit Leadership, and, since 2007, he has served as senior governance consultant for BoardSource. Currently, he manages program and business development for the Presidio Institute at the Presidio Trust. With an extensive background in volunteer development and capacity building, David also worked on the forefront of civic engagement as Senior Director at Points of Light from 2000 to 2007. David has served on many nonprofit boards in all officer positions.

Notes

1. Urban Institute, "Nonprofit Almanac," 2012, www.urban.org/books/nonprofit-almanac-2012.
2. BoardSource, "2014 Leading with Intent," (2014), 1, www.boardsource.org/eweb/images/bds2012/Leading-with-intent-PV.pdf.
3. Ibid., 3.
4. Ibid.
5. Visit the Board Recruitment Center at BoardSource's website at www.boardsource.org/eweb/dynamicpage.aspx?webcode=Board-Recruitment-Center.

PART THREE

Changing Technology

Chapter 11

Volunteer Engagement on the Social Web

Amy Sample Ward
CEO, NTEN: The Nonprofit Technology Network

In August 2014, Nextdoor, an online social network where members are limited based on their physical address and surrounding neighborhood, reported that the site had reached one out of every four American communities.[1] In 2011, German officials explored banning Facebook events because of serious overcrowding at some parties that were posted to public calendars on the site. Each month more than 500,000 events are organized at Meetup.com.[2]

Most of us think of social media as being online phenomena. In reality, social media is just as often produced and consumed as a prelude to actions in the real world. To put it another way, social media can be the bridge between the virtual world and the offline world where the impact of your mission lives.

Usually social media is discussed within the context of raising awareness and generating funds. But done well, social media can also accelerate the traditional three Rs of recruitment, retention, and recognition of volunteers. For most nonprofits, volunteers get involved in what many would consider to be offline activities: producing conferences, setting up events, helping out with fundraisers, office administration, and so on. All these contributions have online components, and the volunteers involved in these efforts have opportunities to engage with each other and with you online.

Alliance for Climate Education (ACE) educates young people about climate science and equips them with the resources and inspiration to take action—small and large—in their homes and schools. ACE educators use school assemblies or classroom presentations to connect with students and a text messaging short code for students to make pledges about the actions they want to take. These personal pledges are added to the database so ACE staff can track and support the various kinds of projects individuals can take at home or volunteer groups can organize for the entire school. Social media, including Facebook, e-mail, and text messaging, connect students and educators that participated together offline in a social channel where they can continue receiving information, reminders, and additional support for making real impact.

Ultimately, none of us will be able to fully meet our missions purely online. With social media, you have the opportunity to create real connection and ongoing relationship development with your community online between offline events. The social web is driven by our offline world—your conferences, programs, galas, and services are all part of it.

In this chapter I'll first put social media into the context of how nonprofits usually operate, and then explore how to use social media effectively and safely to engage volunteers.

How Does Social Media Fit In?

Realistically, social media can't be your only form of communication or information sharing. E-mail still rules and there's no substitute for the phone on a one to one basis. Social media is a valuable and unique channel for volunteer engagement because it brings together five characteristics that directly enhance the volunteer experience:

1. *Real-time*—Social media allows for you and your volunteers to connect and respond immediately.
2. *Public*—Social media operates in public, which means you can connect your volunteers to your greater community, or quickly move content from a small group to a large audience.

3. *Shareable*—Photos, videos, or text in social media are inherently sharable, whether through likes, shares, or retweets.
4. *Multidirectional*—Unlike traditional channels, social media allows for conversations to engage multiple people at the same time, or for content from one network to be easily shared on another platform with a different subgroup.
5. *Personal*—Organizations that succeed on social media share themselves and others. They allow supporters and staff to have a personal voice and encourage them to engage with followers and fans as peers.

When we combine these elements, we have an outlet for creating and sharing information or content that can encourage engagement between volunteers and with the community, easily support calls to action, and create real relationships between volunteers and your organization.

Your Community versus Everyone Else

The same questions always come up when I talk to nonprofits about social media: How can we talk to everyone? How do you make a video go viral? Which channel has the most people? These kinds of responses are natural. We see videos help raise thousands of dollars for organizations with hundreds of thousands of followers. Then we meet people who could benefit from our services and they've never heard of us.

Trying to solve this problem by creating a video we hope goes viral or joining Facebook to talk about all of the work we do is probably not going to get us there, though.

We can't jump from having no volunteers (or donors, or supporters, or participants) to many just by creating a Facebook page or posting a YouTube video. And, because of the nature of their features and audiences, we also can't engage the same way on a Facebook page as with a YouTube video. Recognizing those differences can help us select the best tools and make the most of our time and capacity.

Community, Network, and the Crowd

Although we often use these words interchangeably, there really are differences between the concepts of *community*, *network*, and *crowd*. Recognizing the

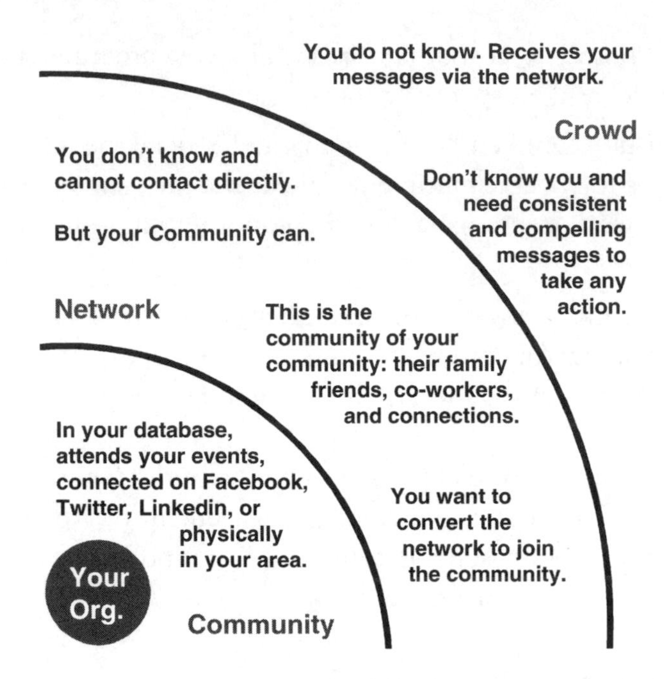

Figure 11.1 The Relationship of Organization to Community, Network, and Crowd
Source: A. Kapin and A. Sample Ward, *Social Change Anytime Anywhere* (San Francisco, CA: Jossey-Bass, 2013).

distinctions can help you better plan for engagement, recruitment, and even ongoing communication with your volunteers. Refer to Figure 11.1 for the specific characteristics of each group.

Community

Your community is the layer closest to your organization and includes everyone who is directly connected to the organization. These are people who have signed up for your newsletters, received your e-mail alerts, followed you on Facebook. The key thing is that you can communicate with your community when you need to (and they can communicate with you). These are the people who already believe your work is important, so you don't need to "sell" them on it every time you communicate.

Network

Your network is made of the friends, family, and co-workers of everyone in your community. You can't directly communicate with your network right now, but you can connect with them by communicating with your community members and asking them to share, invite, or otherwise spread your messages to their own communities. Since you are only able to talk to your network by connecting first with your community, these messages usually need to have some information, links, or other context so that when the community forwards your message to their friends, they'll be able to learn more about your organization.

Crowd

The crowd is, most simply, everyone else; for practical purposes we can categorize this group as all those you are hoping to connect with but haven't reached yet through your community or the immediate network. These people haven't engaged with you and don't know about your work, but that doesn't mean they aren't interested.

Communicating with the crowd requires creating content that is compelling enough that your community will share it with their friends, family, and co-workers (your network), and those people will promote out to their friends, family, and beyond (the crowd).

Volunteers in Your Community

Of course, not every person on your e-mail list, attending your events, giving donations, or even benefiting from your programs or services has the same interest in your mission or the same motivation for participating. Treating everyone on the e-mail list the same sets you up for poor response rates and low engagement.

Mapping your community to understand how it's made up is a simple process:

1. *Identify your groups.* The more specific you can be, the better: not just donors, but maybe monthly donors, first-time donors, annual donors, large-gift donors, and so on.
2. *Articulate each group's goals for their engagement.* A monthly donor, for example, may want to support your mission through regular financial

contributions as well as be recognized as a valuable supporter. Your goal for this group would be to increase their gift size or maybe diversify their participation.

3. *Note the various channels or tools for communicating with your groups.* Each group may have multiple answers! For monthly donors, e-mail and Facebook will probably be a channel with the organization, as well as occasional phone calls at the number you have on file,

Volunteers will probably fall within many different groups in your community map. You may see volunteering as a goal for moving a program participant up the engagement ladder; you may see volunteering as an entry point to becoming a donor. It is crucial to pinpoint where volunteering is positioned within your organization's overall engagement ladder and capacity needs.

When you have a clear picture of your community, you're ready to craft valuable and meaningful plans for working with them.

Learn Where Your Community Is Online

You know your volunteers or your event attendees are using the social web, but which platforms are they on and where should you invest your time? Ask them!

- *Surveys:* Do you have annual surveys about your programs or participants? Add a question or two asking which platforms your supporters prefer.
- *Quick Polls:* Already using some social media tools? Log in and ask your supporters on the platform what content they like or would like to see.
- *Sign-Up Forms:* When someone signs up for your e-mails or newsletter, do they submit a form on your website? Add an optional field to the form asking with which social media tools they would also like to engage with you.

Social Media for Volunteer Recruitment

Recruiting new volunteers with social media starts with having a volunteer listing posted on your own website, as well as leading recruitment platforms like VolunteerMatch.org or Idealist.org. VolunteerMatch has the biggest audience and most participation. Idealist has more international activity. (Check out Chapter 21 to learn how to create a clear, inspiring message that will attract the right prospects.)

Through the community mapping process you were able identify where volunteers are hanging out online. Simply cross posting the links to your volunteer opportunity listings isn't much in the spirit of social media, though. Social media for volunteer recruitment calls for content that highlights the engaging, personal, and immediate value of volunteering for your organization—so think about using photos and videos.

Show the Pathway

Volunteers weren't always your volunteers. Use social media to tell the story of how key supporters decided to volunteer and use those stories to highlight their path to eventually giving their time and energy.

For example, instead of highlighting just the details of a volunteer event, share the story of a few volunteers and how they first got involved. Girls Inc., based in Portland, Oregon, likes to share the kind of work that a volunteer does to show that volunteering is something that working professionals can fit in.

Highlight Rewards

Emotional content is highly engaging and you should use that to your advantage, especially in positioning your volunteer opportunities as rewarding and even life-changing contributions. Post photos of volunteers celebrating a great event, or of volunteers and program participants connecting.

You should also use social media to celebrate your collective impact. Credit your volunteers! This content will also be powerful to share with donors, funders, and other supporters.

Social Media for Volunteer Management

Volunteer management can take many shapes and forms, especially considering that often volunteers are self-organizing, sharing, or collaborating on their own.

Using social media as a component of volunteer management depends more on whom the volunteers are and what they are trying to do, rather than which tools your organization may use.

For example, Carizon Family and Community Services in Kitchener, Ontario, utilizes a private group on Facebook for communicating with volunteers. The organization also has a page on Facebook for sharing content and communicating with other groups in the community, but they wanted somewhere dedicated to their volunteers so they could have their own space to connect. As Volunteer Coordinator Dale Gellately explains, many of their volunteers are university students so creating a closed group on a platform where they were already participating made the most sense.

Current and previous volunteers all participate in the private Facebook group to welcome new people, to share programmatic information or schedule changes, and to have conversations among the volunteers. The biggest contributor for success with the group, in Dale's opinion, is "keeping it fresh without overwhelming it with too many posts."

As you recruit volunteers, ask them what kind of ongoing communication they want with other volunteers. If you mostly have one-off volunteer opportunities, it may be more difficult to mobilize those individuals in a private group because their interest may parallel general interest supporters more than volunteers. If you do create a dedicated online social space for volunteers, like Dale did, be sure to ask the community first what tool or tools they are already using.

Creating Volunteer-to-Volunteer Connections

Recruiting new volunteers for every event, program, and campaign takes much more organizational capacity than retaining the volunteers who have already participated. When you create the sense of community with and among your volunteers, the likelihood of retention increases. (See Chapter 7 for more on how to keep your volunteers.)

Social media is a valuable tool in retention because it can allow you as the organization to create relationships and shared experiences with the volunteers and, especially, connect volunteers to each other to build relationships rooted in a positive experience with you.

Amplify Content and Storytelling

When you aren't actively planning an event or coordinating with your volunteers online, you can still engage them with "ready-to-share" content. Post updates that are packaged to make reposting, retweeting, or forwarding easy. One tip: Volunteers are in a great position to personalize your organization's message because they've participated and contributed to your success. When you ask volunteers to share, encourage them to add their own voice, story, or even photos or videos to the post.

Social Media for Volunteer Retention

The volunteer experience starts with their first contact with your organization—it isn't simply about the day spent volunteering. Having a positive experience, of course, contributes massively to whether that volunteer ever comes back. Social media can support your focus on retention by creating a connection with the volunteer before, during, and after the volunteer opportunity.

Onboarding

If you have a private group, e-mail list, upcoming orientation call, or even simply a page on your website with information for volunteers, inviting new volunteers to check it out should be one of your first steps. Even if you've never had a volunteer and this is your first-ever event, you will ensure a much more positive experience for volunteers by spending some time upfront organizing resources, information about your organization, and expectations for their involvement.

Mentoring

Got a volunteer? Then you're ready to start peer mentoring as part of your next volunteer orientation. Using social media, start highlighting volunteers who have participated before, introducing new volunteers as they join, and even suggesting that experienced volunteers share tips and suggestions.

At NTEN, volunteers organize and run monthly public events focused on technology topics for nonprofits. If an interested community member wants to start a monthly event in their own city, they get added to a private online discussion group with other local organizers. This allows the new local organizer to meet many others tackling the same kind of challenges and have an immediate support network to ask questions, test ideas, or share success. In NTEN's experience, the volunteers who contribute and engage in the organizers' group are almost always the ones who stay on as organizers the longest.

Collaborative Capacity Building

Create ways for your volunteers to regularly edit or contribute to the shared materials that they use. Inviting a volunteer to contribute to "official" resources for your organization's volunteers can be an empowering opportunity as well as a valuable engagement between other volunteering or events. Whether you have documentation on how to run an event, transcripts from training or orientation calls, or ongoing documentation from campaigns, your volunteers are often in a great position to identify what did and didn't work for next time.

Multichannel Strategies for Volunteers

We check Instagram and send text messages while watching television. We read news online and share links on Twitter. Volunteers are no exception to this multichannel reality—they may find out about you from Facebook, a hashtag on Twitter, or even a forwarded e-mail. Jason Shim, at Pathways to Education Canada, uses Google Adwords ads[3] to connect potential volunteers when they search with keywords like *volunteer*, *volunteer with youth*, and *volunteer opportunities in Toronto* (see Figure 11.2).

"This began as an experiment, and it was challenging to track the metrics at first because after people find out about the opportunities, they'll often call," explains Jason. But now staff are reporting "a significant increase" in people mentioning they found out about the opportunities via Google.

Making Sense of Available Platforms

Just as social media doesn't attract the same users, the social web isn't a homogenous landscape where all platforms and applications do the same thing. You don't need to have a profile on every platform—it's probably impossible to do with the thousands of applications there are, anyway! Understanding the actions or content that is of interest to your volunteers will help you anticipate when there may be a new tool that's of interest.

Figure 11.2 Sample Google Ads from Pathways to Education Canada

As you can see in Figure 11.3, the social web can be broken out into categories of platforms based on their function or content type. Choose platforms wisely. If your after-school volunteers like to share photos, choose an application that supports photo sharing like Facebook, Flickr, or Instagram. (Of course, be sure to review privacy and security policies first; sites that allow for private groups or photos may be a better choice for youth or other vulnerable constituencies.)

Adopting New Tools

When adopting a new tool for use with volunteers, listening is key. Often, volunteers will find a new tool first. Regularly check in about the tools that are in use, if they are meeting needs, or if there are opportunities to improve. Participation is the key metric here; if volunteers won't want to log in to a specific site, it doesn't matter if it meets technical needs or not.

Whether the impetus comes from community members or from you, it is best to communicate that there's a change ahead in advance. Explain why you are adding or changing platforms and keep conversation open. Identify who may want to help set up the new platform and champion the change. When it is ready

Figure 11.3 The Social Media Landscape
Source: FredCavazza.net.

for everyone, let your champions announce it and orient others to their new, shared space.

Things to Consider When Selecting Tools

What works for one person may not work for another and it's impossible to find something that everyone loves equally. The following questions can help you find the tools that may work for the most people:

- Does this fill a need that participants have articulated or identified?
- What is the financial cost to download, access, or otherwise use the application?
- What is the "time cost" for learning and using the application?

- How frequently will participants need to access the application?
- Is it accessible across operating systems, devices, and languages?
- What are the privacy options?
- What are the content options?

Evaluating Success

Engaging with you on social media is probably not required for every volunteer role. It can be extremely influential, though, in supporting success and retention. As such, goals for engaging volunteers in social media shouldn't reflect the extremes or be based on 100 percent participation.

Goals should also be tied to the volunteer role's unique function or program. For promoting and marketing events, participation in social media ahead of time may be explicitly required for volunteers. For preparing an event, volunteers may find it valuable to participate in a group or access online resources, but doing so may not be required. Once the event is happening, sharing photos or live highlights would most likely just distract from the day-of-event tasks.

Focus on actions and engagement instead of individual platforms. For example, setting a goal for how many volunteers report feeling supported by and connected to other volunteers may tell you more about your success or what needs to change than how many volunteers shared content on Facebook. (For more about measuring and evaluating volunteer engagement programs, see Chapter 20.)

Putting Safety First in Social Media

Using social media isn't risk-free. Regardless of your technical savvy, there are plenty of examples out there to prove that you may still slip up. Accidentally posting private thoughts on your professional profile is just the start. Unfortunately, there's no foolproof system to protect yourself or your organization. We are all humans, even your volunteers! But you *can* create policies and guidelines that recognize we aren't perfect but do want to do our best.

Staff and Volunteer Policies

Just as you have (or should have!) an employee handbook, you should also develop a volunteer policy—and part of it should deal with social-media use. (Check out Chapter 21 for more on developing volunteer policies.) The focus of this handbook shouldn't be identifying what not to do or say—you will never be able to create an exhaustive list of the things volunteers shouldn't do. Instead, it should include three areas: information about the organization and how it uses social media, suggestions and guidelines for positive social media use, and the consequences of bad behavior.

Security and Safety

One of the biggest security risks you can take is to create a social media account that is managed exclusively by a volunteer. Too often this leaves organizations without login credentials or any way to moderate volunteer activity. The volunteer becomes unresponsive or moves away and they have no way of engaging with community members in those channels. Many, many organizations have done this, and I'm sure that soon I'll be adding more commas to the list!

Your standard practice should require that only staff set up the original profiles or accounts for each service and that a staff e-mail is tied to the password retrieval or reset prompt. The good news is that this also ensures that staff members are the ones to set up the branding and other organizational information in the account—which means it will also be up-to-date and correct.

Another security concern is that of physical location reporting. Social media is rife with geo-location tags, check-ins, and maps. If you have volunteers working in a safe shelter or other sensitive location, show them how to disable location sharing on their devices so that, in their eagerness to share, they do not accidentally endanger others. A general policy for social media at events or with high-profile individuals is to "check out" instead of check in. That is, post content from sensitive places once you've left the location instead of when you arrive.

Engagement Policies

Your social media guidelines should reflect your culture and values. If you have a communications or style guide, include it in the handbook so that volunteers can get a better sense of the voice and priorities of the organization. Additionally, consider including the following policies and modifying them to fit your organization:

Don't be afraid to say no.

If you are using social media on behalf of the organization or personally in promotion of the organization, and other members of the community request to connect with you directly, you are under no obligation to accept. Your personal, private profiles are yours and you can set up the privacy levels that you are comfortable with.

Be honest and transparent.

It is always appropriate to tell someone—whether a community member, interested citizen, news reporter, or otherwise—that you are a volunteer. If you receive messages that you do not have information to address, respond that you are a volunteer and will pass on the questions or the feedback to staff for a complete response.

Be a good ambassador.

Supporting the organization as a volunteer is valuable. You are not expected to share everything we post and know everything we do. Whatever inspires you about our work, whichever programs are most important to you, share them and be a cheerleader.

Give credit.

When sharing information, resources, or even photos, always give credit for the source. This is not only a best practice for content sharing but also a valuable way to demonstrate the diversity of content and contributions.

Be respectful.

The social web has some important obstacles to face when it comes to creating a safe, inclusive, participatory space. Our volunteers should not be part of extending those issues. Please behave and communicate in a way that is consistent with our policies concerning harassment and discrimination as well as the community's values for engagement.

Conclusion

Social media can be instrumental in an organization's volunteer recruitment, management, and retention efforts. It can also bolster the work your staff invests in and create new opportunities for growing the organization's community. Social media can also be a time suck, a frustration, and even a legal liability.

Starting with an understanding of who your volunteers are, why they've come to your organization, and the kinds of content or engagement that makes sense to support them will ensure that your time and energy are put to use in the most effective places.

Ultimately, the social web should be a complement to your website and a supplement to other communication channels. If social media is your only way to reach your volunteers, you may find yourself in trouble if something happens to that account, if the functionality of the tool changes, or even if that social media platform stops providing the service. It can't be everything for you, but it can contribute to a volunteer engagement plan that truly serves both your goals and your volunteers.

Amy Sample Ward is an author and speaker focused on technology and social impact. She works with nonprofits of all sizes around the world to use technology to better meet their missions. She is the co-author, along with Allyson Kapin, of *Social Change Anytime Everywhere: How to Implement Online Multichannel Strategies to Spark Advocacy, Raise Money, and Engage Your Community.* Amy is the CEO of NTEN: The Nonprofit Technology Network, a member organization that believes all nonprofits can make lasting change with the help of technology to be more effective and efficient.

Notes

1. B. Popper, "The Anti-Facebook: One in Four American Neighborhoods Are Now Using This Private Social Network," *The Verge*, August 18, 2014.
2. Meetup.com "About" page, www.meetup.com/about.
3. Google Adwords grants are available as part of the Google for Nonprofits program, providing $10,000 value of Adwords per month to participating nonprofits. Learn more at google.com/nonprofit.

Chapter 12

Microvolunteering for Big Impact

Mike Bright
Founder, Help From Home

The United Nations Volunteers issued a report in late December 2011, describing the state of global volunteerism. In the report, United Nations Volunteers highlighted three of the fastest growing trends in volunteering around the world: corporate volunteer engagement, travel-related volunteering (or "voluntourism"), and the less well-known practice of microvolunteering.[1]

It's ironic that when the report was released, much of the discussion that I was seeing about microvolunteering revolved around whether it was actually just a passing fad or not. I'm pleased to say to those naysayers that, not only was the news of its early demise greatly exaggerated, its staying power now even warrants a chapter in this book!

Although microvolunteering is considered a niche subset within the virtual volunteering sector, it contains within it huge potential to transform the way in which nonprofit tasks and projects can be completed by people who have a spare few minutes or hours on their hands.

Microvolunteering seems to be challenging some of the cherished beliefs held about the need to foster long-term volunteer relationships. This is in part due to the dip-in, dip-out, no-commitment attitude that prevails among microvolunteers.

This is leading some nonprofits to recruit people purely for the sake of participating in a single project, rather than nurturing them for any long-term volunteer involvement.

Microvolunteering can be conducted on the go, on demand, and on a person's own terms. In relation to your life, think of the moments when you're busy doing nothing. Maybe you're at the bus stop, in a doctor's waiting room, or just in bed. These are all times when you could be microvolunteering—or to put it another way these are all times when your nonprofit could be asking people to microvolunteer for you.

But can such a small amount of effort create impact? That depends on the micro-action itself. But by way of a whimsical demonstration, consider this. At any one time, a third of the world's population could be in bed. That's close to 2.41 billion people. If they all spent 10 minutes microvolunteering before they tucked themselves in, it would equate to 45,090 years volunteered. Or, if they microvolunteered via Freerice.com, a website dedicated to feeding the hungry that is owned and operated by the United Nations World Food Programme, their efforts would feed 120,367 hungry people two bowls of rice per day for a whole year.[2]

Sure, there's plenty of other things that a person can do in bed, and although you're not going to learn about them from this book, this chapter will help transform your way of thinking about how to potentially encourage people to volunteer in the spare moments of their life—a time period that is not generally engaged by the traditional volunteering sector.

So What Is Microvolunteering?

There are quite a few definitions out there to describe microvolunteering. These are usually dictated by the remit of the organization promoting the concept, many of whom have clear motivation to either make their own services more attractive to clients or to boost their own sector as being socially innovative. However, the definition I like the most (because it stands out as being more representative of the type of micro-actions available today) is:

> Microvolunteering is bite-size volunteering with no commitment to repeat and with minimum formality, involving short and specific actions that are quick to start and complete.[3]

Characteristics

Although various distinguishing features can be identified within a microvolunteering action, not all of them may be present in any one opportunity. However, they all have one thing in common: the economy of time (thus the prefix *micro*). Different platforms adopt different time criteria—those that promote skilled microvolunteering opportunities tend to place an upper limit of two hours on a task, whereas those that promote unskilled micro-actions tend to restrict it to 30 minutes.

Among its other characteristics, a micro-action is also:

- Able to be performed by a single volunteer.
- One-off or repeatable.
- Conducted online or offline (although it is usually associated with online).
- Either skilled or unskilled.
- Available on demand and on the go.
- Unlikely to require an application process, screening, or special training.
- Not likely to require a formal agreement between volunteer and nonprofit.
- Usually marked by a beginning and an end.
- Free from ongoing commitment.
- Usually crowd-sourced (whether by a few people or by thousands).
- Rarely of critical immediate importance to the organization.
- Not involved in handling sensitive or proprietary data.

Brief History

Microvolunteering has arguably been around for ages—at least as long as nonprofits have asked volunteers to give an hour here or an hour there. Think of nonprofits asking people to be a volunteer taxi driver for the visually impaired, or committing to a shift on a charity stall. They just weren't labeled as such.

Jayne Cravens, the pioneer who helped popularize virtual volunteering, coined the term *byte-sized volunteering* back in the 1990s to describe short-term online volunteering tasks that could be completed in just a few minutes and did not require any ongoing commitment. (For more on virtual volunteering, see Chapter 13.)

Fast-forward to 2008, arguably "The Year of the Microvolunteer."

First, Spain-based Microvoluntarios created what could arguably be defined as the first modern microvolunteering network. It offered an online system for nonprofits to post requests for help with simple actions that people with professional skills could complete in 15 to 120 minutes.

That year the U.S. firm The Extraordinaries (now known as SkillsForChange.com) also set up a skilled microvolunteering brokerage platform. Their efforts went on to ignite the attention of the media and volunteering world and, eventually, popularized the concept we see today.

And for unskilled microvolunteering actions that could be accomplished by the masses regardless of their professional skills, my own organization, Help From Home, first brokered these in the UK in December of 2008.

Today, there are over 30 dedicated microvolunteering platforms around the world. But the term *microvolunteering* has not suited everybody over the years—largely because, since the demise of The Extraordinaries, there has been no real effort by any single organization to "own" the term and popularize it. Various terms have included *snack-sized volunteering*, *byte-sized volunteering*, *mobile volunteering*, *micro-tasking*, *episodic volunteering*, *slacktivism*, *clicktivism*, *ad-hoc volunteering*, *mini-help*, *speed volunteering*, and *micro-actions*. In reality there's no real reason for you to use the term microvolunteering at all; if another one seems more appropriate, go for it!

Action Types

You're probably wondering what a micro-action looks like and how different it might be to a traditional volunteering opportunity. For the purposes of providing examples, microvolunteering actions can be categorized into two distinct types—skilled and unskilled. Some micro-actions may look like traditional volunteering activities, but at the end of the day it all generally boils down to the amount of time it takes to complete, ease of entry, and what level of commitment there is beyond the task at hand.

Skilled Microvolunteering

Here are a few examples of popular skilled microvolunteering opportunities:

Transcribing from administrative forms into e-documents

Brainstorming project slogans

Designing a Twitter account background

Checking a grant-proposal submission

Helping to create e-mail newsletters

Advising on a Google Adwords campaign

Demonstrating new software

Developing a list of cause aligned blogs

Compiling campaign Twitter hashtags

Advising on website SEO rankings

Translating a web page

Unskilled Microvolunteering

Here are some examples of recently publicized "unskilled" microvolunteering opportunities. Note that although some of these actions may *appear* to require substantial skills, in most cases the sponsors have designed them so that no specialized skills are required to participate:

Analyzing tumor images to help cure cancer

Mapping disabled-access issues

Writing a cheery letter to a sick child

Helping marine scientists understand whale song

Donating photos to promote a nonprofit's cause

Providing a one-hour bucket collection stint

Describing pictures to assist the visually impaired

Knitting puppets for disadvantaged children

Making origami cranes for cancer patients

Discovering planets around other stars

Contributing to psychology research surveys

Participating in seed-planting events

Converting public domain literature into eBooks

Playing with robot toys to end animal homelessness

Donating a Tweet to advocate for good causes

Being a meet-and-greeter at a volunteering event

The Rise of Microvolunteering and Why You Should Be Interested

Microvolunteering may or may not be in your comfort zone—yet. Every organization has its own way of engaging with volunteers. But there are too many factors at play that are causing the microvolunteering blip on the radar to become increasingly larger and, eventually, impossible to ignore. Even if you decide to pass up on micro, you should still be interested in what's behind this trend.

Research Studies

The United Nations Volunteers prognostication that microvolunteering will be one of the fast growing sectors in the global volunteering arena is slowly being backed up by research studies that indicate a shift is occurring toward people wanting more shorter-term volunteering opportunities.

For instance, as part of its Third Sector Foresight project, the U.K.-based National Council for Voluntary Organisations published its *Trends in Volunteering* report (2011), stating that, "*Demand for short-term volunteering opportunities and one-off activities is increasing.... Long-term commitment to organisations is falling as people's participation becomes more fluid.... At the extreme, there is a growth in 'micro volunteering' whereby people volunteer for very short periods of time, usually on a non-committal basis.*"[4]

"Mission Driven Volunteer," a white paper published by Sparked Consulting, pointed out "*The large (80+ million) Millennial generation is rapidly entering their 'career years.' . . . They want to contribute in ways that are meaningful to them and make a demonstrable difference, in small bites, and on—and only on—their schedules.*"[5]

The U.K.-based Institute of Volunteering Research concluded their report on microvolunteering, "The Value of Giving a Little Time," (2013) with: "*The demand for microvolunteering from individuals is likely to grow because it meets people's desire to be in control of their time and engagement, and suits their increasingly busy and unpredictable lives.*"[6]

(For more on trends that will impact the future of volunteering, see Chapter 1.)

Engagement Levels

So there's a trend toward shorter term volunteering, but demographically what do we know about people who participate in microvolunteering actions? Studies from both Help From Home and the Institute for Volunteering Research[7] have been conducted in the past few years that provide an insight into their make-up.

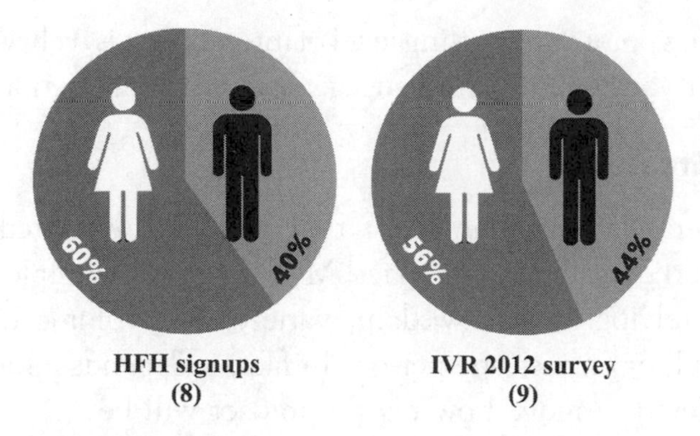

Figure 12.1 Microvolunteers by Gender
Source: Help From Home.

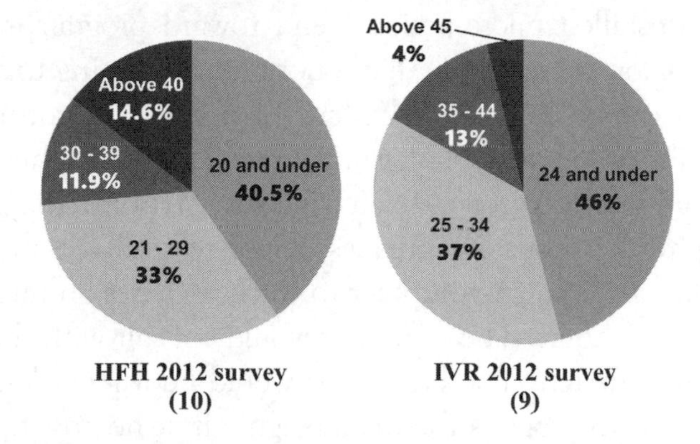

Figure 12.2 Microvolunteers by Age
Source: Help From Home.

The story told by these statistics is that more females microvolunteer than males (see Figure 12.1), more people under the age of 24 microvolunteer than any other age group (see Figure 12.2), and that the vast majority of microvolunteers would recommend similar activities to their friends and family (see Figure 12.3).

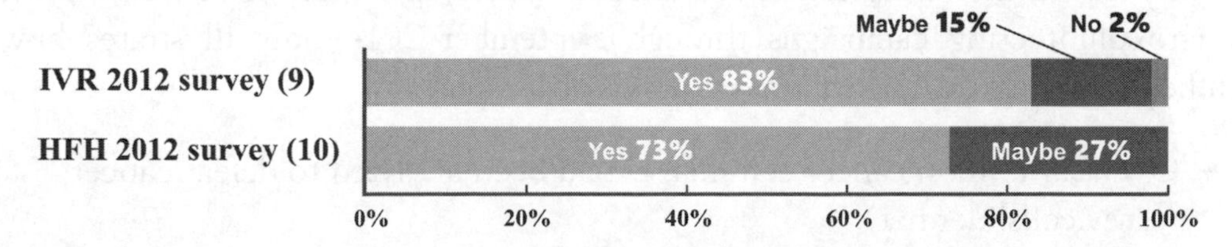

Figure 12.3 Willingness to Recommend Microvolunteering to Others
Source: Help From Home.

These statistics point to a startling level of interest that is well worth taking into consideration for your volunteering engagement program—ignore at your peril!

Impact Being Created

A question I often hear is that an action that could be completed in only several minutes surely can't create much impact! My response: It completely depends on whether you're relying on the wisdom, variety, and volume of the crowd to achieve your goal, or on just one person. In fact, it depends a lot on the type of action being offered to judge how big the impact will be.

Skilled microvolunteering opportunities tend to benefit nonprofits themselves, whereas unskilled micro-actions tend to benefit the beneficiaries of nonprofits. That is, skilled micro-actions usually support the effective running of the organization, whereas unskilled micro-actions tend toward program services for the people or partners "on the ground" that a nonprofit is aiming to help.

In the case of the kinds of skilled microvolunteering opportunities typically posted on the Skills For Change platform, volunteers can post their creative input in response to a call-out for a project-related logo design from a nonprofit. The time taken for a nonprofit to post such a request might typically be about 15 minutes, and the time taken for a microvolunteer to work up a design might typically be between one and two hours. The nonprofit would consult with the responders to perhaps tweak their design. The end result would be a logo design that would enable the nonprofit to progress their campaign, all at no cost to the nonprofit.

On the other hand, unskilled microvolunteering actions as featured typically on the Help From Home platform may vary enormously in the time and cost it takes to develop an action. That's because there is such a huge diversity of actions out there. Unlike skilled actions (which are difficult enough to measure and calculate for impact), no single size fits all. Development costs to set up an unskilled microvolunteer opportunity might range from nothing to tens of thousands of dollars, or from minutes of set-up time to months.

In fact, a list of representative impact stats from a number of well-known microvolunteering campaigns through September 2014 only illustrates how difficult the task of impact reporting is in this area:

- Over 2.4 million cancer cell images had been analyzed to defeat cancer (www.cellslider.net).
- Over 4,000 photos had been donated to enable charities to promote their cause (www.photofoundation.org).

- Over 18 percent more kitten adoptions occurred at participating animal shelters (www.ipetcompanion.com).
- Over 69,000 people had registered to donate a tweet to worthy causes (www.justcoz.org).

For more information regarding the impact of these and 130 other microvolunteering initiatives, refer to Help From Home's "Microvolunteering: Evidence of Impact" report.[8]

Indeed, although most observers agree that microvolunteering, as a brand new category of volunteer engagement, suffers from an obvious lack of research into its overall impact, the anecdotal evidence is growing increasingly clear that micro is making a big difference. The most extensive survey into the arena has been conducted by the Institute of Volunteering Research, whose 2013 study on microvolunteering drew on information obtained from workshops, case studies, focus groups, and literature reviews. As they put it in their 76-page report: "Despite the difficulty of assessing the overall impact of microvolunteering, the evidence highlights that organisations offering microvolunteering have benefited considerably from the experience."[9]

Can Microvolunteering Overcome the Excuses Not to Volunteer?

In my experience there are five main reasons that people give for not volunteering. (See Table 12.1.) Can microvolunteering strip away these barriers to volunteer participation?

The bottom line to microvolunteering is that it can strip away a lot of the barriers to participating in a volunteering activity. As a suggestion it might be useful to embrace some of the preceding counterarguments in your recruitment campaign if (or hopefully when) you decide to start developing and promoting your own microvolunteering actions.

How Do I Tap Into Microvolunteering?

Microvolunteering probably seems quite a bewildering arena to tap into, but fear not. The following section is a brief primer on the practicalities of creating a bite-sized action, in tandem with some mindful references to the uniquely evolving nonprofit-microvolunteer relationship.

Table 12.1 Overcoming the Barriers to Participation in Microvolunteering

Excuse	*Reality*
"I'm too busy."	Some actions, like the click-to-donate ones, can be completed in under 10 seconds. Who doesn't have a spare 10 seconds?
"It's no fun."	Fun is subjective, but there are online games for fundraising and other engaging tasks.
"I'm too tired after work."	Microvolunteering enables volunteers to be tucked in bed and still help a nonprofit via smartphone or tablet.
"There is nothing that interests me."	It's surprising how diversified bite-sized actions can be.
"I can't commit myself."	Dipping in and out is one of the hallmarks of the microvolunteering concept.

Developing a Microvolunteering Action

The process of creating a microvolunteering action is not that much different than creating a traditional volunteering role, except that there may be a few more people to convince about the return of effort needed to develop one.

Start by talking with appropriate staff members and volunteers about the potential for microvolunteering at your organization, and why different staff members and volunteers want or don't want to do this. There may be a few people who would love to try microvolunteering at your organization, but who feel that the other staff or volunteers aren't ready, or are uneasy about the whole idea of it.

Once you've got the ball rolling, you'll probably want some guidance on how best to proceed. The information below is a very simplified list of actions to get started:[10]

1. Start with a great idea. Help From Home and the National Council for Voluntary Organisations (both U.K.-based) can also help as consultants on this.
2. Introduce the idea to other staff members and get buy-in for the microvolunteering concept.

3. Prepare a written plan that includes a mission statement, potential costs, timeline, goals, and objectives.
4. Ensure you have funding in place (if applicable).
5. Create the action—including sorting out text, graphics, web hosts, and analytics tracking (if applicable).
6. Arrange for legal status relevant to the country your program is operating in.
7. Ensure safety measures are in place where minors, the disabled, or senior citizens are involved.
8. Test drive the action with colleagues and interested supporters.
9. Promote and market it via supporters, social media, and other channels.

What to Expect from a Relationship with Microvolunteers

The no-obligation and no-commitment mentality prevalent in a microvolunteering action is changing people's attitudes toward their participation in volunteering. In fact, the Institute of Volunteering Research's study found that participants "conceived the value and role of microvolunteering not so much in terms of the outcomes for themselves or beneficiaries but the convenience *of the activity and opportunity to occupy a short period of time*."

This is also backed up more by their finding that "Retaining microvolunteers and keeping them engaged with the organisation and cause is a challenge because it can be difficult to build a relationship with people who might only dip in and out of activities."[11]

This is the "micro-relationship" in a nutshell, and it doesn't take long to see that when it comes to forming long-term relationships between nonprofits and volunteers, microvolunteering goes against most of what you've probably been trained to work toward in support engagement.

As an example of this "micro-relationship," take a project called Describe Me by the Museum Victoria in Australia. To help the visually impaired access their website, the museum engaged volunteers in providing a few brief word tags that describe an image of an item from its museum collection. Volunteers could choose to log in to complete the action—or not. Both methods will achieve the same outcome.[12]

Clearly, the nonprofits with the most effective microvolunteering programs are placing their focus on achieving a projects outcome, rather than on nurturing retention or a long-term relationship. This "letting go" of long-cherished beliefs and goals within the voluntary sector is indeed a transformative mind shift.

This is not to say that nonprofits should be tossing aside their volunteer relationships; it's just that this "relationship" may increasingly take on a different form over time. In the future, it's not unforeseeable that capturing personal data of microvolunteers may no longer be the driving force it is today.

Marketing Microvolunteering

A wide variety of methods are currently being employed by nonprofits to market their needs and recruit microvolunteers. Many are engaging their own networks, whereas others are using third-party platforms to reach new people. The easiest way to get started is to see what is working.

Inside Audiences

Perhaps sensing the rising momentum of interest (or just wanting to look hip), some nonprofits have rebadged what would normally be considered a traditional volunteer role into microvolunteering.

The U.S.-based Mariner Management, for example, has used the microvolunteering label to recruit Registration Clerks and volunteers for Set Down and Tear Up roles.[13] Meanwhile Canada's Cenovus encouraged volunteers to assemble 1,000 food bags for the homeless in 20 minutes during their "2013 Thanks & Giving Microvolunteering" event.[14] Caring Bridge in America offers weekly microvolunteering challenges to keep supporters motivated.[15] Postpals in the U.K. uses social media (and especially Twitter) to inform their supporters about which sick children need cheery letters to keep their spirits up.[16] And the Indonesia-based Planet Indonesia just uses a static web page to describe its grant-watching microvolunteering role.[17]

Outside Audiences

Many nonprofits are using the 30 or so dedicated microvolunteering platforms around the world to recruit people for their tasks. Here are a few of the best known of these:

Skills For Change	Skilled, crowd-sourced actions up to two hours	www.skillsforchange.com
Help From Home	Mostly unskilled, crowd-sourced or non-crowd-sourced actions up to 30 minutes	www.helpfromhome.org
BrightOne	Media and communication tasks up to three hours	www.brightone.org.uk
Raise5	Fundraising micro-actions up to two hours	www.raise5.com
Crowdcrafting	Citizen science and research projects up to one hour	www.crowdcrafting.org
Fcancer	Donating skills by the hour to cancer charities	www.fcancer.org

Microvolunteering Events

As the interest in the microvolunteering concept continues to grow, I am seeing more and more events that either focus entirely on microvolunteering or include a microvolunteering element as part of their overall activities. Event organizers are experimenting with different names to attract attendees. Recent examples include:

- Volunteer Centre North Kesteven: "30 actions of good in 30 minutes."
- Volunteer Centre Lincoln: "Challenge 30: Microvolunteering coffee morning."
- University of Nottingham Student Union: "Microvolunteering Party."
- Combined Federal Campaign: "Microvolunteer Happy Hour."
- Anchorpoint: "Microvolunteering Speed Dating."
- University of Guelph: "Microvolunteering Fair."

The versatility of the microvolunteering concept has also been experimented, with at times remarkable results. The U.K.-based Jewish Volunteer Network claims to have broken an unofficial world record by enabling all 400-plus attendees at their 2014 Yoni Jesner Award Ceremony to microvolunteer while still in their seats.[18]

Finally, to show just how far microvolunteering has come, it even has its own global awareness day, Microvolunteering Day, now held on April 15 each year.[19] Keep an eye out for hashtag #microday.

What's Next in Microvolunteering

It's a dizzying world we live in, and in the very near future "right-around-the-corner" technologies will open up new ways to microvolunteer. Nonprofits are already experimenting with such concepts as 3D printing, wearable computers, QR codes, and drones.

As for me, I predict nonprofits will explore new ways to integrate microvolunteering within the following areas of society:

- Health and well-being programs to aid convalescing patients
- Social responsibility projects for prisoners aimed at instilling respect for fellow humans
- Empowerment initiatives for disabled people to give back to society
- Socially impactful activities during service club meet-ups (Rotary, Lions Clubs, etc.)

I also see microvolunteering expanding from its current U.S. and U.K. base into more non-English speaking countries. It's possible that this will be propelled by microvolunteering's increasing visibility within employee volunteering, which is driven in part by the needs of global corporations with skilled volunteers in other countries (for more on these trends, see Chapters 15 through 19). Volunteering organizations will experiment with more enticing microvolunteering events. And future smartphone apps may even become the panacea to volunteer engagement, enabling people to microvolunteer on demand and on the go even more!

Heady stuff—the future of microvolunteering is certainly looking bright.

Ride the Wave

In the course of reading this chapter, you've probably had your preconceived concepts about volunteering pushed to the limit. I've stripped away excuse barriers, let go of traditional mindsets, and looked at innovative campaigns that are using microvolunteering to get real work done right now.

Although microvolunteering may have been considered a fad, it is most definitely here to stay.

Certainly, its time as just a talking point is coming to an end. The ease of entry to participate in most microvolunteering opportunities, combined with the premise that people can volunteer in as little as five minutes, now gives any nonprofit the ability to experiment with this innovative new approach to engagement and impact.

Can you afford to ignore those spare moments in people's lives that are just asking to be tapped into? Ride the wave and join the future!

Mike Bright is the Founder of Help From Home, an initiative that promotes and encourages people to participate in easy, no-commitment, microvolunteering opportunities via its tagline, "Change The World in Just Your Pyjamas." Mike has been involved in the microvolunteering arena since 2005, initially as a participant and then more fully from December 2008 with his Help From Home initiative. He is considered one of the pioneers of the microvolunteering concept, as well as the organizer behind Microvolunteering Day that occurs every April 15. He's married with no kids, and continues to use the excuse of microvolunteering as a cover for his fetish of wearing pyjamas.

Notes

1. United Nations Volunteers, "State of the World's Volunteerism Report: Universal Values for Global Well-Being," 2011, 26, www.unric.org/en/images/stories/2011/PDF/SWVR%20Report%20%5BEng%5D.pdf.
2. Based on stats provided by Worldometers and FreeRice.com, www.freerice.com/about/faq.
3. Kristen Stephenson, "Giving a Little Time," National Council of Voluntary Organisations (November 2013), 4, http://blogs.ncvo.org.uk/wp-content/uploads/kristen-stephenson/ncvo_guidance_giving_a_little_time_micro-volunteering.pdf.
4. National Council for Voluntary Organisations, "Trends in Volunteering," 2011, ncvoforesight.org/drivers/trends-in-volunteering.
5. Sparked Consulting, p. 20, http://getmespark.com/wp-content/uploads/MissionDrivenVol.pdf.

6. Institute of Volunteering Research, "The Value of Giving a Little Time: Understanding the Potential of Micro-Volunteering," 61, www.ivr.org.uk/images/stories/micro_volunteering_full_report_071113.pdf.
7. Ibid.
8. Help From Home, "Evidence of Impact," helpfromhome.org/impact_micro-2012.pdf.
9. Institute of Volunteering Research, "The Value of Giving a Little Time."
10. For a much more comprehensive guide, check out Help From Home's "How to Develop a Microvolunteering Action Guide," www.helpfromhome.org/microvolunteering-project.pdf.
11. Institute of Volunteering Research, "The Value of Giving a Little Time," 53.
12. To see "Describe Me in Action," visit: describeme.museumvictoria.com.au.
13. http://associationsnow.com/2013/10/micro-volunteering-all-hands-on-deck/
14. www.facebook.com/media/set/?set=a.724022144278584.1073741841.219930134687790&type=3.
15. amplifierhub.caringbridge.org/amptivities/share/microvolunteering.html.
16. www.twitter.com/postpals.
17. www.planetindonesia.org/get-invovled/microvolunteering/.
18. "400 'Microvolunteers' Set New Record at Yoni Jesner Awards," *Jewish News Online*, July 10, 2014, www.jewishnews.co.uk/yoni-jesner-awards.
19. Learn more about Microvolunteering Day at microvolunteeringday.weebly.com.

Chapter 13

Virtual Volunteering: Are We Finally Ready to Talk about Direct Service?

Jayne Cravens
Consultant, Researcher

As I write this chapter, I'm in Kyiv, Ukraine, where I have been working for the last two months. Here in Eastern Europe, I've encountered many non-governmental organizations or NGOs, which is the global equivalent for the term *nonprofit* organization used in the United States. These organizations don't use the same label, but they have much in common with U.S. nonprofits: these organizations are started by passionate people who are committed to a cause—people who, often, have little experience running a cause-based organization. Just like in the United States, they involve volunteers. And, just like in the United States, some of these organizations flourish and last for years, while some flounder and don't last long at all.

That said, there's one big difference I regularly encounter with NGOs from Europe: Many, and maybe most, are engaged in virtual volunteering, often without ever having heard the term. They have integrated using the Internet completely into their support and involvement of *all* volunteers, and they are perplexed when I try to talk about virtual volunteering as something distinct.

These organizations involve volunteers, period—they don't segregate online from onsite.

Back in the United States, I regularly encounter nonprofits that still think of using the Internet to involve and support volunteers as something entirely separate from their overall involvement of volunteers. I meet managers of volunteers who assure me, after seeing me present virtual volunteering yet again, as I've been doing since 1994, that they will eventually "get around to do this stuff." I smile—and wonder if their organization will be around much longer.

Even among organizations that claim to not involve online volunteers, it is rare that I find this to be true: usually, they are using some Internet tool to allow volunteers to select their onsite shifts and provide feedback on those shifts; they ask their volunteers via e-mail or an online discussion group for ideas on new events (also known as *crowdsourcing*); they engage unpaid interns in designing web pages from home; they allow *pro bono* graphic artists to design new logos from the workplace; their board members have online discussions; and on and on.

In *The Last Virtual Volunteering Guidebook*, my co-author Susan J. Ellis and I say, "It is time—even long overdue—to consider virtual service as fully integrated with all sorts of real-world volunteering, not off on its own in an isolated silo."[1] In truth, the idea of including a chapter on virtual volunteering for *Volunteer Engagement 2.0* goes against everything I believe about virtual volunteering because I believe *any* book about volunteer engagement should have virtual volunteering threaded, inextricably, throughout each and every chapter. How can anyone talk about volunteer engagement today without also talking about using the Internet for every aspect of volunteer involvement and support: recruitment, screening, supervision, support, recognition, and monitoring? It's long been time for virtual volunteering to be a part of all our talk about volunteer engagement, period.

There is, however, one aspect of virtual volunteering that remains largely unsupported and undiscussed and, therefore, does warrant special attention: *virtual volunteering as a primary part of an organization's service delivery to meet its mission.*

It's easy to think about online volunteers supporting staff with graphic design, researching projects, managing social media, developing marketing strategies, and on and on; it's much harder to think about online volunteers actually working with those who the nonprofit serves and playing a central role in an organization meeting its mission. However, it's a role that many volunteers desire. Yes, there are many volunteers who want the no-commitment, just-show-up experience of an onsite, one-time group event or online microvolunteering, but there are many online volunteers who are hungry for a more substantial experience, great responsibility, and ultimately a deeper relationship with your organization. And there are tasks that are actually better done online than onsite.

This chapter explores direct-service virtual volunteering, and will, I hope, help you:

- Empower and support current, onsite volunteers who work with clients to also provide support for those clients online, where appropriate.
- Explore the idea of creating Internet-based programs that bring volunteers and clients or the general public together in ways that meet your mission.
- Improve such practices that may already be happening at your organization.

A Well-Established Practice

What Is Virtual Volunteering?

In this book, *virtual volunteering* refers to activities that are completed, in whole or in part, using the Internet and an off-site work computer, smartphone, or other device.

Because there is no organization tracking direct-service virtual volunteering, there is no way to say how many such programs exist. Some of my favorite, well-established online mentoring programs include:

Bpeace (http://www.bpeace.org)

A U.S.-based nonprofit that recruits business professionals as volunteers to help entrepreneurs in countries emerging from war to create and expand businesses and employment, particularly for women.

Cherie Blair Foundation (http://www.cherieblairfoundation.org/mentoring/)

This online mentoring program recruits successful businesswomen in the United Kingdom to work online with women entrepreneurs in developing countries.

GoodProspects (https://goodprospects.goodwill.org/volunteer/)

This is an online mentoring program by Goodwill. Mentors coach people who are entering or re-entering the workplace, including those with criminal backgrounds or disabilities, young adults, veterans, older workers, women, and immigrants.

IMAlive (https://www.imalive.org/)

IMAlive is a live online crisis network staffed by screened, trained, online volunteers. It's a project by the Kristin Brooks Hope Center, To Write Love On Her Arms, and PostSecret.

Infinite Family (http://www.infinitefamily.org/)

An international online mentoring program matching adults and families in the United States with at-risk, impoverished children in South Africa.

Sidelines (http://www.sidelines.org/)

A U.S.-based nonprofit organization providing international support for women and their families experiencing complicated pregnancies and premature births. Much of this support is provided by online volunteers who have experienced complicated pregnancies themselves.

Trevor Project (http://www.thetrevorproject.org/pages/volunteer)

Trevor Project operates an online, social networking community for lesbian, gay, bisexual, transgender, and questioning (LGBTQ) youth ages 13 through 24, and their friends and allies. Online volunteers monitor the interactive site to maintain a safe space for young people online.

Using a variety of asynchronous and synchronous Internet tools, direct-service virtual volunteering includes:

- Electronic visiting with someone who is homebound, in a hospital, or in an assisted living facility.
- Online mentoring and instruction, such as helping young students with homework questions or supporting adults learning a skill or finding a job.
- Teaching people to use a particular technology tool.
- One-time counseling by volunteers, such as staffing online crisis support lines.
- Facilitating online discussion groups for people with specific questions or needs on childcare, organic gardening, travel to a particular area, or almost any subject humans are capable of discussing.

- Offering legal, medical, business, or other expertise to clients.
- Working on a project together with clients and other volunteers as a part of meeting the organization's mission, such as writing about the news of their neighborhood, school, or special-interest group.

Some of these direct-service virtual volunteering activities may already be happening at your organization. Consider that most volunteers use e-mail, smartphones, and the Internet in almost every facet of their personal and professional lives and, to a large extent, so do your clients or customers. If you already have a traditional face-to-face mentoring program, for instance, how do you know virtual creep—the slow, even unremarkable addition of online contact—isn't already happening at your organization? Or perhaps you have a friendly visitors program, in which volunteers visit and call homebound people to check that all is well; it's likely that there are some volunteers who are incorporating Skype or other online calling platforms that include webcam video with those homebound people with Internet access.

Is It Right for Your Organization?

There are questions you need to answer for your organization in order to decide if direct-service virtual volunteering would be a good fit, or if you need to start formalizing or better supporting such activities already happening at your organization:

- Could direct-service virtual volunteering help to further your organization's mission? Could it be a central part of meeting that mission? Could it improve service for current clients or new clients, rather than offering service only onsite during regular business hours? If it's already happening, what impact is it having on your organization and its goals?
- Would you be able to attract highly qualified, highly committed volunteers if they had this option for helping—and support them? Or, if this is already happening, are volunteers fully supported in these activities?
- Do you have the in-house expertise to launch or expand such a program?

The rest of this chapter will help you to be able to accurately answer these questions for your organization.

Keys to Success

Just like any nonprofit initiative of any kind, some direct-service virtual volunteering initiatives thrive—they have high impact, they attract great press and other attention, and they last for years—whereas others don't make it more than a few months. Why do some thrive and others fizzle?

When volunteers interact with clients directly, it quickly becomes a highly personal activity, no matter the mission of the organization. Whether onsite or online, these interactions are human, not technical—you are connecting people, not computers and smartphones. The most important things to remember when planning to bring volunteers together online with clients are not the technical aspects but the human aspects: building and maintaining trust, cultivating interactions, encouraging buy-in, keeping everyone safe, and enjoying the effort.

Some organizations look to direct-service virtual volunteering as an expansion of traditional onsite, face-to-face services. Others want to make practicing direct-service virtual volunteering a central part of their organization's services to meet their mission.

For the former, a successful direct-service virtual volunteering is a fully integrated part of an organization's mission, not an add-on, something kept separate from other volunteer engagement and client support. For instance, there isn't entirely separate staffing for the online component: The organization's mentoring support staff supports all mentoring, online or off; the counseling experts work with all volunteers, onsite and face-to-face; the experts regarding small-business development or infant care or teen depression work with all staff and volunteers, regardless of whether their role is primarily online or onsite, and so forth.

In both scenarios, a successful program has experts for offline versions of what the organization wants to achieve online: mentoring, counseling, tutoring, support, and so forth. For instance, if your organization does not have staff with experience regarding mentoring teens, how are you going to effectively mentor teens online? If your organization does not have staff with experience in small-business development in high-poverty countries, how are you going to successfully mentor people in those countries regarding starting or expanding their own businesses?

For either scenario of starting or expanding direct-service virtual volunteering to be successful, exactly what the program will look like, and what success might look like, has to be mapped out:

- What will online interactions between a volunteer and client look and feel like? Will they be text-based? Include video? Will interactions be synchronous or asynchronous? Will it allow for informal banter and off-topic discussions, or will it be highly focused, with off-topic discussions discouraged?
- How much time will an online volunteer be expected to devote to training? And what will that training look like?
- How much time will a client be expected to devote to training in preparation for interaction with an online volunteer—if any?
- How will interactions be tracked by the organization?
- How will you know volunteers and clients are having satisfactory experiences—or that they need guidance or an intervention by someone from your organization?
- How will you measure and communicate success?
- How will you identify, address, and communicate challenges?

Only you, the representative of a nonprofit organization, can answer these questions, and the answers are different for every organization.

Training for Success

One thing is a constant across all direct-service virtual volunteering: Training is key to the success of volunteers engaging with clients and customers online.

Consider that traditional volunteers for a sexual assault or domestic violence phone hotline typically go through around 30 hours of onsite training, and then are heavily supervised during a probationary period of several weeks when they start answering calls. Volunteering candidates who will work with clients online may need to come in for intensive training in-person first, not only to ensure they have actually completed the training (it is much harder to determine if an online volunteering candidate has watched a training video online, for instance), but also because the training may involve role-playing and other exercises that cannot be translated online.

In your training of online volunteers, you will have to clearly define how they should interact with clients and customers, including: how to introduce themselves online, suggestions for building rapport, how to deal with common issues and problems (for instance, what to do when faced with hostile or inappropriate communications), how to transition a client to another online volunteer, and even how to end an online relationship.

Volunteers, clients, and even parents or adult children of any participants should be fully aware of any supervision taking place regarding online exchanges, your organization's policy regarding face-to-face meetings, your policy concerning what constitutes inappropriate online behavior, and what your organization will do if inappropriate online behavior is exhibited—by either party. Also, if online exchanges between adult volunteers and youth are archived, volunteers, youth, and their parents should be aware of who will (and will not) have access to these archives.

Remember that all training points must be referenced frequently with all participants—not simply covered once at the start of a program bringing together online volunteers and clients.

Notifications

Silence is deadly to any online relationship. It can be absolutely destructive to the goals of an online mentoring program, for instance, that is focused on helping a teen have a positive, trusting relationship with an adult. You will have to explore ways to be notified quickly if an online volunteer working with clients has gone silent and to quickly meet the clients' needs through a new volunteer or an employee. Such a notification system can easily be automated if you create a private online platform where all volunteer and client interactions take place; for example, the system could notify you if a client does not receive a response to a message within a set number of days.

Consider an internal online mentoring scheme that matches experienced online volunteers to new ones, encouraging them to be in contact by e-mail or phone, especially in the first few months of the newbie's service. An online community for all online volunteers can also provide a great question-and-answer forum for peer support. You will want employees involved in client services on such a forum as well, giving everyone a safe, private place where they can discuss client-related issues without violating confidentiality.

Your organization may want to offer an off-hours phone number so direct-service online volunteers can immediately reach appropriate staff if they face critical or emergency issues outside of normal business hours.

In the same vein, clients and customers must know who to contact at your organization if there is any problem or issue with an online volunteer. Frequently reach out to those being served or supported by online volunteers to learn how things are going and to identify any concerns or complaints. It is important for them to know that issues will immediately reach the appropriate staff at the organization, that these concerns and complaints cannot be blocked by the volunteer, and that they will be dealt with promptly.

Safety and Screening

Although most people have a fun, safe trip on the Internet, including young people, when it comes to online volunteers who interact with clients or customers, no list of suggestions would be complete without a discussion of online safety, confidentiality, and privacy.

Relatively speaking, the Internet is no more or less safe than any other public space, such as a school, faith community, or sports stadium. Fears of exploitation, abuse, or exposure to sexually explicit or violent material should not prevent an agency from engaging in virtual volunteering, any more than such fears should prevent the involvement of volunteers on site. The challenge is to minimize and manage such risk.

Safety measures for direct-service virtual volunteering have four goals:

1. To prevent opportunities for abuse or exploitation of any participants.
2. To protect youth and other vulnerable clients from inappropriate or harmful activities or information.
3. To screen out people who would abuse or exploit participants or the computer systems they use.
4. To protect participants' privacy and personal information (whether clients, volunteers, employees, parents, or anyone else).

Just as you do when considering someone for face-to-face client service, you will probably need to do background checks on someone volunteering virtually that will work directly with clients: personal and/or professional references, criminal background checks, child abuse history clearance, or even credit checks.

An interview, which can be done online, can test for desired skills and attitudes. In addition, you will have to screen candidates for online abilities.

Engage a candidate online with all of the tools you intend for the volunteer to use (e-mail, video conferencing, text messaging, etc.) to ensure the person writes well, responds to messages quickly, responds appropriately, really knows how to use the tools, or anything else that will be needed.

If your organization brings volunteers together onsite, face-to-face with clients, and you have practices in place to screen out people who might be inappropriate as volunteers, you have already established the procedures to screen out people who might be inappropriate as online volunteers. But, of course, no system is perfect and supervision is vital to keep clients and volunteers safe.

How do you currently ensure that face-to-face volunteer-client interaction, whether in your facility or elsewhere in the field, is appropriate, that everyone feels safe, that confidential information is not being shared with family and friends, and so on? The answer to that question will help you identify what needs to be done for an online version of your program to ensure safety.

Should your online volunteers and clients use a software platform that provides ways for parties to remain anonymous to each other while allowing you, the host organization, to know who all participants are? Should you use a platform that allows a moderator to read and even edit any message from a volunteer to a client (or vice versa), ensuring that no inappropriate information is ever shared?

Keep in mind that no technology tool can guarantee safety; policy and practice will protect the safety of participants as much as, if not more than, the tech tools you choose.

Also, if you are going to monitor and archive volunteer-client online interactions, it is imperative that you communicate this to clients frequently, and that you clearly state who will and will not have access to these interactions. Of course, your motivation is safety for all parties involved, but it often feels like a gross violation of privacy to know that a third party can read one's written communications, no matter what the motivation to do so. Having volunteers and clients help craft the policy together can help prevent negative feelings later.

As mentioned earlier, there are many software platforms that provide ways for parties to remain anonymous, and anonymous interactions between volunteers and clients may be best for your organization, depending on the focus of your work. But while it may be appropriate for volunteers to be anonymous from each other, it is never appropriate for volunteers in a direct-service virtual volunteering scheme to be anonymous from the organization itself. If volunteers are providing service on your organization's behalf, you need to know exactly who is doing what online.

Example of Balancing Program and Safety

Here is a true story of an online mentoring program that illustrates the difficulty in achieving the balance between safety and goals. It's one I cite in *The Last Virtual Volunteering Guidebook*, and which I use frequently in trainings, as I was the designer of this particular online mentoring program:

There were two classes at Sanchez Elementary School, in Austin, Texas, that partnered with the Virtual Volunteering Project at the University of Texas at Austin to pilot an online mentoring program in the late 1990s. The project had a goal of not only bringing together adults from all over the USA with students online for one-on-one interactions; it was also meant to test suggested practices in online mentoring from various sources, including the National Mentoring Partnership.

To ensure the safety of all participants, the Sanchez program was designed to be fully moderated; no message could get to a student from a mentor, or vice versa, without being read first by one of the three program directors, two of whom were the classroom teachers. To further ensure safely, only students' and mentors' first names were used in exchanges. Also, all messages were sent and tracked via a private (password protected), customized website (designed by an online volunteer!). Any message sent that had personally identifying information in it, like an e-mail address or a phone number, was rejected by a moderator before the intended recipient received such, and the moderator would advise how the message needed to be altered in order to be approved.

The system worked very well from a safety point of view: there was no way mentors and students could contact each other outside the system because of the absolute moderating of all messages, and that prevented any inappropriate communications or interactions. There was also no way for online mentors and students to meet face-to-face, secretly, because of this absolute moderating. But the system did not work well from the student's point of view: students did not understand that two of the moderators would be their own teachers. Although students had been told at the start that all messages would be read by the moderators, and that two of those moderators would be teachers, several students realized it only after the project was underway, and after they had made comments about their teachers. The students felt betrayed and hurt. Although the program did a great job from a safety point of view, it almost completely defeated one of the primary goals of the mentoring program regarding trust!

Although it may have been appropriate for the Sanchez program to moderate every message, it would have been better (1) if the moderators were not teachers, and (2) if students had been briefed several times that teachers could have access to their messages at some point.[2]

If you bring together volunteers and clients online, you have two options: You can set up a private system through which all messages are sent, reviewed before they can be read by the intended recipient, stripped of all personal identifying information by the moderator, archived for the record, and so forth. But if you decide against such a cumbersome, moderated, and anonymous system, you need to employ all the suggested practices and legal requirements associated with bringing volunteers and clients together onsite.

Conclusion

I have not only designed and managed direct-service virtual volunteering programs; I've also been a volunteer in half a dozen online mentoring programs. These experiences were, at times, emotionally intense, even draining. And this volunteering was never something I could do "from anywhere"—my interactions with those being served by the program required all my attention; I had to make time and be in the right setting to fulfill my role as a supportive, informative, trustworthy online mentor.

But I also must say: I loved it! Of all of the online volunteering I have done, it has been the most satisfying. Unlike in my online microvolunteering experiences, I've gained an emotional attachment to the organizations I've supported, eventually even working to recruit other volunteers and, at times, soliciting donations on the organization's behalf.

Yes, sometimes I want a quick, one-time online volunteer gig that requires no ongoing commitment. But sometimes, I want something long term, substantial, even intense. And I'm not alone in that desire. Many other virtual volunteers would love to provide direct service for their favorite nonprofits. Are you ready for us?

Jayne Cravens is an internationally recognized trainer, researcher, and consultant. She is a pioneer regarding the research and practice of virtual volunteering, and a veteran manager of various local and international initiatives. She has been quoted in articles in the *New York Times*, the *Wall Street Journal*, and the Associated Press, as well as for reports by CNN, Deutsche Well, BBC, and various local radio and TV stations. Resources from her website, coyotecommunications.com, are frequently cited in reports and articles by a variety of organizations, online and in print. She is currently based near Portland, Oregon.

Notes

1. Jayne Cravens and Susan J. Ellis, *The* Last *Virtual Volunteering Guidebook* (Philadelphia, PA: Energize, 2014).
2. The materials for teachers, mentors, and parents who participated in the Sanchez Elementary School online mentoring program can be found at www.coyotecommunications.com/sanchezov/index.html.

Chapter 14

Getting the Most Out of Hackathons for Social Good

Scott Henderson
CEO and Founder, Sandbox Communities

Hackathons are the solution to every problem. Hackathons solve nothing. Hackathons are a fad. Hackathons are here to stay. Hackathons are just for the technology savvy. Hackathons are for everyone.

Well, one thing is for sure: there are a lot of strong opinions about hackathons. And as someone who has helped to organize and promote many hackathons in recent years, I wouldn't necessarily disagree with any of these perspectives—no matter how bewildering that sounds. It's difficult to understand these crowdsourced volunteer events unless you've participated in one, and it's practically impossible to know if hosting or signing up your organization as a beneficiary in a hackathon would be helpful for your organization without hands-on experience. It's one thing to see the pudding and an entirely different thing to taste it.

Hackathons aren't going away. If anything, the circumstances making them popular today are only bound to grow. As technology continues to dominate much of how the world works these days, the ability to attract and work with talented software developers, designers, and product experts may become vital if your organization depends on it to perform your mission.

Although you may appreciate the importance of these highly paid professionals, you probably won't have the budget to have a large team of technologists on your payroll.

According to a recent national survey by NTEN, the average nonprofit employs 4.4 technology-responsible staff members each supporting 30.6 staff members.[1] Hackathons offer you the opportunity to augment your technology team for short periods of time without breaking the bank—and potentially a chance to work with some of the best talent in the field.

By applying the insights I'll share in this chapter, you can use hackathons as a new way for you to attract skilled volunteers to your cause—and then keep them engaged through periodic direct service, organized pro bono consulting teams, virtual volunteering, and even web-based microvolunteering.

What Is a Hackathon?

I like to think of a hackathon as a bunch of kids playing around in the sandbox or with a big box of Legos. Each kid has different skills, and here they can explore and collaborate in a safe environment that encourages creativity and risk-taking. At least, that's a hackathon in analog form—minus the sand in your shoes.

Although hackathons come in different shapes and sizes, they adhere to the same general formula:

- The hackathon is scheduled for a specific amount of time—usually 24 to 56 hours over a weekend or holiday to avoid conflicts with work or school obligations.
- As participants arrive and check in, they're encouraged to mingle and become acquainted with each other either informally or through structured icebreakers.
- At the official kickoff, organizers welcome the participants and present an overview of the hackathon's focus, logistics, and partners. Sometimes, technology partners showcase new technologies they're offering to the participants to experiment with during the hackathon.
- One by one, participants with ideas for projects pitch them in front of the group.

- After each idea has been pitched, teams form around the most compelling ideas; ideas that don't attract a critical mass of people are set aside.
- Then, everyone gets to work building out their team's idea within the hackathon period. It can become pretty intense, with teams working around the clock in pursuit of their goal (cue the pizza, caffeine, and sleeping bags!).
- Periodically, volunteer mentors and technology partners check in with each team to see what help they might need.
- At the end of the hackathon, teams gather and present what they built—usually with a panel of judges reviewing and awarding prizes to the top teams.

As you can see, hackathons aren't about hacking into secure data or stealing anything. That's a common misperception. The word "hack" is actually technology sector slang for finding quick solutions. The suffix *-athon* (think *marathon*) is used to describe extended periods of a focused activity.

Hackathons are appealing to developers, designers, and other technologists because they are opportunities to try out new skills, play with cutting-edge technologies, and apply their existing skills to solve problems they don't normally get to solve.

Increasingly, they're very popular on college campuses, which are experiencing a wave of student-organized hackathons. Students view them as an opportunity to acquire practical experience using their skills and abilities in ways the classroom can't provide. Sponsors—which could include investors, technology companies, or foundations who supply the space, promotion, food and drinks, and prizes—love them because they are an efficient way to identify top talent, get their new technologies in the hands of developers, or engage the community in problem solving.

How Did Hackathons for Good Originate?

Dev days, hack fests, code fests, and hackathons emerged in the late 1990s. The first documented use of the word "hackathon" occurred in 1999 by two separate organizations. Over the next decade, companies, venture capitalists, and web-developer communities helped spread the hackathon as a way to prototype new technologies and help attract talented developers to projects—often for the purpose of recruiting them for paid positions at startups.

Within the software developer community, hackathons also became an important tool for the "open source" movement. Open source methodologies are based on the belief that an open network of collaborators can accomplish more work faster and with greater resiliency than a traditional top-down hierarchical organizational structure. Instead of protecting the code behind the castle's proverbial "moat and walls," open source developers put the code out into the open and let anyone work with it.

This ardent belief in open collaboration was successfully applied to many of the conferences and workshops of the open source movement. Rather than have event organizers make the big decisions about the event, attendees could submit their own ideas for panels, workshops, and presentation topics when they first checked in. Through various combinations of sorting and attendee voting, the program for these "unconferences" and "camps" are decided and slotted in real time. Within this culture of open source coding, crowdsourcing, and wiki-style collaboration, the hackathon for good was born.

Like all species, it is difficult to pin down the exact moment the hackathons for good became distinct from its ancestors. The earliest instances were sporadic, isolated gatherings of developers organized in response to large-scale disasters. One was attempted after the 1995 Oklahoma City bombing but did not happen. The first successful one was for the 1988 Armenian earthquake with other gatherings following suit in wake of the September 11 attacks, 2004 Indian Ocean tsunami, Hurricane Katrina in 2005, and Hurricane Gustav in 2008.[2,3] They each popped up in different cities disconnected from each other.

In 2006, the organizers of BarCamp, an unconference, launched a variation on the format that brought the usual collection of open source technologists together with representatives from the nonprofit sector. In early 2008, a Microsoft developer evangelist organized GiveCamp, a weekend-long event format that eventually spread to different cities across the world but were held as individual events, not synchronized to the same date and focus.[4]

Around this time, civic-minded technologists began to collaborate with government leaders to enlist the help of other technologists through app contests. This variant opened the challenge up for a longer period of time than a weekend, did not require participants to gather in-person, and awarded cash prizes for the best solutions to specific problems. Technologist Vivek Kundra (who later became the nation's first Chief Information Officer under President Barack Obama) and iStrategyLabs launched the first "Apps for Democracy" contest in 2008, which then helped inspire similar contests in over 50 countries and cities around the world.[5]

CrisisCamp held a panel discussion of technology leaders in June 2009, which led to Microsoft, Google, Yahoo!, NASA, and the World Bank coming together in November 2009 to launch Random Hacks of Kindness (RHoK) for the purpose of gathering subject matter experts in crisis management with developers and technologists to create new solutions.[6]

The Sunlight Foundation held the Great American Hackathon in December 2009 as a "get-together of developers interested in opening up government."[7] The first iteration of RHoK was held as in-person event in Mountain View, California, while the Great American Hackathon attracted volunteer groups in 20 different U.S. cities each averaging about 10 developers, who worked collaboratively over the same weekend.

The following month on January 12, 2010, the 7.0 magnitude Haiti Earthquake became a watershed moment for hackathons for good. The lessons of RHoK and the Great American Hackathon helped give individuals in different communities a framework for how they, too, could collaborate and respond, almost in real time.

With the leadership of the CrisisCamp team and the network effects of social media, hackathons sprouted up just two days after the initial earthquake in six different cities with everyone working "to create technology projects that provide data, information, maps and technical assistance to non-governmental organizations, relief agencies and the public."[8] Tangible outcomes included a Creole/English iPhone translation app, the We Need/We Have Exchange, open sourcing mapping, and a Crisis Wiki to serve as a Yellow Pages of sorts for people supporting the relief efforts.[9]

For hackathons for social good this was, well, kind of like the "gig that changed the world" when an unknown band called the Sex Pistols played to a small crowd in Manchester, England, and launched the punk movement. Many of the people in that crowd would go on to create the most influential bands of their generation.

The Haiti Earthquake effort introduced hackathons for good to a new wave of tech folks who would later go on to create a wide variety of social good innovations. Today many of these volunteers hold key leadership positions in the private, governmental, and nonprofit sectors.

The Opportunity of Hackathons for Good

Regardless of how tech savvy your organization is, hackathons offer you ample opportunity to grow and evolve. As software continues to eat the world (as entrepreneur and venture capitalist Marc Andreessen predicted[10]), every organization is feeling this disruption. Those who are prepared will not only survive but also thrive within this new reality.

Your organization exists to achieve a vision and mission. These matter to your staff, donors, and volunteers. Making them relevant to people with the skills and talents to help you adjust to the technological shifts underway is of great strategic importance.

Hackathons can give your organization the ability to introduce your cause to software developers, designers, entrepreneurs, and other technologists who participate in hackathons and even inspire them to become involved directly—whether for 24 hours or for months and years to come.

Hackathons and Long-Term Engagement

The greatest and most important opportunity is for your organization to tie hackathons to a larger skilled volunteer engagement strategy. I like to think of hackathons as an open-house-type event at which you can learn from skilled people and they can learn about your cause.

For those volunteers who take a deeper interest, you've spent 24 to 56 intense hours with them building rapport and mutual understanding. An easy posthackathon ask is to invite volunteers to continue to flesh out the prototype into something your staff can integrate into its normal operations.

As you move the project from prototype to working tool, you can encourage them to get more involved through other project-related volunteer opportunities or by sharing their knowledge with your staff and board members. The more you learn about their interests and expertise, the more opportunities for ongoing volunteer service will emerge. Entice and intrigue them; don't hard-sell them.

At a minimum, hackathons can help you educate cause-minded technologists. On the high side, they can help you form meaningful long-term relationships with a new class of volunteers who can serve as a force multiplier for your existing "tech person" without breaking the bank.

The Challenge of Hackathons for Good

With all this technology flying around, it is very easy to lose sight of having a clearly stated purpose/challenge for the hackathon. This will ensure the participants produce solutions that meet your needs and are focused on solving real problems. Otherwise, you risk having an event that sprays around like a fire hose with no one guiding it.

What most people quickly discover is that organizing hackathons requires a significant amount of time and energy. Pulling together the logistics, assembling relevant data sets, writing out the specific problems and challenges your organization wants to solve, and rounding up prizes and sponsorships can be overwhelming.

Managing expectations is another challenge. Rome wasn't built in a day and hackathons will never be able to deliver fully baked solutions to highly complex problems. In fact, this is worth emphasizing: because they tackle highly complex problems with solutions that are often pulled together under extreme conditions, *hackathons will never be able to deliver fully baked solutions*. Hackathons must always be thought of as ways to prototype or test ideas. Making sure leadership and staff understand from the start that a hackathon is a step toward finding solutions—even if it only proves that prospective solutions won't work—is a critical first step.

Another easy element to overlook is having a champion at the highest levels of the organization—board or staff—who can help remove obstacles and free up resources for the hackathon. This includes making sure the most tech-savvy team members are available and directly engaged, regardless of where they sit on the organizational chart and how many fires they might be fighting.

Perhaps the most intractable challenge is having the will to fight the organizational tendency to control. You need to trust the process. Inviting relative strangers who likely don't have the depth of subject matter expertise in your cause area and giving them license to pull back the kimono and do their thing can be quite unsettling. For those of you who do overcome this, you'll find the experience quite energizing and stimulating.

The Impact of Hackathons for Good

From the hackathons I've participated in and organized, I have seen impact take shape in two key ways—the first benefiting the organization and the second, the volunteers.

Organization's benefit. In addition to engaging skilled volunteers, hackathons are Trojan horses for innovative thinking and problem solving to infiltrate your organization's culture. Joeli Brearley of CultureCode, an arts and culture organization in the U.K., crystallized this natural by-product in a piece she wrote for *The Guardian*:

> Hacking takes us away from our organisational constraints; it lets us play and experiment with minimal risk and without a rigid agenda. It is in the hacking itself where the real dynamism lies. The common mistake often made is to evaluate how effective a hack event was by exploring the prototypes it generated, but this almost entirely misses the point. The magic is in the "how"—not the "what".[11]

Even if the only thing to come from hackathons is that you find yourself with staff and volunteers who are dynamic problem solvers, I'd say that's a pretty good return on investment.

Volunteer's benefit. Through the local, national, or global hackathons for good I've organized and participated in, I typically see common volunteer archetypes. To help explain the benefit to the volunteers, let's view it from the eyes of four people I've worked with in the Atlanta hackathon-for-good community.

Linda S. heads a family design firm and is a young Latina with a passion for design and making her community better. As the owner of a family business, she is always searching for new client work. The benefit she enjoys is demonstrating her design abilities that directly help impact a social issue and indirectly helps her attract participants and partners who might need to engage her for client work.

Jon M. is a top-notch mobile developer who's worked for a variety of Fortune 500 companies as a contractor and is currently an employee of one. Married with children, he has a healthy respect for a steady paycheck and having time to spend with his family. The benefit he derives is working on projects that have greater meaning and purpose over a short, defined period of time.

Terry A. is a talented UX/UI designer who works for a growing startup. He's married with grown children and has been a longtime organizer of hackathons for good. He's the go-to guy when it comes to conceiving and running these events within Atlanta. All of which he does because of the satisfaction he gets from bridging the technology community with city government and local nonprofits. Plus, he enjoys designing the t-shirts for attendees to wear.

Kurt R. is a serial tech entrepreneur who recently had a successful exit and now mentors and coaches social good entrepreneurs. He serves on a number of nonprofit boards and regularly participates in charitable races. The benefit he gets from participating is finding new people and ventures to mentor, as well as enrolling ad-hoc teams to help him develop specific social good initiatives he's involved with.

When Does a Hackathon Make Sense (and When Doesn't It?)

As the old saw goes, when you have a hammer, everything begins to look like a nail. A hackathon is not the panacea. It is one of many tools you can use. As any serious craftsman knows, the right tool at the right time can make all the difference. By no means is this an exhaustive guide, but here is something to help give you a rule of thumb.

When It Does

- Your organization has specific problems to solve using technology.
- Your organization can provide direct access to subject matter experts.
- Your organization knows it doesn't have all the answers.
- Your organization is open to frank feedback and critical analysis.
- Your organization has a plan for how the hackathon ties to a larger skilled volunteer engagement strategy.
- Your organization likes attracting new volunteers, donors, and partners.

When It Doesn't

- Your organization lacks a strategic vision with clear organizational objectives.
- Your organization is fractured internally and is full of strife.
- Your organization requires complete ownership and control of the hackathon's output.
- Your organization is adverse to collaboration and openness.

- Your organization is in crisis.
- Your organization hasn't mapped the hackathon to an ongoing engagement strategy.

Inside a Typical Hackathon

Every component of a hackathon offers you an opportunity to engage skilled volunteers, because a successful hackathon happens only through the effort of a core team of dedicated staff and volunteer producers. What's beautiful is that you can ask nontechnical volunteers to do what they're good at to help the technical volunteers work their magic. Here are a few typical roles volunteers might play in bringing off a successful hackathon:

Theme/Challenges/Sponsors/Partners

You need volunteers to help you make the hackathon fun and playful. Tap people who can help you frame the hackathon that makes people lean forward in their chairs. Who do you know who's great at game plans, marketing, sponsorships, and partnerships?

Opening and Closing Segments

Here's where a seasoned event coordinator can help you make sure all the details are taken care of and things are working smoothly. Who loves to plan and host events for you?

Mentor Input/Group Check-Ins

This is where you can reach out to new technology savvy people and business and nonprofit leaders. You're only asking them to come for a two- to four-hour window during the hackathon to meet with teams and provide them with feedback on their project and offer insights and resources that could help them.

Subject Matter Experts

Who do you know that can provide hackathon participants with real-world perspective on the challenges they are trying to solve? Are there volunteers, community members, other service and nonprofit organizations, or corporations who can give guidance and perspective?

Judging Panel

It's always easier to entice highly successful and visible people to participate when you're asking them to serve in a prominent role.

Rounding up your volunteer judges is a great way for you to introduce them to your organization and the issues you're aiming to solve. You can reach to elected officials, prominent business leaders, and other thought leaders.

Getting Your Hack On

Okay, you've seen the light and you have realistic expectations for how a hackathon can benefit your organization in the short- and long-term. What's the best first step?

Sand in Your Toes

If you haven't already, find a hackathon near you and attend one—either as an observer or a participant. Everyone has skills that are useful to a hackathon team. Project management, guiding team strategy, and the ability to prioritize are often the difference makers for teams—and those are skills the volunteer sector has in spades. Search online for startup and student event calendars. They're often the best starting point to find hackathons in your area.

Sponsor a Prize Challenge

Maybe you're not ready to organize your own hackathon but you want to find an easier way to leverage the energy and enthusiasm they offer. The simplest way is to sponsor/issue a prize challenge at an existing hackathon. This approach is used often by technology companies and would give you the experience of defining a specific problem and providing teams with the context they'll need to solve it. Student-organized hackathons and Code for America hacking events would be good opportunities for you to try this.

Share the Fun with a Partner

As mentioned earlier, hackathons are a great way to partner with like-minded organizations and companies. The very first hackathon my colleagues Brian Reich, Anne Bertelsen, and I organized at the SXSW Interactive Festival in 2010 brought Share Our Strength, Feeding America, and the local food bank in Austin together with corporate sponsors and conference attendees.[12,13] No one person or organization owns a social issue like hunger, and working with partners helped each organization focus on its strengths while leveraging the other partners' strengths. Along the way, partners developed stronger relationships with each other and learned how to run a successful hackathon.

Now that you've read this chapter, you've got pretty much all you'll need to get started. Let the brilliance begin.

Parting Thoughts

As we come to a close on this chapter, I want you to take a moment to imagine you have just wrapped up your latest annual report that includes a short summary of your organization's first hackathon experience. Whether it was one you hosted or one you attended, what were the surprising insights you gained from it? What new technologies did it uncover? What new skilled volunteers have emerged and are now engaged in helping your cause?

Perhaps more importantly, who are these new volunteers and what did they say about their experiences and observations working with you? How did they come to know about your cause and the unique assets and solutions your organization brings to the world?

Although it is natural to consider all of this from your organization's perspective, hackathons for good help you see the world from the perspective of the skilled volunteers who will play an increasingly important role in your ongoing operations. They require a willingness to collaborate, a tolerance for risk taking, and a persistent desire to learn from experience regardless if the experiment succeeded or failed.

I hope you have fun playing in the sandbox.

Scott Henderson helps produce experiences and events that create community, collaboration, and commerce. He's organized numerous hackathons—traditional and cause-oriented—including SXSW's Hunger CauseLab. Over the past five years, he has also helped to launch campaigns including UN's 7 Billion Actions, Speak Justice Now, and the Startup America Partnership, while providing strategic counsel to P&G, UNICEF, SXSW, Discovery Channel, Aetna, and the City of Louisville. Scott is currently helping create a stronger sense of identity for Atlanta's burgeoning technology scene through the Sandbox Crew social club and Square on Fifth apartment tower. He is proud to be a Nebraskan by birth and an Atlantan by choice.

Notes

1. NTEN, *The 8th Annual Nonprofit Technology Staffing and Investments Report*, 2014, 5, www.nten.org/sites/default/files/staffing_report2014_final1.pdf.
2. The *Katrina Aftermath* blog is one example: katrina05.blogspot.com/.
3. Al Tompkins, "NPR's Andy Carvin on the Role of Social Media in Gustav Coverage," Poynter, 2008, www.poynter.org/mediawire/als-morning-meeting/91234/nprs-andy-carvin-on-the-role-of-social-media-in-gustav-coverage.
4. For more information on GiveCamp: www.givecamp.org/faq.
5. For more on the history of Apps for Democracy: http://istrategylabs.com/work/apps-for-democracy-contest.
6. See Wikipedia, http://en.wikipedia.org/wiki/Random_Hacks_of_Kindness.
7. Clay Johnson, "Great American Hackathon Wrap-Up," Sunlight Foundation, December 22, 2009, http://sunlightfoundation.com/blog/2009/12/22/great-american-hackathon-wrap/.
8. Jolie Odell, "Hackers Helping Haiti: Find or Organize a Hackathon Near You," ReadWrite.com, January 15, 2010, www.readwrite.com/2010/01/14/hackers_helping_haiti.
9. "Hackathons Aim to Improve Aid Distribution and Coordination in Haiti," ForumOne, www.forumone.com/insights/hackathons-aim-improve-aid-distribution-and-coordination-haiti.
10. Marc Andreessen, "Why Software Is Eating the World," *Wall Street Journal*, August 20, 2011, online.wsj.com/articles/SB10001424053111903480904576512250915629460.
11. Joeli Brearley, "Art a Hack: Is Hacking Yesterday's News?," *The Guardian*, October 24, 2014, www.theguardian.com/culture-professionals-network/culture-professionals-blog/2014/oct/24/-sp-art-hack-hacking-innovation-culture.
12. Adam Hirsch, "3 Ways to Support the WeCanEndThis #EndHunger Campaign [SXSW]," Mashable, March 11, 2010, www.mashable.com/2010/03/11/wecanendthis.
13. Scott Henderson, "No Fear of Failure: WeCanEndThis.com to Use Innovation and Amplification to Help End Hunger in America," Case Foundation Blog, March 11, 2010, https://causeshift.wordpress.com/2010/03/11/471/

PART FOUR

Changing Corporate Perspectives

Chapter 15

The Power and Unrealized Promise of Skilled Volunteering

Meg Garlinghouse
Director, LinkedIn for Good

Alison Dorsey
Manager, LinkedIn for Good

Sherri Lewis Wood is the national founder and board chair of an extraordinary nonprofit called One Warm Coat. The mission of One Warm Coat is to provide a coat, free of charge, to anyone in need. It was founded in 1992 as a coat drive held in San Francisco's Union Square over Thanksgiving weekend. Not quite a decade later, while driving into the city, Sherri heard a radio interview with a woman who came over on the train to deliver 10 coats. The caller was committed to bringing the coats but had logistical issues getting them into the heart of downtown San Francisco. Listening in, Sherri decided at that moment to aggressively scale up the program with more donation sites and, ultimately, more people helping keep others warm. Now, 13 years later, One Warm Coat has distributed more than 4 million coats to people who need them across the country.

What is especially remarkable about Sherri and One Warm Coat is that until recently, they had no full-time staff. Out of necessity and Sherri's resourceful mindset, One Warm Coat identified and recruited both board members and skilled volunteers to help her run a successful organization.

And One Warm Coat continues to grow its impact. Recently, while creating a three-year strategic plan, the board wondered if they could engage a skilled volunteer to help them facilitate the process. Somewhat skeptical they could find the ideal person, they put aside $15,000 to hire someone, just in case. Sherri posted a volunteer opportunity on LinkedIn and received six applications in the first two days. The quality of applicants was so high that she ended up bringing on two women who happened to work together as strategic planners at an international pharmaceutical company. The women were thrilled to bring to One Warm Coat what they were experts at in their day jobs.

Unfortunately, there's another way in which Sherri's story is remarkable: The vast majority of nonprofits have been unable, or unwilling, to tap the abundance of skilled volunteers to support their organizations. Although more than 92 percent of nonprofits say that they would like to use a skilled volunteer, only 8 percent actively do.[1] At the same time, there is a growing tidal wave of interest from professionals to apply their skills for good.

Volunteerism: An Abundant—and Largely Untapped—Resource

Today volunteerism is well on its way to becoming a "norm" in terms of one's professional identity. Employees, driven in part by the growing numbers of working millennials, expect their employer to provide ways for them to find purpose at work. Many corporations have formal, staffed volunteer programs to help their employees find meaningful work in their communities to make an impact beyond their day jobs.

Volunteering is also increasingly valued as credible work experience. According to a recent LinkedIn survey, 41 percent of hiring managers consider volunteer work equally valuable to paid work experience when evaluating candidates; 20 percent of hiring managers in the United States say they've hired a candidate *because* of their volunteer work experience.[2]

Recognizing these trends, a few years ago LinkedIn added the ability for professionals to include their volunteer work and nonprofit interests as part of their profile, under the "Volunteer Experience and Causes" section. As this book goes to press, more than ten million members have done so. And perhaps more impressive, more than four million LinkedIn members have signaled they want to volunteer their skills or serve on a board.

The time is ripe for nonprofits to take advantage of this trend and meet this demand. In addition to providing valuable skills to a specific project at your nonprofit, volunteers are potential donors—or even staff—in the making. It's well known in the sector that the most reliable and coveted donors—those who write repeat checks and are passionate advocates—often have been initially exposed to an organization as volunteers.

In this chapter, we will help you learn how to identify and best leverage skilled volunteers for your organization by exploring three questions:

1. Who are the professionals who want to volunteer their skills?
2. Are skilled volunteers really for everyone?
3. How do I find the right skilled volunteer for my organization?

Ready to find valuable and free talent to help your organization succeed?

Who Are the Professionals Who Want to Volunteer Their Skills?

Your dentist, your nephew, and the person you sit next to on the bus may all want to give their time and talent to support nonprofits.

In a recent LinkedIn survey, 82 percent of LinkedIn members said they wanted to volunteer their skills.[3]

So the chances are good that the tax accountant with nonprofit 990 reporting experience who you're hoping will help your organization is in fact interested in doing so.

These volunteer-inclined professionals are not only in every industry, but also of all ages. Although millennials are volunteering by the millions and providing the most social influence to one another and their employers, baby boomers are also among the most active volunteers. (For more on millennial and boomer volunteer engagement, see Chapters 5 and 6.)

Millennials entering the workforce are used to school-based service programs and are holding their employers to the same standards as their schools. In fact, 46 percent of U.S. high schools require community service hours. And with many students ranking service programs high on their list of criteria for selecting a school, universities are investing more in their own community engagement programs.

Immersed in structured and institutionally supported service opportunities throughout their academic lives, millennials are now selecting companies to work for based in part on their volunteer offerings. According to Case Foundation research on millennials at work, over 50 percent "were influenced to accept a job based on the company's involvement with causes." Furthermore, of millennial employees who volunteer, 94 percent want to use their accumulated skills to volunteer.[4]

Both boomers and millennials no longer think of volunteer service as something extracurricular to their professional life—but rather as *essential* to finding purpose, as core to who they are. So what are the implications?

Professionals used to keep their volunteer work separate from their community service. They would work nine to five from Monday through Friday and then serve lunch at a food bank on Sundays. Today, things are different: Many of us don't close out work when we leave the office anymore, and we also don't turn off our passions, interests, and external involvements when we enter the office in the morning. And that's encouraged. We bring our whole selves to our work, our social lives, our families, and our service.

Although these skilled volunteering programs are driven by millennials, they are supported by the vast majority of employees of all ages. Recognizing that 82 percent of professionals want to volunteer and 26 percent of Americans do volunteer,[5] companies are creating corporate volunteering programs to connect their employees with service opportunities. Now, 95 percent of Fortune 250 companies release sustainability reports.[6]

Knowing that there is less of a division around the work life and social impact life of skilled volunteers, there are some significant implications for nonprofits in engaging volunteers.

You may still be wondering if skilled volunteers are right for my organization. Do I actually have the capacity to manage a skilled volunteer, and do I really want to hand over my most important projects to a new person who's not on staff (or the board)? Let's think through what capacity is necessary and how you might approach project scoping for volunteers.

Are Skilled Volunteers Really for Everyone?

This is a great question. As mentioned earlier, the majority of nonprofits are currently not using skilled volunteers. As you can read in Chapter 17, 92 percent of nonprofits say they want to use skilled volunteers but only 8 percent actually use them.

At LinkedIn we've spent a great deal of time trying to understand this. Why are some nonprofits more prone to engage in skilled volunteering than others? Is it the size of the organization? The mindset of the leadership? The perceived access to talent? In the spirit of transparency, although definitive answers continue to elude us, we do have a few theories.

Theory 1: It's All About the Capacity of the Organization

This is probably the prevailing theory. There is no question that U.S. nonprofits are some of the most underresourced entities. Although they certainly could use skilled volunteers, it does take a real commitment of time and energy to find and optimally leverage these people.

However, anecdotally we have seen what we call the "barbell effect," in which early adopters of skilled volunteers tend to fall on opposite sides of the capacity spectrum—scarce or abundant.

On the scarce side, One Warm Coat is a great example of the idea that "necessity is the mother of invention"—or in this instance the mother of early adoption. With this example, Sherri did not have staff and was reluctant to use programmatic dollars to hire a strategic facilitator. Her limited capacity was her incentive to find a solution through skilled volunteers.

On the other side sit nonprofits that have a full-time person (or a team) whose job it is to manage volunteers. Many of today's best-known nonprofits such as Rebuilding Together and Habitat for Humanity rely heavily on volunteers as part of their core value and function; it's how they run. Therefore, these organizations often already have an internal culture and capacity set up to utilize skilled volunteers.

Theory 2: It's the Mindset of the Leader

Until the notion of using a skilled volunteer becomes standard operating procedure at a nonprofit, it does require a certain mindset to be open to trying it. And this is especially true when involving a skilled volunteer who was not already in your known network. The most common way skilled volunteers are identified is through an existing network—usually your board of directors, staff, or community. This is a terrific way to find the right person, but is inherently limiting.

At LinkedIn we are working on surfacing the extraordinary talent in your network that is often in your second- or third-degree of connections. These are sometimes referred to as "weak ties" and have been identified by Adam Grant and other researchers as often being the most valuable.[7] And the magic of these "weak ties" is that you have a connection to them—it just isn't direct.

Theory 3: It's About Finding the Right Value at the Right Time

When LinkedIn first launched our program to connect members with skilled volunteer opportunities, we sent an e-mail out to nonprofit leaders with the offer to post a skilled volunteer opportunity for free on LinkedIn. The response was low—as in, close to zero. However, when we sent an e-mail with a specific offer to help them find a social media expert to volunteer at their organization, adoption increased significantly.

In other words, we are learning that nonprofit adoption of skilled volunteer practices often depends more on the specific need for a certain volunteer than on the embrace of skilled volunteering as an overall strategy. Reinforcing this, the second piece of the e-mail that we think helped drive conversion is that we included profiles of people in their network who were social media experts and had signaled they wanted to do skilled volunteering. Moving from the generic ("Sure, I'd like a social media expert") to the specific ("Yes, I'd like Sarah") also helped move the needle.

So, yes, we think skilled volunteers *should* be for everyone. Our hope is that all organizations will start thinking about how to leverage skilled volunteers not as a last but as a first resort—baked into their planning process. It is such a powerful tool to absorb the enormous appetite of professionals to use their skills to change the world and get them up the ladder of engagement.

Okay—feeling inspired to try this? Let's find that perfect skilled volunteer!

How to Find the Right Skilled Volunteers for Your Organization

Supporting skilled volunteers does take significant preparation. But the good news is that there are several great organizations that exist to help you identify your skilled volunteering needs, scope projects, and recruit talented professionals to lend their skills to those projects. Catchafire, Taproot Foundation, and NPower are just a few that are national in scope. Many cities also have local or regional services affiliated with volunteer centers and other capacity-building support systems.

Four Steps for Sourcing Skilled Volunteering Candidates

1. Tap a volunteer support intermediary for help with your needs assessment and project scoping preparation.
2. Post your scoped project description on services like LinkedIn, VolunteerMatch, and Taproot+ (some of the intermediaries will do that for you).
3. Use LinkedIn to search for professionals with the skills you need as well as a stated interest in skilled volunteering.
4. Leverage your network for introductions to the professionals who interest you.

On the board side (in our view, the highest form of skilled volunteering), BoardSource helps nonprofits both to recruit board members and to manage their boards once they exist. They also provide a community of fellow nonprofits and a wealth of resources on governance best practices.

Some nonprofits are building large skilled volunteering elements as programmatic offerings. These organizations have made volunteer recruitment and management core to what they do. Nepris, for example, is an organization matching kindergarten through 12th-grade teachers with classroom speakers. Nepris recruits professionals to speak about their area of expertise and matches the professionals with the teachers. The entire model relies on the supply of skilled volunteers to support classroom needs.

Using LinkedIn to identify great volunteers. LinkedIn makes finding these professionals easy. With Nepris, for example, teachers can quickly generate project descriptions that are posted as volunteer opportunities. LinkedIn's job-matching algorithm gets these speaking opportunities in front of the professionals with the requisite desire, skills, and experience, who are in turn delighted to be presented with specific, time-bound opportunities to use their skills for good. VolunteerMatch also has a similar service.

There are really two sides of recruiting: posting and searching. In addition to posting volunteer job descriptions, we recommend searching for professionals who meet your needs and directly reaching out to them. LinkedIn is designed to enable highly targeted searching. You can search by industry, title, years of experience, location, and so on to find the right professional to volunteer for your organization.

More recently (and also part of the free advanced-search experience), we added the ability for you to filter your search results by nonprofit interest. You could always use LinkedIn to search for graphic designers who work in Memphis and went to the University of Tennessee, and now you can narrow that list of professionals by viewing only those interested in skilled volunteering. These people are particularly excited to hear from nonprofits about service opportunities because they have already signaled to their network—and to organizations like yours—that they want to donate their time and talent.

LinkedIn search results are ordered by the strength of your relationship with the professionals listed. When you're not directly connected to an individual LinkedIn member, but you're only one degree away, we tell you who you know in common. If you know well-connected professionals (maybe your board members!), you can see into their networks on LinkedIn and use them as a bridge to new relationships to benefit your organization.

Frequently, we all rely on our strong connections, the people with whom we have personal relationships. However, many times your most valuable contacts are one connection away. LinkedIn enables you to see these connections in an efficient way. To fully tap the power of LinkedIn's network effects, think broadly about who you connect with on behalf of your organization.

Finding volunteer talent, assessing fit. With posting and searching, both sides of the volunteer engagement have an opportunity to take action: Professionals apply to volunteer opportunities and nonprofits search for and directly contact potential volunteers. The tools exist to connect with the right professionals for your organization, with a fairly minimal investment of time. And myriad support organizations are there to help in your preparation for those volunteers.

Once you identify candidates, it's critical to spend time assessing which candidates have both skill and culture fits for your organization. Some of the support organizations we mentioned also help in the selection process. Many nonprofits are uncomfortable with the rejection part of screening candidates. Our recommendation is to have a backup plan for the professionals you do not ultimately select as volunteers. For example, send them information on your next event or invite them to follow your social media channels; let them know you still want them to be involved in your cause. Keep them in the fold. You never know what future needs will surface—or who might end up being a future donor.

Skilled Volunteering Success Stories

Great Nonprofits: Don't Be Afraid to Think Big

Lessons Learned

1. Engage skilled volunteers deeply. Treat them like employees, give them strategic projects that matter, and bring them into the fold to get a true taste of your culture.
2. Make the engagement about volunteers' needs, too, not just yours.
3. Don't be afraid to make a bold ask.

As a leading developer of tools that allow people to find, review, and share information about nonprofits and charities, GreatNonprofits isn't afraid to think big. Today users can rate more than 1.2 million organizations on its site and partner sites. Maintaining and growing the service can be a big challenge given its small staff and budget. This is especially true when it comes to technical talent.

Founder and CEO Perla Ni had a bold product vision. She posted two pro bono product manager positions—each with an explicit minimum of eight hours a week, six-month commitment—on VolunteerMatch, which were automatically cross-posted to LinkedIn.

Turning up in LinkedIn's Volunteer Marketplace reaped immediate benefits. In short order, Ni had four qualified candidates apply. She moved forward with two of them, on separate and highly strategic projects for the organization. One focuses on product development to help nonprofits showcase their reviews, and the other is working on a statement of social impact and partner nonprofit videos. Both have day jobs as product managers for tech companies.

According to Ni, in both cases, the match was superb. "These volunteers had time, had energy, and were very interested in our work," she said. "And since both came from enterprise software backgrounds, we're offering them a very different experience to learn and expand their skill sets into the consumer web."

Both volunteers physically come into the GreatNonprofits office one day per week, which Ni feels enriches their experience, connects them more deeply to the organization, and leads to a high-quality work product. "In our experience, volunteers get the most out of the experience if they are a part of the team. They are more energized when they come into our office and are working alongside other smart and interesting people working hard to make a difference" said Ni. "The volunteers are both creative and analytical, and are engaging with staff and asking questions. Especially for product management, it is critical that they interact with the team of marketers, program managers, and designers to be successful."

One month in, both volunteers are already making a material impact. Ni is encouraged about the new features in the pipeline that the volunteers are developing. "So far it's been terrific and our staff has been impressed with the caliber of the volunteers," she said. Ni said that if she had to pay for these skilled volunteers, the market value would be $80,000 per year.

Artreach: Engage Skilled Volunteers as Professional Coaches for the Skills You Want

Lessons Learned

1. Be self-aware—reflect on your own abilities and know where you need help.
2. Have a growth mindset—know that your strengths and weaknesses are not set in stone. You can develop a new strength.
3. Ask for fishing lessons—don't just find volunteers to do things for you, but consider having them teach you a new ability you can use on your own.

Artreach is a cultural organization that supports personal growth for underserved communities through engagement in arts and culture.

Becca Atkins, the executive director of Artreach, is recognized for her leadership in the arts therapy space and gets asked to give public presentations about the organization, but she was not confident in her public-speaking abilities. Not wanting her fear to make her turn down opportunities that could benefit Artreach, Atkins realized she needed a public-speaking coach and turned to Catchafire for help scoping the project and recruiting a professional.

Arthur, a professional between jobs with an extensive theater background and a passion to serve, saw this Catchfire project posted on LinkedIn and applied to coach Atkins. After six structured training sessions, daily skill-building homework, and a best-practices guide for the future that Atkins can use to pull out main points for her presentations, Atkins was ready for her upcoming presentation as well as those in the future, now eager to accept speaking engagements and present on behalf of Artreach.

Skilled Volunteering *Is* for Everyone

We hope that we have left you both inspired and empowered to find a skilled volunteer to help your organization succeed. These professionals exist in droves, and are eager to lend their time and talent to advance your mission. We want to reiterate three takeaways:

1. Leverage your networks to find the perfect person to help. There is currently more demand from professionals to help than there is a supply of active opportunities.
2. Think creatively about how to leverage skilled volunteers. They can be invaluable for both short-term projects (i.e., a photographer at an event) and longer-term commitments (product manager for a new feature). Either way, take a cue from GreatNonprofits and scope volunteer job descriptions thoughtfully and don't be afraid to ask for an up-front commitment.
3. Make skilled volunteering part of your annual planning process. Build it into your budget and make someone on your staff or board at least part-time responsible for volunteer recruitment and engagement.

We have seen firsthand the power of skilled volunteers. When used right, they provide immeasurable benefit to both the nonprofit as well as the professional.

At LinkedIn we remain committed to ensuring we help realize the full potential of skilled volunteers. It's clear that we have only scratched the surface.

Our vision is that 10 years from now, the notion of using skilled volunteers will become so accepted that it will be a standard line item in the Form 990, reported on annually. And that, just as you would ask a new acquaintance where they went to school, you would also inquire where they do their skilled volunteering. We envision a day in which skilled volunteering is ubiquitous and seamless—and core to who we are as professionals.

Meg Garlinghouse leads the Social Impact programs at LinkedIn, where she is responsible for programs that leverage the LinkedIn platform to create positive social impact. Meg has nearly 20 years of experience working in the technology and philanthropy sector. She spent almost 10 years building and leading Yahoo!'s global community relations function. She has a background in international development, working in the private sector development department of the World Bank, and served as a Peace Corps volunteer in Niger. Meg received her Bachelor's degree in public policy from Duke and Master's in public policy from the John F. Kennedy School of Government at Harvard. She currently serves on the boards of VolunteerMatch and Zynga.org.

Alison Dorsey is the Social Impact Manager at LinkedIn, focused on supporting nonprofits to recruit skilled volunteers and board members through LinkedIn's Volunteer Marketplace. Alison also leads LinkedIn's Veterans Initiative to connect U.S. veterans with customized training, a curated community, and advanced job-search tools. Before joining LinkedIn, Alison worked in early-stage social venture support in North Carolina, where she founded an incubator and a student recruiting platform. She currently serves on the board of that incubator, Bull City Forward. Dorsey received her Bachelor's degree in public policy from Duke University.

Notes

1. FTI Consulting and the Taproot Foundation, "Nonprofit Survey: Leveraging Pro Bono Resources," 2001 (unpublished data).
2. LinkedIn member survey, 2011, https://volunteer.linkedin.com.

3. Ibid.
4. D. Feldmann, *2014 Millennial Impact Report*, Achieve, 2014, http://cdn.trustedpartner.com/docs/library/AchieveMCON2013/MIR_2014.pdf.
5. Corporation for National and Community Service, "Volunteering and Civic Life in America 2014," www.nationalservice.gov/impact-our-nation/research-and-reports/volunteering-america.
6. C. Zukin and N. Szeltner, "Talent Report: What Workers Want in 2012," Net Impact, May 2012, https://netimpact.org/sites/default/files/documents/what-workers-want-2012.pdf.
7. Adam Grant, *Give and Take* (New York: Penguin Group, 2013), 49–50.

Chapter 16

Partnering with Workplace Volunteer Programs

Angela Parker and Chris Jarvis
Co-Founders, Realized Worth

Corporations weren't created to do good—much less send their employees out to volunteer on company time. Rather, companies were created to maximize shareholder returns. Right or wrong, this fundamental *raison d'être* is written into the DNA of corporations and inevitably influences their relationship with the social sector.

The responsibility of the social sector, on the other hand, is to organize and harness available resources to address social and environmental concerns—resources that are usually so scarce as to cripple our ability to respond to these challenges effectively.

So while corporations hurry to make the rich richer, nonprofit organizations scramble to piece together just enough sustenance to sustain at-risk populations, light our souls with art and culture, and help nurture our relationship with the world around us.

But perhaps things have changed. . . .

In recent years, the phrase *corporate social responsibility* (CSR) has taken on increasing weight. In most corporate circles, the term now carries with it important implications—implications that could make or break the future profitability of a company.

At the same time, many nonprofit organizations are becoming increasingly savvy corporate partners. They are launching profitable products and services, selling partnerships in high-profile campaigns, influencing public policy and opinion, and building valuable brands that compete in the marketplace.

Are we entering an era in which it's possible to bridge the gap between great power and great responsibility? When nonprofit organizations are prepared to usher their corporate partners into a better understanding of societal needs and the strategic opportunities to address those needs, both groups can begin moving together toward achieving a shared purpose. And in that process, individuals from companies find that when they are "giving back," they also receive—and sometimes, they receive far more than they expected.

Take Jim, for example.

Case Study: Jim

Jim had been joining a group of us downtown to volunteer for a couple of months. He never said much. All I knew about him was that he was an executive at a collections company—and by the looks of him, he hadn't spent much time serving food at men's missions. But still, he came every week and did whatever was asked of him.

Every week before we served the meal, I would gather everyone together to set expectations and remind everyone about our greater purpose. I gave a brief history of the organization, went over some basic parameters like, "Don't give out your phone number (or money or lend people your phone)—no matter how nicely the men ask for it," and then talked about why we were there.

"We're not going to solve hunger with one meal," I would say. "The 'poor' aren't a problem to be solved. These men are told on a daily basis to get off the stoop, get out of the way, get a job. They are told by everyone around them that they are worthless. So today, we're going to treat them as though they are the most important person we've met all week. That's our contribution. Not the food, but being here—that they are worth our time."

And then I would say, "Some of you will serve today and then go home and go about your business, relatively unaffected. And that's fine. We appreciate you being here today. Others may have a different experience. As we serve these men and comprehend everyone's value we may remember that we too have great value. And it's not tied to our salary or our home or our success. Today isn't about how much we get done. It's about allowing ourselves to be affected—as much as we're ready for—by what we experience here. Take time today to sit down with these men, listen to their stories, and share your own. If you're not ready for that, no problem. But if you are, you may find you get more out of volunteering than you expected."

I gave that speech every week. And every week, Jim was there, listening, nodding. But still, he didn't have much to say. I think it was six months later when he came up to me at the end of a meal, his brow furrowed. He said, "Chris, can I talk to you for a second?" This made me a little anxious, of course—I must have done something wrong. But I said sure.

"What's on your mind, Jim?"

"I just need . . . I uh . . . something's been bothering me for a few weeks."

I waited.

"I've been coming here for a while . . . but you might not know why I started here. About six months ago, I was at home with my family when I heard a loud knock at the door. It was two policeman. I knew something was wrong. They said, 'Is your son here?' He was upstairs. I barely let them in before they pushed past me into his room. Before I knew it he was in the back of the squad car. He's 16 years old. At the station I found out he had been selling drugs at school. Third strike.

"I was destroyed. I had no idea what to do. I couldn't relate to what my son was going through. I didn't know anything about drug abuse or jail. I couldn't talk to anyone. I was ashamed. . . . The only thing I could think to do was put myself around people who've been there before—people who have been where my son is. And so I came here.

"A few weeks ago, I decided to try what you suggested—sit down and talk to one of the guys. So I sat down across from Paul—you know that huge, black guy from Mississippi with the booming voice?—and just asked him how he was doing. He told me about his time in jail, his work to get his life back together, and his own son. And then he asked me about my life: 'What about you, Jim? Do you have any kids?' The whole story just poured out of me. And you know what he did? He took my hand and said, 'Jim, I'm gonna say a prayer for you.' And when he did, I was crying. I got up after that and walked away . . . and I felt like everything is going to be okay.

"So that's the problem, Chris. Since then I've been coming here for me. Now I'm worried I'm getting more out of this than I'm giving. What should I do?"

We don't volunteer just to create change, but to be changed. We become a better version of ourselves. And the world changes because of it.

From *Chris Jarvis*.

If we can agree that, in addition to addressing a big need, the act of volunteering itself has the potential to give life to the individual volunteer, then we can also agree that the power of partnering with workplace giving programs is nearly boundless. The challenge is finding the time and energy to determine *how* without ever losing sight of *why*.

How to Be a Great Partner (and Get Everything You Want in Return)

Despite the fact that companies were not created to do good, the number of workplace giving programs is increasing every year.

According to CECP's 2014 *Giving in Numbers* report (highly recommended for readers from any sector), from 2010 to 2013 "a majority of companies increased both total contributions (64 percent of companies) and giving as a percentage of revenue (66 percent of companies)." Corporate volunteering is on the rise as well and has been consistently since 2008.[1]

This gain shouldn't imply that the company's program managers have a lot of internal support. Although senior leadership staff members typically understand the value of philanthropy and even sustainability, their attitudes toward workplace giving and volunteering still tend to be doubtful, if not cynical.

Because nonprofits professionals are all too familiar with this attitude—it's a basic barrier in most fundraising campaigns, after all—you can help CSR practitioners break through this reticence by educating, equipping, and empowering them to make the case for the support they need.

First, Know Your Stuff

For better or for worse, the social and private sectors sometimes display a lack of respect for each other that comes from a simple language barrier. Nonprofits don't always understand the challenges companies face on a daily basis and companies don't always appreciate the immense pressure nonprofits are under. Like any language barrier, making an effort to learn just a few words can make all the difference.

The Basics

Although the definition of *corporate volunteering*—and even *workplace giving*—is constantly evolving, a typical definition is something like "the encouragement and facilitation of volunteering in the community through the organization by which an individual is employed."

Some of the first examples of this can be traced to the early twentieth century. Now, almost one-third of U.S. corporations embrace some form of employee volunteering, a growth of nearly 150 percent in the past three decades.[2]

Let's be clear: If a company's CSR manager simply slaps their colleague on the back as they walk out the door on Friday afternoon, and says "Good luck volunteering—don't forget to track your hours!" without offering any support (like matching the hours with corporate dollars or providing transportation to the volunteer activity), this isn't corporate volunteering. The time employees spend on their own—with no contribution from the company—should not be reported as time the company donated to the community.

The Benefits

Because it's an effective strategy for addressing negative reputation in society (meaning, it's good public relations), corporate volunteering is usually considered part of a company's corporate social responsibility efforts.[3] Although this is true for some companies, many are now moving to a more strategic approach that promises a myriad of potential benefits for not only the company, but also for the employees and the community, as well.

In recent years, the inclusion of volunteering within CSR is motivated strongly by the positive effect it has on individual employees. As HR managers will tell you, increasing employee engagement is the name of the game these days. Volunteering is a powerful path to engagement in part because it demonstrates support of the employee's interests outside of the workplace environment. It also can provide the achievement, recognition, new responsibility, opportunity for advancement, and personal growth that makes people happy at work.[4]

These concepts each relate directly to personal fulfillment and basic humanity. When a company takes time to formally offer an opportunity for community involvement, they are creating space for people to bring *who they are* to work, ultimately enabling employees to integrate their lives with their jobs. The more your volunteer program can speak to not only improving a company's public reputation—but also adding value to the recruitment, retention, training, development, loyalty, and overall satisfaction of employees—the more valuable the partnership will be.

Trends and Challenges

At times, CSR program managers can feel like no more than t-shirt vendors—and those are the good days! The bad days are when it seems like everyone in the office is asking for proof of the value of their position. Nonprofit professionals can offer both sympathy and empathy. Although the challenges CSR managers face are rapidly evolving, in general there are five key trends that make their job hard:

1. *Measuring Impact*

   CSR practitioners are often idealists—many of them came from the social sector. When corporate volunteering was new, impact was measured by how many people participated in the program. Now, companies are getting smarter. What difference are these programs making? What is volunteering doing for employees? Are they more engaged? How do we know? Is there any ROI? How are we helping the community? Companies need help measuring success and tracking and reporting their impact.

2. *Workplace Giving Software*

   You know how nonprofit professionals like to complain about technology? Well, so do CSR practitioners! Corporations depend on specialized software to connect, communicate, track, measure, and report on their volunteer programs. Every software provider says their tool can do almost anything under the sun—and they're usually not lying. The problem is, the vendor's understanding of what's being asked and the practitioners' intended questions are entirely different things. Since most workplace giving tools allow nonprofits to create profiles, upload their volunteer activities, and receive funds from employees, nonprofits should be as familiar as possible with them and be ready to encourage employee volunteers to use them.

3. *Increasing Participation*

   Corporate volunteer programs typically see the same volunteers again and again. Nonprofits have this problem, too. What's the secret to involving new people and keeping them? With this challenge, nonprofits and companies have to work together to create a program that provides space for people to fall in love with volunteering and then meets them at their highest level of contribution.

4. *Implementing Skills-Based Volunteering*

   Companies and nonprofits are in the same boat on this. Nonprofits need more skilled volunteers doing real work that moves the organization's mission forward in a significant way. Companies need to show how volunteering connects with their core business and increases the knowledge and abilities of employees. Partnerships are the perfect environment in which to address the needs of both parties. Two great examples are PwC's "3-Tiered Strategy for Community Investment"[5] and Edelman's "The Little Give."[6]

5. *Vetting Nonprofit Partners*

   According to a recent survey by LBG Associates, vetting a nonprofit outside the home country is the biggest challenge of all. As the report puts it, "The process includes deciding whether to even get involved in vetting local NGOs . . . and if the company does decide to vet, how deeply it wants to vet for different programs, who will do the vetting, and how much it is willing to pay for that."[7] Nonprofits can provide valuable insight into what it takes to crack this nut.

Know Your Story

Before any of this—before diving into research on corporate social responsibility or learning to empathize with the challenges program managers face—take a moment to consider whether you know your own stuff. I'm not talking about your organization's mission or metrics. I'm talking about *your* story, your fundamental *why*.

Why does any of this work matter to you? What compelled you to commit your life to the cause you now stand behind? Who helped? Where were you when your life changed? And if you're unsure of how it happened, take the time to look for it, and listen. Otherwise, we promise, the strain and exhaustion of a life that deals with fundamental needs of others will be too much to bear. Know your own story. There may be no practice more important.

Case Study: Mike and Greg

I didn't get into volunteering because I wanted to make a difference. I didn't get into it for any particular reason at all. It all started when everything I understood about the world was completely uprooted one afternoon on a street corner in Toronto. But let me back up. . . .

I had just completed my Master of Divinity and I was working at a tiny church in Milton, Ontario. It was a safe little suburb of Toronto with a predominantly elderly population who believed all teenagers were hoodlums and any group of more than three was a gang. Needless to say, they didn't like it when teenagers started to hang out outside the local mini mart after school. Between our white-haired community and the church, it was decided that Milton needed a drop-in center. And somehow I found myself volunteering for the task.

I had no idea what a drop-in center was. So, I began searching for someone who knew what they were doing—and that's how I met Mike. Mike was running a drop-in in Mississauga and his friend Greg ran a community center in downtown Toronto. The two of them invited me to come to Toronto. We met at a 24-hour greasy spoon to grab some breakfast. I explained the task, asked questions, and they answered as well as they could.

Mike and Greg walked me around the city. They wanted to introduce me to kids they knew—kids who were sleeping outside on cardboard, and as haggard as someone who'd lived a thousand lives.

"15,000 kids come in from the suburbs every summer," Mike told me. "And more than 5,000 stay. Too many. They think they'll spend the summer here, have an adventure, get into some harmless trouble, and go back home. But they get sucked in. Next thing they know, they're doing things they never thought they'd do—indescribable things. And they can't go back home because they feel ashamed."

We walked up and down alleys and backstreets for three hours. After awhile, they must have realized that I was overwhelmed with what I was seeing, because we stopped. Mike looked at me. "Chris, we've been talking non-stop for three hours. Can I ask you a question?" I nodded and he asked, "Your church in Milton—how many families are members there?"

"Probably about 25."

"Do any have basement apartments? Or spare bedrooms?"

"Yeah. Yes, I'm sure they do."

"Well, one of these kids—Sally—has been prostituting since she was 16. We were having coffee with her last week and she's ready to get her life together. She's got two kids, 2 and 4, and she's got a debt to pay. She's got a good head on her shoulders. If she could get a place to stay, a loan, some help getting her GED, she could really make a life for herself. Do you think any of those families would be willing to help Sally out?

I thought about it. I mean, I really thought hard. One by one, the faces of the families in my congregation cycled through my mind.

"Honestly, Mike—I can't think of anyone. I don't think anyone would be comfortable with that."

"Think harder. There's got to be someone. Just a little help. For a couple months."

"I'm sorry, Mike." I remember looking down at my feet.

Mike looked me hard in the eyes, pushed his finger into my chest, and asked, "Then what the hell good is your god to anybody?"

He may as well have punched me in the gut.

That afternoon I had an epiphany and it changed the course of my life. Here I was, an educated, decent person who believed in doing good. I believed in helping people. I had faith. But for someone who needed real help, I had nothing to offer. Neither did my community. I felt powerless.

I didn't know it at the time, but I made a simple and important decision that night. I decided to relearn my faith. Rebuild my beliefs. To do that, I would take every opportunity I could to interact with those who had been left behind. These men and women became my friends, my colleagues, my teachers—and they are, to this day, the reason I do the work that I do through Realized Worth.

From *Chris Jarvis*.

Next, Let Them Fall in Love

When corporations discuss volunteering partnerships with nonprofit organizations, they're usually referring to one of two categories of volunteering:

1. *General Volunteering*

   Also known as nonskilled or hands-on volunteering, general volunteering basically involves activities that require minimal skill and no long-term commitment.

2. *Skills-Based Volunteering*

   Also known as pro-bono volunteering (when it comes from employer programs), skills-based volunteering harnesses a specific skill such as accounting or marketing and often requires a sustained commitment over a period of time.

   Skills-based volunteering naturally appears more beneficial for both nonprofit and corporation. For example, let's assume a marketing director has the option to: (a) paint a fence, or (b) work with the nonprofit to create a marketing plan. Which does more for the nonprofit?

   In reality this contrast is meaningless. The litmus test for effective corporate volunteering isn't skilled versus nonskilled—it's the impact of the contribution on the mission of the organization. The real test: If you remove the company or the nonprofit from the equation, does it matter? Can a volunteer still do the same activity and achieve the same outcome on her own time with her own resources without the help of the nonprofit or the company? If so, the impact of the company's or the nonprofit's involvement is low.

   For the company, this kind of volunteering is really just a fun day out of the office. For the nonprofit, the partnership won't result in any long-term impacts.

A "Both/and" Approach

Companies and nonprofits that intend to generate high levels of impact together need to face two important realities.

Most Employees Don't Volunteer

On average, only about one in three employees volunteer on a regular basis (in the U.K., United States, and Canada). So companies have the amazing opportunity to promote volunteerism through their internal programs. According to the University of Toronto[8] in 2009, 42 percent of surveyed employees in Canada *volunteered for the first time in their lives* through their company's volunteer program. Great corporate-nonprofit partnerships have the opportunity to provide an experience that will significantly increase civic engagement in the communities where they operate.

Work together with corporate partners to establish high-quality volunteer experiences that will enable them to explore a bit before committing. This may involve skills-based activities, but at this stage it's not about immediate impact—it's about conversion. Give volunteers the chance to fall in love and then commit long-term.

But Some Employees Do

On the other hand, about one in three employees already volunteer regularly. In fact, many will view volunteering as a personal choice having nothing to do with their workplace. These volunteers have already made a connection with a cause that fits their interests. A significant number will also already be performing skills-based activities and want to remain committed to their nonprofit.

Follow their lead. Work with your corporate partners to identify employees who are already volunteering and empower them to help lead volunteering and giving. These employees are influential because they possess the experience, knowledge, and compelling stories to convince their colleagues (who have never volunteered) to get involved. Most corporations will have lists of employees who participate regularly in existing giving and volunteering events—start with this. These volunteers are the greatest asset of a corporate-nonprofit partnership.

Finally, the First Stage

The importance of a first step—where volunteers can fall in love with the organization—cannot be overemphasized. We call this a "First Stage" space.

What is First Stage space?

1. It is a low-commitment volunteer activity, usually one to three hours.
2. It takes place on a regular basis. Same time, same day, once a month or once a quarter—more than once a year!

3. Volunteers aren't required to commit to anything—no training, no e-mail list, no commitment. (Of course, these options should be available to those who ask for them.)
4. Friends and family are welcome.
5. A briefing is held at the beginning of the activity in which participants are told what to expect, why it matters, and most importantly, for whom.
6. A debrief is held at the end to give volunteers a chance to reflect. This isn't an evaluation of the event—it's a reflection on personal experience.

First Stage space enables volunteers to begin or continue a journey of leadership development that takes place through volunteering. New volunteers have the freedom to decide if they're ready for what the nonprofit offers, experienced volunteers can take on responsibility and help direct activities, and seasoned volunteers can offer leadership so new volunteers have a great experience.

Through this process, volunteers lead and recruit other volunteers, and both can ultimately gain personal connections to the nonprofit and become committed, long-term program advocates. These are the volunteers both corporations and nonprofit organizations are seeking.

A High Calling

Corporations weren't created to do good, but for better or worse doing good is now an important avenue to profitability—as well as a legitimate distribution of power and resources. Whether or not nonprofit and CSR professionals realize it, the rise of the practice of corporate social responsibility has positioned them as gatekeepers to civic engagement. More people will experience volunteering for the first time in their lives this year at work than anywhere else.

This is a high calling. Volunteering and giving is never just about stacking boxes, raising money, and collecting cans. These aren't transactional moments where someone gives an order to get something. These are moments where individuals can become involved in their communities and real transformation can occur.

When we volunteer, we transform into better versions of ourselves. If companies and nonprofit organizations can work together to enable more people in the workplace to realize better versions of themselves, the world will—over time—become a better place, too.

Angela Parker Co-founded Realized Worth with Chris Jarvis in 2008 to help corporations around the world develop workplace volunteer programs. Today the company's clients include Estée Lauder, Microsoft, Abbott Labs, Ball Corporation, AstraZeneca, and others. At Realized Worth, Angela is working to expand Realized Worth's global thought leadership through client work, workshops, webinars, and speaking engagements. Prior to launching Realized Worth, Angela spent more than 10 years addressing the challenge of building programs relevant to both the volunteer and the community being served. She is currently an MBA candidate at IE Business School in Madrid, Spain.

Chris Jarvis is Co-founder of Realized Worth, a global company that helps firms develop workplace volunteer programs. Before launching Realized Worth in 2008 with Angela Parker, he spent more than two decades working with nonprofits ranging from urban centers in North America to informal settlements in Africa. Widely known for his thought leadership, Chris was asked by the United Nations Office of Partnerships to design and launch Impact2030, the first private sector-led initiative to achieve the post-millennial Sustainable Development Goals through corporate volunteering.

Notes

1. Junior Achievement, *A 2009 Summary Report*, www.juniorachievement.org/documents/20009/36541/Benefits-of-Employee-Volunteer-Programs.pdf/8de7c97e-246c-4165-900d-b4a84f28c228.
2. John Peloza, Simon Hudson, and Derek Hassay, "The Marketing of Employee Volunteerism," *Journal of Business Ethics* 85/Supplement 2 (2009): 371–386.
3. Gian-Claudio Gentile, Christian Lorenz, and Theo Wehner, "Introduction: A Humanistic Stance towards CV—Taking a Critical Perspective on the Role of Business in Society," *International Journal of Business Environment* 4, no. 2 (2011).
4. "Two-Factor Theory," Wikipedia, September 24, 2014, http://en.wikipedia.org/w/index.php?title=Two-factor_theory.
5. Chris Jarvis, "PwC's 3-Tiered Strategy for Community Investment (USA)," Realized Worth, June 16, 2010, www.realizedworth.com/2010/06/pwcs-3-tiered-strategy-for-community.html.
6. For more, see www.thelittlegive.ca/2014.

7. LBG Associates, *Global Employee Engagement: Challenges and Solutions*, 2014 www.lbg-associates.com/publications/201408151108099CFDF1_LBG-Global%20Employee%20Engagement%20FINAL-ReducedSize.pdf.
8. The Southern Ontario Social Economy Community University Research Alliance, "Employer Supported Volunteering: Corporate Participation in the Social Economy," 2009, http://sec.oise.utoronto.ca/english/pdfs/factsheets/factsheet22F.pdf.

Chapter 17

Becoming Powered by Pro Bono

Alethea Hannemann
Vice President of Product and National Programs, The Taproot Foundation

Imagine if you had all the skills you needed to fully empower the talent you have on staff, run the best programs possible, stay in touch with clients, and report out in a way that made your story shine? Imagine if you felt like you were fully engaging the volunteer resources in your community? Imagine if you could motivate your board in new ways by asking them for more than a check? Imagine if you were getting your share of the $15 billion in value that professionals donate in time and talent each year?[1]

Imagine if, like Year Up (a national organization that empowers low-income urban adults to go from poverty to a professional career in one year), you were adding an additional 5 to 20 percent in value to your budget through high-quality, high-value pro bono? This is the potential of pro bono today.

When Aaron Hurst founded the Taproot Foundation in 2001, he had to prove that pro bono was a reliable, valuable way for nonprofits to engage their communities. People doubted that professionals would ever give their skills for free; they doubted that nonprofits would put in the effort to truly take advantage of those skills without "skin in the game"—unless they paid for it. In the early years, Taproot often asked our nonprofit partners and clients, "Is there any area or topic for which you wouldn't want to engage pro bono?" They always had an answer, typically having to do with finances, or organizational culture, or evaluation, or their clients—areas they thought were too nonprofit-specific, too sensitive, or too mission-critical to entrust to pro bono.

Times have changed. When we ask that same question today, we almost always get a resounding "no." Pro bono is seen as reliable and valuable, wherever a nonprofit sees a need—at least when it's done right. The question on people's minds is no longer "What is pro bono?" or "How can pro bono help me?" but rather, "How can I make pro bono an even bigger part of what I do with my community?" Pro bono is a way to bring top talent to the organization in areas where you can't or shouldn't have full-time staff. That's why Taproot calls the people who do pro bono "pro bono consultants"—because they're consultants brought in for special engagements in key areas, to augment the skills and talent of your team.

Since 2001, Taproot has brought high-quality pro bono service to thousands of nonprofits across the country and helped to design pro bono programs for dozens of companies. We know it works, and we know how it works. In this chapter, we'll help you understand how to turn on or tune up your pro bono efforts. You'll get the basics and background of pro bono, the wide range of organizational benefits, and the critical how-tos. We'll also show you how to scale your efforts across your team or organization. When you're done with this chapter, you'll have a better idea of the potential of pro bono to accelerate your progress and make the most of the resources you have on staff, as well as how to get there.

Defining Pro Bono

Pro bono—short for *pro bono publico*, which means "for the public good"—has come to mean the donation of professional services to advance public good. For the purposes of this chapter, we define it as professional services (marketing, legal guidance, human resources, technology, and so on) donated to a social change organization to further their mission.

What Is Pro Bono Today?

When people hear the words "pro bono," they often think of legal assistance. Legal pro bono is an important part of life in the nonprofit sector, bringing many millions of dollars of value to organizations across the United States and the world. And it's institutionalized; most lawyers think of giving pro bono as part of their professional responsibility, and top law firms compete on pro bono stats so that they can attract the best candidates.

Legal pro bono, however, has only been happening in a standardized, regular way since the 1980s. It grew quickly because the needs and rewards (on both sides) were so clear. Now the same thing is happening with other professions and functions. Pro bono today is a nonprofit COO getting ongoing technology advice from a business sector CTO. It's a nonprofit marketing team getting feedback on key messages and website copy from a company's branding team over a video chat. It's a nonprofit ED working with a PhD student to get insight into her 10 years of client data. And it's making a big difference in the nonprofit sector.

Why Do We Need Pro Bono?

Running a nonprofit today is an increasingly complex operation. New technologies bring great possibilities for efficiency and effectiveness, but also an abundance of choice (for example, try making a quick decision about volunteer management software!) and a whole new set of tasks and responsibilities (if you're not on social media, for example, you're likely feeling an anxiety that you should be). Funders are exploring powerful new partnerships with their grantees, but also demanding more in terms of program measurement and outcomes evaluation. And the rise of B Corps and for-profit social enterprises is adding to the war for talent and money.

In this environment, many nonprofit organizations need access to increasingly specialized skills, and often in project-based work. For example, take that technology issue. According to a 2014 study by the Nonprofit Finance Fund, in the previous year, 40 percent of nonprofits had upgraded hardware or software to increase organizational efficiency.[2] If you need to upgrade your Salesforce installation, you're not necessarily going to bring on a full-time, highly specialized consultant, but you do need expertise initially to make sure the installation meets your needs.

Pro Bono Facts

Seventy-seven percent of nonprofits believe skilled volunteers could significantly improve their organization's business practices.[3]

Pro bono service is considered a cash-equivalent donation and is valued at an average of $120 per hour.[4]

In this environment, it's not surprising that 92 percent of organizations tell us they want to use more pro bono services,[5] and not just as a response to scarcity. In addition to covering critical needs for your organization, pro bono can help you:

- *Engage partners in a new way.* Corporations and foundations often tell us how excited they are when nonprofit partners raise the possibility of talent donations, not just grants.
- *Bring unique professional development opportunities to your team.* It's impossible to engage a pro bono team and not learn from the experience, whether it's management coaching or subject matter expertise.
- *Develop a more agile, less siloed organization.* In thinking beyond the staff box, you'll see your community, and your own organizational capabilities, in a new way.

With these benefits in mind, pro bono today fits in a spectrum of volunteer engagement, as described in Figure 17.1—part of a robust volunteer engagement strategy that matches donated labor to critical organizational work. As millennials

Spectrum of Corporate Community Engagement

Nonprofit Needs	MAKING BUDGET	"EXTRA HANDS" TO DELIVER SERVICES/PROGRAMS		INFRASTRUCTURE AND LEADERSHIP	
Types of Support	FINANCIAL SUPPORT	HANDS-ON VOLUNTEERING	SKILLS-BASED VOLUNTEERING		
			GENERAL SKILLS	BOARD SERVICE	PRO BONO PROFESSIONAL EXPERTISE
Examples of Common Activities	▸ Cash grants ▸ Dollars for Doers ▸ Matching gifts	▸ Playground clean-up ▸ Soup kitchen ▸ Planting a garden	▸ Tutoring ▸ Literacy programs ▸ Career mentoring	▸ Board placement ▸ Board member training	▸ IT assistance ▸ Marketing collateral design ▸ HR consulting ▸ Legal counsel

Taproot Foundation, 2008.

taproot FOUNDATION

Figure 17.1 Where Pro Bono Fits In

Source: Taproot Foundation, 2008.

Table 17.1 Number of U.S. Professionals Working in Key Functional Areas

Functional Area	*Number of Professionals*
Finance	1,816,290
Human Resources	523,870
Information Technology	1,742,050
Legal	1,247,000
Marketing	742,330
Strategy	642,350

Source: BLS.gov, 2012.

in the workforce increasingly demand to give back in careers and corporate social responsibility programs embrace giving talent in addition to grants and in-kind donations, the pro bono part of the spectrum becomes more and more accessible.

The Nonprofit Professional's New Swiss Army Knife

What skills do you need today? And in what type of engagement? You can use pro bono in a variety of ways depending on your goals, your team, and your existing volunteer strategy.

Let's start with the expertise available in different functional areas. As you can see in Table 17.1, pro bono may have gotten its strongest start in legal, but today it reaches far beyond the legal profession.

The skills you need can come from different types of providers, as well. For example, corporations and professional services firms can offer a wide range of talent, regardless of the industry or product type in which they specialize. Individual pro bono consultants can support as many different types of engagements as there are professions and roles. Professional schools of all kinds often incorporate pro bono into the curriculum to attract top students or help prepare them for better post-graduation outcomes. And more and more organizations similar to Taproot—nonprofits that specialize in bringing pro bono to social change organizations—are launching every year and offering structured pro bono to nonprofits.

Finally, people often think that skills-based engagement by volunteers has to come in a big package, or it's not pro bono. But pro bono doesn't have to be team-based, or long-term. When Taproot talks to a new nonprofit partner, the organization's leaders sometimes tell us that they don't really use pro bono. Then they describe the HR strategist in their volunteer ranks who talked them through a big HR systems decision, or how a class from the local business school delivered an environmental scan before their last strategic plan, or the time they went to a Meetup group for local graphic designers to get feedback on their new brochure design. All those interactions are valuable pro bono work!

Year Up: Getting Good Pro Bono from the Get-Go

When an organization is really tapping into the pro bono potential in their community, we call it being "powered by pro bono"—and many of the top organizations you know are there.

One good example is Year Up, the organization we mentioned in the introduction. Year Up is one of the most successful nonprofits in the United States; as of 2014, they've worked with over 10,000 young adults in 12 cities. They also produce successful outcomes (85 percent of program graduates are working or in school full-time within four months of graduation), operate with a staff of over 400 people and an annual budget of over $70 million, and have been voted one of the top nonprofits to work for in the United States.[6]

Part of their secret lies in their ability to harness pro bono from the private sector, starting with legal services: Wilmer Hale, Latham & Watkins, and Goodwin Proctor have all provided critical analysis. Over the years, Year Up has also successfully locked in pro bono support from New Profit, Alta Communications (which provided initial start-up space and administrative help), and Monitor Group (whose four strategic planning projects have helped make Year Up the organization it is today)—along with countless creatives, event planners, and marketers who facilitate events with Year Up's corporate partners.

"I've never been afraid to make a polite ask," says Gerald Chertavian, Year Up's Founder and CEO. "Millennials and many other employees want more than just a paycheck. I ran a for-profit business for a number of years, and if a nonprofit could make that easy for me, they were doing me a favor. It's not just a one-way value exchange."

Hallmarks of Good Pro Bono

Organizations that make the most of pro bono are successful because they follow proven best practices. Here are five basic principles we share with our partners and clients.

Principle One: Know and Define Your Needs

Like all good initiatives, successful pro bono projects start with a clear need, articulated in a way that shows measurable goals and endpoints. This isn't always easy—most nonprofits who come to Taproot need and want help diagnosing their needs. Don't worry if all you can describe at first is a pain point, rather than the remedy. The right pro bono provider will eventually help you think through the possible remedies before you kick off the project.

Principle Two: Get the Right Resource for the Right Job

Once you know what you need, you can think about who can address it. Remember that the best pro bono is engaged proactively in response to your organizational plans and priorities. Savvy nonprofit leaders are as opportunistic with pro bono as they are in other areas, but don't create a project just to use a resource, or to keep a contact happy!

Principle Three: Be Realistic About Deadlines

Be thoughtful about which projects you can address with pro bono. Even small tasks can take longer than expected, and pro bono is rarely a good solution for urgent needs. As a general rule of thumb, count on pro bono to take 50% longer than in-house projects.

Principle Four: Act Like a Paying Client

You want your pro bono consultants to treat you like a paying client, so you need to treat them as if you are paying, with all the expectations and responsibilities that go along with it. Be flexible and appreciative, yes, but taking the project seriously, and insisting that your pro bono provider does too, is the only way to get what you need. The pro bono consultants you work with will appreciate that framing and attitude; it shows them their work is valuable, not an extra that you can afford to do without.

Principle Five: Learning Goes Both Ways

A pro bono project is a partnership in which you supply knowledge of your organization and field while the pro bono consultants bring their functional expertise. Different consultants have different motivations, but one of the most valuable things you can give any volunteer is new knowledge and new experience. Don't underestimate the value you're providing by enabling consultants to flex their skills in new contexts.

Making Pro Bono Work for You

So how do you put those best practices to work for you? Organizations that want to engage pro bono, or get more pro bono, face three basic challenges: articulating their needs, accessing or assessing potential providers, and finding the right way to manage projects (because like all volunteer work, pro bono projects definitely don't manage themselves).

To address those challenges, you can use Taproot's formula for good pro bono: scope, secure, manage, and scale.

Scope	*Secure*	*Manage*	*Scale*
Prioritize your list of possible pro bono projects; select one that is both feasible and high-priority; then define a scope of work so you and your pro bono partner know what will and won't be done.	Find the pro bono providers who are right for your needs and a good fit for your organization.	Manage your pro bono resources to ensure high-impact results. And be a good client! That can make all the difference.	Increase the use of pro bono across your organization, using pro bono as a key resource to grow your impact year after year.

Scoping: Setting Clear Goals for Pro Bono

The first step in scoping a project is selecting the right one. In choosing a project, you'll want to make sure that the project is a good fit for your organization, and that now is the right time. These four tests can help you answer those questions.

One Size Does Not Fit All

If you're new to pro bono, we highly recommend beginning with a "starter" project—one with less complexity but plenty of potential for impact. We have a catalog of over 130 projects on our website, taprootfoundation.org, all rated by level of difficulty.

1. *Is it bigger than a breadbox?* Can you clearly define the work that needs to be done? Ideally, your chosen project can be done by one or two people in no more than a few weeks or a couple of months. One person is easier to recruit, manage, and retain than a full team. (Bigger projects, such as websites, are often best for a known corporate partner, a nonprofit pro bono specialist, dedicated resources such as a loaned employee, or a nonprofit pro bono provider.) You can also break bigger projects down into smaller, standalone chunks so that you don't overwhelm your team or potential providers.
2. *Is it a burning need, or a flaming one?* When do you need to complete this project? What are the consequences of not hitting the deadline? If it needed to be done yesterday, it's likely not a good match for pro bono.
3. *Would you need to be an insider to be successful?* What will a consultant need to know about your field, clients, and so on? Certain projects, such as recommending a new organization name, require significant sector or organization-specific knowledge.
4. *Are your staff and board ready for this project?* Is your internal team open to this project (and having it done pro bono)? Do they have the time to be engaged on the project? Internal buy-in for the engagement is key, as is planning for what happens postengagement. And you'll want to select a project that is important, but not so strategic that your board needs to be

involved in every decision—those projects are difficult to socialize and close no matter who is doing the work.

Once you have a good project in mind, you need to set the parameters of the project so that everyone—both your internal team and the consultants you bring on board—has the right expectations. Get it on paper! In doing so, you want to be as specific as possible in scoping the work you need done, but stay open to input: the first step in a project is typically finalizing or confirming the project scope with your chosen provider. The most important thing at this stage is to clearly identify and prioritize your goals.

Elements of a Good Scope Document

- In scope. What will this project accomplish, and why is it important?
- Out of scope. What you won't do is just as important as what you will.
- Measuring success. How will you measure the impact of this engagement?
- Logistics. What resources are available or needed? What are the timing considerations?

Securing Resources: Getting the Right Pro Bono Provider

Securing pro bono resources can feel like one of the biggest challenges for nonprofits. We suggest you bring the same considerations to this type of resource-raising as you would to any other development process. For example, you'll want to use connections wherever possible and be specific about the ask you're making.

Three Tips for Securing Resources

1. Don't underestimate the value of relationships. Social capital is your best bet for finding and retaining pro bono talent.

2. Don't underestimate your own networks. Think about not just who you know, but who your staff, volunteers, and board members know. LinkedIn is a great tool for exploring your extended network.
3. Don't be afraid to ask! We hear over and over how pleasantly surprised clients are when they start advertising their needs.

You'll also want to tailor your outreach and pitch to your audience. The following table describes the pros, cons, and driving needs for each type of pro bono provider.

Source	*Motivation*	*Considerations*
Corporations	Pro bono helps them retain top employees, develop talent, and have a deeper impact in the communities in which they operate.	Have a lot of translatable core competencies in infrastructure support. May deprioritize pro bono if they have a sudden increase in workload. Most employees aren't consultants and aren't primed to work with external clients.
Professional services firms	Pro bono helps them attract, retain, and grow their talent—their main asset as a company.	Offer experienced consultants and niche or technical experts. May deprioritize pro bono if billable work increases. Often have a particular and preferred approach to their work.
Individuals	Pro bono helps them find personal satisfaction by giving back while growing their skills.	Are motivated by mission, so can be very dedicated. A single provider often means a single perspective (and a potential single point of failure). Requires screening capability by the nonprofit.

Professional schools	Pro bono helps them attract and train top students looking for real-world opportunities that augment the classroom experience.	Students have flexible schedules and offer insight into the newest best practices. Projects must fit into the academic calendar. The client is often the professor or advisor, not the nonprofit. Must be careful to focus on skill sets students currently have, not what they are learning about.
Nonprofit pro bono specialists	Pro bono is their mission.	They know a lot about pro bono. Can be an efficient connector. May have restrictions on who they can work with, and how.

At the end of the day, you engage pro bono talent for the skills ability they bring to the job. For more on getting the right pro bono expertise for the job, see Chapter 18.

Managing: Keeping a Project Rolling

Managing a pro bono gig can be more challenging than a typical consulting engagement (which is no small task itself!). Here are some of the most critical components to making it work.

1. Be prepared to invest time. To be successful, you must prepare your team or organization for the work, make sure the pro bono consultants know enough about your organization to be helpful, and be ready to take over the results when the consultants finish their work.
2. Understand your role as client. Check in regularly with your provider, hold him or her accountable to meeting deadlines, and give and receive feedback in a timely and considered manner.
3. Foster effective communications among your internal team. Keep them up to date, even if they aren't involved in day-to-day project decisions. This will help with both buy-in and implementation.

4. Create the space for you and your provider to share both good and bad news. And be prepared to listen to them!
5. Celebrate before, during, and after the project is complete. Recognition is one form of payment for your consultant team, and keeping everyone motivated will improve both process and results.

Scaling: Making a Habit of Pro Bono

When you use pro bono consistently, it stays top of mind, just like other volunteering opportunities you support. You're constantly on the lookout for opportunities to engage your community in ways that are rewarding for both volunteers and your organization. Here are some ways you can build some structure around pro bono as a core strategy.

Make pro bono part of the conversation.

Proactive pro bono is good pro bono! If you make pro bono part of the conversation, particularly in strategic planning and operational planning, you'll know where you can bring in help. With a thoughtful, vetted list of engagements, you can both seek resources proactively and react with confidence when good fortune brings you a skilled resource unexpectedly.

Integrate pro bono at all levels of the organization.

To make pro bono a priority, you have to track and support it. For example, you might adapt your volunteer database to track pro bono consultants and skill sets, and ensure that pro bono consultants are included in your recognition practices. To make sure that everyone is thinking of pro bono opportunities, you can train your staff and board on pro bono basics and opportunities, and publicly celebrate pro bono projects. Finally, you'll want to use evaluation to ensure you get good return on your investment and learn from each engagement.

Build strategic partnerships to support pro bono.

When pro bono is a core strategy for engagement, leadership thinks about resource-raising, not just fundraising. You're helping your partners to consider a full range of needs and opportunities, from financial and hands-on volunteer support to pro bono. Understanding pro bono is an option can be very rewarding for a funder or partner; when they believe in your mission, they often want to provide truly holistic support. (For more on partnering with workplace volunteer programs, see Chapter 16.)

Think resource-conscious, not resource-constrained.

Pro bono should never be used to fill in gaps or cover areas that require financial investment, no matter what the cost. With good pro bono, you're not looking to replace paid staff, you're looking to amplify their efforts. Doing that can start with a simple question about every project you take on: Would additional (pro bono) resources help us do this more, or better?

Next Steps: Where Do You Go from Here?

Pro bono is always an investment, but it's one that we believe pays back in spades. Whether you're doing pro bono for the first time or ramping up your pro bono engagements, you will see great returns in employee engagement, community involvement, and progress toward your mission. The best way to get started is, well, to get started! Here are a few smaller ways to dive right in:

1. Think about the pro bono you've done or experienced. What worked well and not so well? What can you learn from these experiences?
2. Learn from your peers. Can you talk to people at other organizations who are engaging pro bono?
3. Understand the possibilities. Look at your organizational plan with your management team to brainstorm some areas that might be ripe for pro bono.
4. Engage your board. Talk to your board chair about pro bono possibilities, and making pro bono a priority.
5. For more information about anything in this chapter, see our website, www.taprootfoundation.org.

Pro bono is a serious investment, but your existing volunteer practice can provide a jumpstart— and it gets easier every time you do it.

Alethea Hannemann is Vice President of product and national programs at the Taproot Foundation, where she uses pro bono services to turn complexity into opportunity for social entrepreneurs and social change organizations. The programs she's built at the Taproot Foundation have helped to mobilize thousands of professionals in pro bono work and delivered more than $140 million in consulting services to thousands of nonprofits. Alethea speaks regularly about pro bono and service development, and how professionals can join together to build social change. Before joining Taproot, she worked in product and content management for technology firms, and as a college instructor.

Notes

1. Corporation for National and Community Service, "Capitalizing on Volunteers' Skills: Volunteering by Occupation in America," Issue Brief, September 2008, www.nationalservice.gov/pdf/08_0908_rpd_volunteer_occupation.pdf.
2. "2014 State of the Nonprofit Sector Survey," Nonprofit Finance Fund, 2014, nonprofitfinancefund.org/state-of-the-sector-surveys.
3. "2006 Volunteer IMPACT Study," Deloitte & Touche USA LLP and the Points of Light Foundation, 2006.
4. "Defining and Valuing Pro Bono Service," Committee Encouraging Corporate Philanthropy and the Taproot Foundation, 2009.
5. FTI Consulting and the Taproot Foundation, "Nonprofit Survey: Leveraging Pro Bono Resources," 2001, (unpublished data).
6. Aaron Hurst, "Year Up Is Powered by Pro Bono," *Huffington Post*, October 17, 2012, www.huffingtonpost.com/aaron-hurst/year-up-is-powered-by-pro_b_1973402.html.

Chapter 18

How to Get the Right Pro Bono Expertise for the Job

Deirdre White
CEO, PYXERA Global

Amanda MacArthur
VP, Global Pro Bono & Engagement, PYXERA Global

Is volunteering *truly* a free service? Oxford Dictionary defines free as "something given or available without charge."

Volunteers are excited to give. They are motivated, talented, and make themselves available to you at no charge. They *willingly* give you their hearts and minds to help you in your mission to make the world a better place. Sometimes, a volunteer's motivation is professional in nature. The experience helps him or her to develop new skills and advance their careers. On a fundamental level, however, volunteering one's time and talent makes people feel good. As the pace of life intensifies every year, the experience fulfills a vital social connection, nourishes a sense of purpose, and encourages individuals to tap into something larger than themselves.

Yet, is this infusion of goodwill and talent really free? We propose that, much like the proverbial free lunch, it is not. It is, rather, *an exchange* grounded in a mutually beneficial experience for your volunteers and your organization. As part of this exchange, volunteers offer their time, energy, and abilities for an experience that produces a change inside, however small or large. The experience even induces the helper's high, a term coined by psychologists to describe a euphoric feeling that arises after performing a kind act. In exchange for this influx of talent, a nonprofit offers up valuable time and resources for a deliverable that has the potential to be game-changing.

For the purposes of this chapter, we will be speaking about pro bono volunteering, which we define as the giving of one's professional skills to deliver a product that improves organizational capacity. This can be a new marketing plan, a recommendation for a new technology, or a talent development strategy. It can be a pro bono team funded by a corporation or a single professional with a passion for giving back. This is different from the traditional hearts-and-hands volunteerism. Hearts-and-hands is when people give back through non-job-related skills through activities like building a new house for an underserved community, feeding the homeless at a soup kitchen, or walking for a cause. Pro bono volunteering requires a different level of resource allocation and an alternative approach.

So if pro bono is an exchange, how can you be sure you're getting what you need rather than the person or team that happens to be available? It's critical that you look at what your organization is willing to invest in a pro bono project *and* evaluate what you will achieve after the volunteers leave. Once you've looked at this scenario, ask yourself is this exchange equitable? Considering the resources you have available, is this project investment-worthy?

As a 25-year-old nonprofit, our organization, PYXERA Global, has facilitated thousands of pro bono projects, most international in scope. Today, we design and manage global pro bono programs for over a dozen multinational corporations and send their employees into emerging economies throughout Africa, Asia, Europe, South America, and now here in the United States. Consistently, the organizations that commit their time and talent to a pro bono project in a structured way have reaped tremendous dividends.

As a companion to Chapter 17, which looks at how to evolve your organization's entire pro bono outlook, this chapter will be looking specifically at how to make sure you get the right pro bono volunteer or team for a specific project. First, to understand the potential let's first look at what's taking place in the pro bono landscape.

The State of Pro Bono Today

> *"My pro bono assignments in Africa changed my mindset and my life. It's amazing what can happen in a few weeks in a foreign place with organizations and colleagues you don't know, but come to trust. I'll never look at my work or the world the same way again."*

This is Matt Berry, vice president of IBM Marketing for Cloud and Smarter Infrastructure. Matt had the opportunity to take part in two pro bono assignments in Nigeria and Tanzania. *Changed my life. Amazing. Transformational.* We hear words like these all the time. Experiences like Matt's are just one reason pro bono is on the rise.

From a company's perspective, there are many clear benefits to pro bono. According to a study on skills-based volunteering by True Impact,[1] employees who participate in pro bono are 47 percent more likely to report high satisfaction than traditional volunteers and 142 percent more likely to report job-related skills gains. Pro bono volunteering also provides far more cost-effective leadership development than traditional executive training programs. And it answers the boisterous call of millennials to inject a social purpose into their jobs and at the places they work. In fact, according to CECP, 71 percent of millennials would likely take a job with a company with a commitment to the community if all other factors were equal.[2]

Although hearts-and-hands or service volunteer rates actually decreased between 2012 and 2013,[3] pro bono continues to grow. Recently, PYXERA Global administered a benchmarking study to 26 of 39 known corporations with active global pro bono programs.[4] In 2006, just five major corporations had global pro bono programs. At that time, these five companies sent just 280 employees on pro bono assignments overseas. In 2013, the 26 companies that participated in PYXERA Global's study reported that they sent a combined 2,000-plus employees abroad. Additionally, the 13 companies who did not participate in the study sent many others employees abroad. These numbers consistently climbed each year.

Moreover, strong performers are choosing to stay with their companies over time as a result of participating in pro bono initiatives. IBM, for example, found that, in a survey of 575 employees who participated in the company's global pro bono program, the Corporate Service Corps, 76 percent reported that the experience boosted their desire to complete their careers at IBM.[5] It's for reasons like these that companies are increasing their investments in these kinds of programs.

Despite a mountain of evidence that workers love engaging their professional skills in doing good, most nonprofits say they simply aren't getting enough pro bono help. Confidence in pro bono work is increasing, but many organizations continue to have difficulty defining their needs and gaining access to pro bono providers.[6]

One thing nonprofits can do to address this gap is to create the kind of experience that individuals want to come back to and share with their colleagues and friends. Remember, as a nonprofit, you have a valuable commodity—the ability to create meaningful experiences that inspire and ignite the passion of pro bono volunteers. This may require a leap of faith on your part. Rather than approaching your volunteers from the mindset of "I'll take all the help I can get!," what if you thought of yourself as a provider of incredible journeys of purpose and impact? You have an opportunity to offer your volunteers!

AWESOME Cause: Investing in Pro Bono

One Chilean nonprofit we worked with took this idea of investing in pro bono from the start straight to heart. It paid off in a big way. For the sake of anonymity, let's call this organization AWESOME Cause. Despite its amazing work in social services and education, AWESOME Cause was having a hard time communicating what it achieved on behalf of many communities. Many of the people it had been helping for over a decade were unaware that it even existed. This was a real problem.

AWESOME Cause had worked with pro bono volunteers on a skills-based project in the past, but it wasn't the experience they had hoped for. This time, PYXERA Global worked with the organization's management to carefully think through where professional expertise would be most helpful in the long-term as opposed to just considering immediate, though perhaps not strategic, needs. Together, we determined that a new marketing strategy was mission critical. AWESOME Cause's executive team was prepared to dedicate staff to the project and some financial resources to implement the recommendation.

Before the real work of the assignment even began, the staff introduced the pro bono team to the organization, its staff, and culture through virtual meetings. The volunteers came to understand AWESOME Cause's programs and services. They also learned why the brand was so misunderstood early on. As a result of this immersion, the volunteers designed and presented a contemporary marketing strategy that fit the small organization's budget. They even set up social-media channels like a Facebook page and a Twitter feed and trained employees to manage these accounts.

After the pro bono team returned to their day jobs, AWESOME Cause immediately went to work on the team's recommendations. They had no in-house marketing staff, so they hired a freelance designer to redesign their website and brochure based on the team's suggestions. Today, their organization has garnered much more community attention. This sparked deeper community engagements and even local press, leading to more funding opportunities and allowing them to serve more people. It's a wonderful circle of success!

AWESOME Cause is our favorite kind of success story because its management invested in the project early by identifying the most strategic need and engaging with their volunteers and staff. They then partnered with the volunteers to develop a plan that could be put into action immediately.

Road Map for Pro Bono

A big part of preparing your volunteers to work with you is to give them a road map that defines how you will work together as well as the project focus. One of the most effective ways to do this is through the scope of work. A good scope of work outlines the organizational background, the project objective, the existing challenge, the requested deliverables, and the perceived impact. Share the scope of work with your volunteers before you begin working together. This will help them to absorb the project. At the same time, it sets expectations and defines the operational parameters for everyone involved.

To get the skilled volunteers you need, you must first be clear about what you want. Define what issue is most important to your organization. For example, are you lacking the right staff to carry out your organization's key priorities? In that case, the project may be a new employee recruiting plan. Is budget a key issue? Then you may want volunteers to focus on a new fundraising strategy. Decide what is *most important* for your organization.

How do you decide this when there are so many competing priorities? Strong projects often have a definitive answer to these questions:

Priorities—What is a project that you have always wanted to accomplish but have not been able to? Why do you want to accomplish it now?

Resources—What materials do you have available to address this project? What resources are you able to dedicate to this project *after* the volunteers depart?

Experience—Have you started this project before? If so, why hasn't it succeeded yet?

Bring in key organizational decision makers to provide input into these questions. This will help to ensure that your leaders are onboard with the project and invested in what the volunteers recommend.

Use the answers to these questions to help you define the scope of work. This will help your volunteers understand where your capacity gaps are and to work according to what's available. Here are other questions to consider incorporating into your scope of work:

Your Organization—What makes your organization unique? Provide a brief background on your organization. How and when were you founded? What are your values? Your vision and mission? What are some of your proudest moments?

Services—Provide a brief description of your services. What are your top programs and success stories?

Stakeholders—Who are your stakeholders? Provide a brief description of your target stakeholder profile and geographic coverage.

Background—Provide the history and basis of the proposed project. Try to paint the picture of the situation for the volunteers. What are the main concerns and problems? How were they identified? What has been done to address them so far? What are the consequences if the project is not a success?

Project Influencers—Who will the volunteers need to communicate with in order to be successful? Are they internal or external to the organization? Why are they important?

Project Challenge and Deliverable—In two to three sentences, explain the challenge. Be specific and concrete about what you would you like delivered at the end of the assignment. Are you looking for a slide presentation describing the project outcomes and methodology, a written report, or perhaps staff training? Outline these.

Your Definition of Success—What does a successful project mean to you? What is the potential short- and long-term impact of this assignment to your organization? Describe the community or economic impact you expect as a result of this engagement.

Execution—What opportunities exist for your organization to execute the volunteer's recommendations? Briefly explain what funding sources exist or might be available. Is this part of a larger initiative that is already underway?

Success Metrics—How will you use measure success?

Now once you've defined these areas, what will your volunteers actually do when they work with you? Outline the major activities you anticipate are necessary to accomplish the project objectives. Here are a few examples of the kind of activities to include:

- Hold an initial meeting with management to review the scope of work, understand mutual expectations, and determine the action plan.
- Revise the scope of work, if needed.
- Provide regularly updated briefings on the assignment's progress with the working group and your organization's management, including a final summary presentation with project results and recommended next steps.

What Skills Do You Expect Your Volunteers to Provide?

This is a critical, if often overlooked, part of developing a successful scope of work. Think carefully about where your internal talent gaps are and what professional expertise you want a volunteer to bring to the project. Be as specific as you can. Don't compromise if you feel like the appropriate skills aren't available. Either reconsider your scope of work or wait for a more appropriate group of volunteers to be available for what your organization really needs. As a nonprofit, we well understand the difficulty of saying no to "free expertise." But moving forward on a project with volunteers who do not have the appropriate skill set will only lead to a frustrating experience for everyone involved.

Before the Assignment Begins

The more prepared your organization is, the more efficiently a project can run. The preparation process is crucial to success. Here are some things you can do to prepare the best working environment for pro bono volunteers:

Make sure the right people are onboard.

Make sure key decision makers participate in major consulting sessions, like the initial meeting and the final pro bono recommendations. Appoint a liaison. This person doesn't need to be a decision maker, but he or she should have access to decision makers and enough knowledge to provide information and context to the volunteers. And be sure they have time in their schedule to dedicate to the project. This might mean other tasks need to be reassigned.

Schedule meetings in advance.

Have the initial schedule of meetings established before work begins so that the volunteers can get started immediately. Any schedule changes or times when leadership won't be available should be communicated early and clearly. The reverse is true as well. Request that your volunteers communicate their schedule to you and ensure that you know as early as possible about any changes.

Get to know each other.

Send the scope of work and electronic copies of any reading materials or relevant article links to your volunteers. To better understand who you'll be working with, research their company and business culture. Also, prepare a virtual or live orientation for the start of the engagement. Here, you can introduce the volunteers to your staff, your organization, and your mission.

Partnership: How to Get to the Happy Place

Up until now, we've talked mostly about tactical ways to get the kind of pro bono expertise you need—from volunteer preparation to the activities your staff will need to undertake. But there is another equally important aspect: partnership.

Corporations and nonprofits work differently. Conflict and misunderstanding are a real possibility between any pro bono volunteer and a nonprofit. Diverse backgrounds, cultures, pace of work, environments, organizational structures, and efficiency levels will inevitably lead to frustration. You can count on it.

To avoid these kinds of problems, it helps to have an honest conversation about expectations at the start of the project. Here are four fundamental principles to guide the working relationship with your volunteers toward partnership.

1. *Commit to the project.*

   Prioritizing your time is critical when building a sustainable partnership with volunteers. To maximize the time your volunteers are investing in your organization, make time for them. Dedicate as much time as possible to the project.

2. *Leave room for dialogue and transparency.*

   Help the volunteers understand your needs and goals. Whenever possible, try to provide them with access to the information they need to successfully complete the project.

   Don't hesitate to share your feedback—even complaints—and comments along the way. You should feel comfortable asking for a non-disclosure agreement if you feel like it's appropriate given the type of information the volunteer will be accessing. This level of structure creates the framework in which everyone can be comfortable operating.

3. *Keep an open mind.*

   Volunteers will encounter new ways of working during their project. Working in a nonprofit where there is often an all-hands-on-deck mentality is very different from working in a private sector company where it is often more structured and siloed. At the same time, your organization may come across different cultural approaches when working alongside pro bono volunteers—like the process through which volunteers approach the work. Keep a positive attitude and you'll be likelier to respect and embrace new perspectives and work styles. The best way to deal with difference is simply to be open-minded and communicate clearly if and when lines are crossed.

4. *Be flexible.*

   Expect the unexpected, and be ready to adapt quickly to changes. Having a work plan is important to ensure that the project is completed within the agreed-upon timeline. However, work plans are meant to be modified and should be adapted (with mutual agreement) to meet new priorities or fresh developments.

It really takes a partnership to bring the deliverables to life! In addition to these four principles, here is a phased approach by which to structure the project:

- *Phase 1: Fact Gathering*—The first phase is about immersion. Review the scope of work together to clarify project objectives and deliverables. Talk about responsibilities and expectations. Give volunteers access to pertinent data and reports and have them meet with leadership, staff, and key stakeholders. If you can, arrange for volunteers to meet with community stakeholders and perform site visits. This all provides context and increases the volunteers' understanding of your mission.
- *Phase 2: Data Analysis*—This is when access to your staff is most critical. Volunteers analyze findings from the first phase. Ask questions and provide consistent feedback during this period. Let them know if they are going down the wrong path, but remember, be flexible—it's possible they see something you don't.
- *Phase 3: Initial Recommendations*—Here, volunteers continue analysis and develop initial recommendations based within your available resources. Develop a specific action plan together for what will happen after the project with both immediate and long-term implementing steps.
- *Phase 4: Deliverable Finalization*—Volunteers finalize the deliverable and present these findings to leadership and relevant stakeholders, either in person or virtually.

Lastly, make the volunteers a part of your organization! This will enrich your experience and strengthen relationships, resulting in a stronger final product.

What You Need to Know About Corporate Culture

Although working cultures vary within each company, some common attitudes about time and resources can be fundamentally different from those of a smaller, mission-driven organization:

- Corporate volunteers working for large businesses have abundant financial and human resources. Help the volunteers to understand your resource constraints. Talk openly with them about your human, financial, and technical limitations.
- Because corporations are driven by profit, their working style usually is based on high productivity and specialization. Pro bono volunteers often focus on finding effective solutions as quickly and efficiently as possible. Be honest and open if you need a change in pace.
- It may be necessary to educate pro bono volunteers on what it means to be a mission-driven organization. Make sure they understand any "untouchable" or mission-critical programs.
- Time is a critical resource in the corporate world. Therefore, corporate volunteers typically show up early or on time to meetings.
- It may be difficult for corporate volunteers to adapt to a different professional climate in the beginning. Extend hospitality and explain your office culture. Spend time to integrate volunteers into your organization, especially if they are working in person.

Engage with Purpose

How can you transform your volunteer resources for a successful outcome? *Engage purposefully in the pro bono relationship*. Partnership starts by investing with intentionality. This begins long before volunteers arrive eager to work together. Be goal-driven. Acknowledge and openly communicate about your organizational needs and resources. At the same time, stretch to meet your pro bono volunteers where they are. Give them a structured approach similar to the one we've outlined in this chapter.

Remember you have something precious to offer a rich and diverse community of pro bono professionals who want to give back: a meaningful and authentic experience! If you take time to invest upfront in pro bono, you can create the kind of experience that your volunteers will be hungry for and want to repeat!

Deirdre White is CEO of PYXERA Global and an internationally recognized leader in the field of economic development. Spearheading the growth of the global pro bono practice, she guides companies such as IBM, SAP, PepsiCo, and Pfizer as they provide skilled expertise to build organizational capacity in emerging and frontier economies. Widely cited for her thought leadership, Deirdre has contributed to *The Washington Post, MarketWatch*, and *Stanford Social Innovation Review*. She has been quoted in the *Wall Street Journal, Bloomberg, Forbes*, and *Fast Company*, and served as judge on the 2014 HULT Prize and facilitator of The Clinton Global Initiative's Employee Engagement Action Network.

Amanda MacArthur is Vice President of Global Pro Bono & Engagement for PYXERA Global, where she designs and implements corporate social responsibility programs for the public and private sector focused on skills-based volunteerism in emerging markets, leadership development, and sustainable economic impact. Amanda leads the organization's Global Pro Bono and MBAs Without Borders programs, as well as The Center for Citizen Diplomacy. Amanda played a key role in designing IBM's Corporate Service Corps, while overseeing Global Pro Bono programs for PepsiCo, Pfizer, FedEx, and several other multinational corporations. Amanda has been published in *Organizational Dynamics* and *Stanford Social Innovation Review*.

Notes

1. True Impact, "3rd Annual Volunteerism ROI Tracker Report," 2012, www.trueimpact.com/2013-volunteer-roi-tracker-activity-whitepaper.
2. CECP, "CECP Celebrates 15 Years of Growth: Good Corporate Values Brings Good Business," http://cecp.co/cecp_infographic.html#.VCQqufldXyZ.
3. Bureau of Labor Statistics, "Volunteering in the United States, 2013," www.bls.gov/news.release/volun.nr0.htm.
4. A. MacArthur and A. Bonner Ness, "Benchmarking Survey: Corporate Global Pro Bono: The State of the Practice," PYXERA Global Report, August 28, 2014, http://bit.ly/1vq8j9A.

5. "IBM's Corporate Service Corps: A New Model for Leadership Development, Market Expansion, and Citizenship," IBM, 2011, www.ibm.com/ibm/responsibility/corporateservicecorps/pdf/IBM_Corporate_Service_Corps_Essay.pdf.
6. Z. Halper, "Taproot Foundation Announces Pro Bono Marketplace," *The NonProfit Times*, January 23, 2013, www.thenonprofittimes.com/news-articles/taproot-foundation-announces-pro-bono-marketplace.

Chapter 19

Volunteering and the Future of Cause Marketing

Joe Waters
Author, Founder of SelfishGiving.com

I was surprised when VolunteerMatch asked me to contribute a chapter. I just didn't view cause marketing as connected to volunteering—and I thought Robert Rosenthal and I agreed on this point!

You see, Robert was the one who practically convinced me to not include volunteering in my latest book on nonprofit fundraising, *Fundraising with Businesses* (2013). I had considered several volunteer-related strategies for the book, but in the end I only included one: volunteer grants, also known as "Dollars for Doers" programs, which match a corporate volunteer's time with a small grant from the company to the nonprofit.

So, why would I now write a chapter on cause marketing for a book on volunteering?

Because Robert actually had a much better grasp of what volunteering is and where it's headed than I do. Although he was right to nix volunteering from a book on fundraising tactics, he was also right that volunteering would have a major impact on cause marketing. Robert challenged me to adjust my perspective on the connection between volunteering and cause marketing.

A major hurdle for me was realizing that volunteering was more than just those little old ladies who used to stuff envelopes at my last nonprofit job.

No, volunteering was so much more.

Volunteering is when a person freely chooses to spend his or her time—unpaid—supporting a needy group or individual. A volunteer's goal is to have a meaningful, measurable impact.

Using my new lens on volunteering, I peered out and discovered something incredible: Volunteering is not just connected to cause marketing; it's the future of cause marketing. As focused as I was on defining cause marketing as a partnership between a nonprofit and for profit, I neglected the spark that makes these pacts ignite: individuals. These motivated and empowered do-gooders will be the key drivers of growth over the next generation.

I am excited to share with you what I learned. Here's how the chapter is structured:

1. I start with an overview of what cause marketing is and how it's currently practiced.
2. I argue that cause marketing's traditional approach is changing because of four key factors: millennials, social business, mobile, and social media.
3. I discuss the rise of new, digitally savvy and empowered volunteer fundraisers who are changing the traditional model of nonprofit and for-profit partnerships. I call them "Halopreneurs."
4. I offer some specific advice for nonprofits on how to position themselves for success with Halopreneurs and their business partners.

The last point will be critical for nonprofits. Although I was excited to discover the next shift in cause marketing, I quickly realized these new trends wouldn't favor nonprofits. Competing in a world turned right-side up will require self-awareness, focus, new staff, and of course, money.

To keep up, nonprofits will need to act boldly to thrive in a world where do-gooders and companies are clearly in charge.

What Is Cause Marketing?

Cause Marketing 101

This chapter assumes you know little about cause marketing. If you have more questions about cause marketing after reading it, you should visit my website, Selfishgiving.com. You can also find many examples of cause marketing campaigns on Pinterest at Pinterest.com/joewaters, where I have over 3,000 cause marketing pins.

Although cause marketing (sometimes called cause-related marketing) has been around since the late 1970s, most nonprofits still don't have a good handle on what the term means. They think cause marketing means anything related to the marketing of causes, or to business giving in general.

On social media, someone will post, "Great example of cause marketing!" with a link to some clever piece of nonprofit marketing in print or video. No wonder people are confused.

But I define cause marketing as a partnership between a nonprofit and a for-profit for mutual profit.

Cause marketing is win-win. The nonprofit raises money and awareness and the for-profit earns a halo that enhances their favorability with consumers, which may increase sales.

Cause marketing partnerships are also work-work, which means neither partner gets a free ride. The nonprofit doesn't receive an unexpected check, and the business doesn't write one as part of its annual holiday giving program.

Good partnerships between a nonprofit and for-profit are engaging, ongoing, and valued.

After writing my first book, *Cause Marketing For Dummies*, questions persisted on what exactly cause marketing was. I vowed not to use the phrase in my next book! That's why I chose *Fundraising with Businesses* for the title of my second book. But in practice, I use the two terms interchangeably.

Remember: Cause marketing = Fundraising with Businesses

In *Fundraising with Businesses*, I identified 40 strategies for how nonprofits can work with business. That may seem like a lot, but you probably would recognize most of these. They range from collection drives to Facebook contests to matching gifts.

However, the most popular and lucrative cause marketing strategies are called point-of-sale. They include:

- Pinups: These paper icons are sold at the register for a buck or two. The cashier will ask, "Would you like to donate a dollar to ____"
- Register Programs: Like pinups, register programs happen at the register, but there is no ask from the cashier and no pinup. Instead participation is requested within the transaction process or via signage.
- Percentage-of-Sales (POS): These programs can range from a product that donates a portion or percentage from each sale to a "donate profits" day for everything in the store. Many of the cause-related products for sale during Breast Cancer Awareness Month in October are POS programs.
- Donation Boxes: Donation boxes—also called coin canisters—are one of the simplest and cheapest ways to raise money from businesses. Again, the action takes place at the register where customers can drop a few coins, or a buck or two, into a donation box.

These simple but effective point-of-sale programs have raised millions for nonprofits.

- McDonald's worldwide donation box program annually raises $50 million for Ronald McDonald House Charities.[1]
- In 2013, Kmart stores raised a whopping $22 million for St. Jude's Children's Hospital with a register program.[2]
- On World AIDS Day, Starbucks donates a dime from every handcrafted drink sold. They've raised over $12 million for Product (RED) since 2008.[3]

In 2012, the Cause Marketing Forum did a study of point-of-sale fundraisers and found that the top 64 cause marketing programs raised $358 million. Cause marketing is fundraising gold!

As Charles Best, the founder of Donorschoose.org, has said: "The key to cause marketing is the brand enabling the consumer to be a philanthropist."[4]

Instead of fighting over the charitable-giving scraps from a company foundation, cause marketing lets nonprofits feast on the largest piece of the philanthropic pie—individual donors. It's this important connection between individuals and businesses that will drive the future of cause marketing, which we will discuss next.

Goodpocalypse: The Future of Cause Marketing

In looking for what's next for cause marketing, I might have stumbled on what's next for humankind: the Goodpocalypse. Although I've spent years watching zombie movies and TV shows to get ready for the zombie apocalypse, it turns out all my hard work has been in vain. The future isn't the walking dead: it's GOOD!

The Goodpocalypse will be a golden age of social responsibility. In the near future, some nonprofits will raise more money than they ever dreamed, and, closely working with businesses, society will address and solve some of the world's most serious problems.

The Goodpocalypse will be driven by four key factors (or horsemen!): millennials, social business, mobile, and social media.

Millennials

For more on engaging millennials, see Chapter 5 in this book. But let me first share a few words about why they are driving the Goodpocalypse.

Millennials—men and women ages 18 to 34—are the most socially conscious generation in American history. They expect companies—and nonprofits—to meet their high standards with responsible and impactful programs.

For companies that heed the call of millennials, the benefits are clear. According to the Cone Millennial Cause Study,[5] once they've learned that a company is socially and/or environmentally responsible:

- 83 percent of millennials are likely to trust the company more.
- 79 percent are likely to purchase that company's products.
- 44 percent are likely to actively pursue working at that company.
- 74 percent are more likely to pay attention to that company's message because it has a deep commitment to a cause.

These stats make things clear: Organizations that ignore this generation, and its commitment to social causes, do so at their own peril. Earlier this year, lower-than-expected earnings for warehouse club Costco raised shareholder concerns that its customer base doesn't include enough millennial shoppers. Another victim is golf. Millennials playing golf fell 13 percent over the past five years.

Golf for a cause, anyone?

Millennials are natural do-gooders, but they are not alone. Baby boomers and Gen Xers are not far behind in their commitment to supporting causes. A global survey by public relations giant Edelman showed that 87 percent of human beings believe businesses should place at least equal weight on profit and purpose.[6]

Social Business

What social problem are you trying to solve?

It's a question even businesses will one day have to answer, as every organization will need to be a social organization. Companies will be as deeply committed to social change as they are to turning a profit. Consumers—no, the people of the planet!—will demand it.

Kellogg's, for example, is committed to hunger relief. Through its "Breakfasts for Better Days" initiative, the company plans to donate one billion servings of cereal and snacks in support of global hunger relief by the end of 2016.[7]

Yes, companies will play a major role in solving social problems, and most of these gains won't be accomplished with the corporate checkbook. Right now U.S. companies donate $16 billion to charitable causes each year. This seems impressive, but regular people contribute several hundred billion dollars each year.[8]

The real opportunity is when companies look at every part of their business operation for opportunities to be more sustainable and responsible. These changes will come in all shapes and sizes.

Britain's Marks & Spencer stores, offices, delivery fleets, and warehouses in the U.K. and Ireland are now carbon-neutral. Overall, their CO_2 emissions are down 23 percent since 2007.[9] Meanwhile, General Motors discovered an opportunity in its trash: To support the Empowerment Plan, a Detroit-based nonprofit that employs homeless women to make coats for the needy, GM donated scrap sound-absorption material from its cars to make insulation for the coats.[10]

I can't predict the future, but I can tell you this: More companies will be like Tom's Shoes, Warby Parker, and Chipotle than not.

Mobile

Mobile is the future of, well, everything, and that includes fundraising with businesses. Chapter 1 in this book, which explores future trends that will impact volunteering, goes into this more. But it's important to understand how mobile tech will affect cause marketing, too.

The future of fundraising is targeting donors where they are and where they care. New technologies like Apple's iBeacon are showing how this is now a reality.

iBeacon is "micro-location," in that it works in a physical location (like a store) with the apps on your smartphone. Through an iBeacon transmitter, businesses can better interact with consumers in and/or near their business. They can not only push coupons to you when you walk in the door, but they can also give you one when you linger in a particular aisle or over a specific product.

Companies can even push reminders to consumers: "Last time you were on our website you were searching for a blend of coffee that we have in stock."

Think about the possibilities for cause marketing. Companies can tell consumers which causes they support, which products are eligible for a donation, and consumers can donate while in the checkout line.

Another powerful feature of iBeacon is that it turns consumers into beacons. When you support a cause at the register, the business can update others in the store of the new grand total raised for its favorite charity, which may encourage consumers to give when it's their turn at the register.

iBeacon sounds futuristic, but it's really just the beginning. Soon everything will be connected to the Internet. Cities, cars, buildings, for sure. But also toothbrushes, blenders and, yes, even your dog.

A product called TAGG attaches to your dog's collar and you get an e-mail or text when your pooch strays outside your yard. Think about the potential for good. A tag that keeps track of your dog means fewer chances for mischief and unwanted offspring. That's a good thing, right? And because TAGG is a supporter of ASPCA, one day you could get smartphone alerts on cute dogs at nearby shelters, or make a donation to ASPCA every time your dog strays outside the area—or stays in it!

We currently have around 20 billion things connected to the Internet.[11] This Internet of things will be an Internet of good things, too.

Social Media

If social impact is the fire, social media is the gasoline. (Check out Chapter 11 for more from on social media and volunteering.) But here's why social media will continue to light up the Goodpocalypse.

According to a recent social influence research paper from Crowdtap, millennials spend almost five hours a day on content created by family, friends, and others they know. They also prioritize social networking above all other media types, with 71 percent saying they engage in social media every day.[12]

To connect with millennials on social issues, organizations need to look beyond traditional advertising, which millennials consume irregularly and is not influential. Social networks are where you can find millennials and where you can earn their attention and trust.

In addition to being the current among millennials, social business, and mobile, social media is a nonprofit's best tool to communicate their impact and earn the attention of stakeholders. Although it's easier to discuss millennials, social business, mobile technology, and social media separately, don't forget their interconnectedness. You can't afford to ignore any of these pieces.

A New Breed of Volunteers: Halopreneurs

The convergence of millennials, social business, mobile, and social media has produced a hybrid volunteer-fundraiser who is making The Goodpocalypse a reality. I call them "Halopreneurs."

I created the term after I witnessed the efforts of two college students to help the victims of the Boston Marathon Bombings in 2013.

Nick Reynolds and Chris Dobens are great examples of Halopreneurs, and they certainly fit the description of people who freely choose to spend their time—unpaid—supporting a needy group or individual with the goal of having a meaningful, measurable impact.

As you'll see, Nick and Chris are at the vanguard of The Goodpocalypse. They are smartphone-toting millennials who are savvy social media users. They also partnered with a social business: Milwaukee-based Ink to the People, a company that is as committed to purpose as they are to profit.

Like many Bostonians, Emerson college students Nick and Chris were glued to their television after two bombs exploded at the Boston Marathon finish line on April 15, 2013. Several people died, including a child, and hundreds were injured.

"I looked at Nick and said, 'Why don't we come up with a t-shirt?'" Chris recalled in an interview with Boston's CBS affiliate WBZ-TV.[13]

Working with Ink to the People, the two picked a blue shirt with yellow letters that said "Boston Strong." Their goal was to sell 110 shirts. Each shirt sold for $20 with $15 going to the victims. They promoted the shirts all over campus, but it was social media—especially Facebook with its high number of mobile users—that propelled the fundraiser.

Nick and Chris didn't realize what they had started. Not only did they turn the phrase "Boston Strong" into a battle cry for an angry city and a united nation, but when the campaign concluded two months later they had sold 59,000 shirts!

A fundraiser created on a whim ultimately raised over $1 million for The One Fund, the nonprofit established after the bombings to support the victims.

This accomplishment couldn't have been achieved without two millennial do-gooders, social media savvy, and a social business equipped to meet the challenge of making, printing, and distributing tens of thousands of t-shirts.

Halopreneurs, a hybrid volunteer-fundraiser, was born!

What Nonprofits Need to Do Now

If you're a nonprofit professional who has been carefully reading this chapter, you should be worried. Very worried. Here's why.

Businesses are acting like nonprofits.

Companies are evolving into quasi-nonprofits with their own social missions and infrastructure. Take the example of Panera Bread, a chain of casual restaurants. In 2009, the company's nonprofit foundation created Panera Cares, a nonprofit "pay what you can" restaurant in its home market of St. Louis. Meant to fight hunger by giving the poor a low- or no-cost option, the program has expanded to six other cities.

Another challenge is businesses that are raising money for the company's foundation, and not for a specific nonprofit. For example, in September 2014, Boston-based Dunkin Donuts launched a national campaign in its stores to raise money for its own foundation.[14] Companies like Dunkin are focused on building their own philanthropic brands, and not the brands of their nonprofit partners.

Donors are acting like businesses.

A lot of people think that the Ice Bucket Challenge, which raised over $100 million in the summer of 2014, started with the ALS Association.[15] But it didn't. It actually started with one individual supporter. There are many things that contributed to the success of the Ice Bucket Challenge. But two things it couldn't have succeeded without were social media sites—especially Facebook—and mobile technology. These are the same two things that drove t-shirt sales after the Boston Marathon Bombings.

Supporters can communicate their cause messages like never before, and without the aid of advertising or traditional media. This is powerful stuff, and businesses—as demonstrated by the number of CEOs who participated in the Ice Bucket Challenge—are eager to align themselves and serve the efforts of do-gooders. In short, businesses can bypass nonprofits and go right to the people that nonprofits used to give them access to.

Nonprofits don't have their act together.

With the Goodpocalypse looming, most nonprofits are short on just about everything they need to thrive:

- They're limited on how much they can invest in themselves because donors and watchdogs are carefully tracking their expenses.
- They lack the staff and technology needed to engage on social-media sites and build publishing platforms.
- They're not adept at targeting younger donors, like millennials. Their communication and outreach efforts reflect their preference for baby boomers—despite the fact that, in 15 years, baby boomers will comprise just 30 percent of the workforce.

To review: Businesses don't necessarily need nonprofits to achieve their social missions. They can bypass nonprofits and work directly with do-gooders. And supporters don't need nonprofits to organize fundraisers. On top of this, nonprofits don't have the money, time, resources, or talent to change any of this.

Businesses and Halopreneurs might be the only survivors of the Goodpocalypse.

I'm not saying that nonprofits are going out of business—although some certainly will. We'll always need and have nonprofits. But the competition will be stiff from purpose-driven businesses that are acting like nonprofits and from Halopreneurs who can raise money independently of nonprofits.

The challenge for nonprofits is to build a powerful brand that attracts support from businesses and Halopreneurs. As comedian Steve Martin has said, "Be so good they can't ignore you."

How to Thrive in a World Turned Right-Side Up

Nonprofits give me a perplexed look when I first tell them they can raise more money for their organizations by creating and publishing quality content.

"Content marketing?" they ask. "You mean like blog posts, videos, white papers, and those crazy infographics?"

"Yep," I say. "You can either attract supporters through useful content or you can make endless cold calls. Which do you prefer?"

Silence. Now I have their attention.

Content creation may be the most important thing you can do to attract cause marketing partners and ultimately connect with supporters and raise more money. That is because content is the best thing in the world for communicating your nonprofit brand—which is what corporations are ultimately hoping to hitch a ride on.

As nonprofit brand expert Jeff Brooks has taught me, a nonprofit brand makes two promises:

- To have an impact.
- To communicate that impact clearly and powerfully.

The number-one priority for a nonprofit is to build its brand. Although most nonprofits are having an impact, they do a terrible job communicating that impact clearly and powerfully. This is why creating and publishing content is so critical to the success of your organization.

It's not like you have a choice. Creating quality content about your organization isn't an option. Generating useful content that informs, educates, and inspires is a requirement for three reasons:

It's Part of Being a Top Nonprofit Brand

Share Our Strength, charity: water, March of Dimes, Make-A-Wish, and many other top nonprofits are all content creators. The Water Log—the blog for charity: water, one of the best cause marketing nonprofits on the planet—features stories on successes and failures.[16] But it always keeps its readers informed and inspired.

It doesn't matter if you're smaller than these organizations. The benefits of content creation apply to everyone, regardless of size or budget. Mark Horvath of Invisible People TV has developed a national reputation for his small nonprofit by filming the stories of the largely "invisible" homeless population.[17] Horvath's nonprofit is just him, but his videos have spread the news of his work and caught the attention of many large companies, including Virgin Mobile, Ford, and Hanes.

You Need to Stand Out

According to the National Center for Charitable Statistics, more than 1.5 million nonprofit organizations are registered in the United States.[18] Tiny Rhode Island has more than 7,000 nonprofits alone! Content is a key tool in separating your nonprofit from the rest of the pack.

This is especially important as people use search engines to find and research organizations. Several factors determine how search engines rank and deliver search results, but one thing is clear: If you don't produce high-quality content and links, online searchers won't find you. Period.

You Can't Just Do Good Work Anymore

Sorry, but making the world a better place isn't enough anymore. If you're as old as I am, you may remember the days when there were only a handful of television stations to watch. These days, there are hundreds of stations to choose from, and the competition is brutal.

It's the same with nonprofits. Charities such as the Salvation Army, the American Red Cross, and St. Jude Children's Research Hospital were all lucky to establish their brands during simpler times.

Charities that have quickly succeeded in the past decade or so have been largely driven by celebrities, such as U2's Bono for (RED) and Lance Armstrong for LIVESTRONG. For most of us, Oprah isn't calling. And, as we learned from the LIVESTRONG fallout, having a celebrity ambassador isn't all it's cracked up to be. That's why you need to fall back on yourself and tell your own story with text, pictures, audio, and video. Focus on being interesting, useful, and credible. Publishing is your path to stardom and cause marketing success.

The Rising Tide That Lifts All Boats

I frequently write and speak on how cause marketing can help nonprofit organizations succeed. I speak from experience. I started my blog, Selfish Giving, in 2004 shortly after I was hired to launch the cause marketing program for a Boston hospital. During my tenure, we partnered with dozens of businesses and raised millions of dollars.

Cause marketing is the rising tide that lifts all boats. The better you communicate your impact, the more your organization will become a magnet for all forms of giving. You'll raise more money from businesses, individuals, and foundations.

If you're like most nonprofits I know, you're stuck in the shallows with no current or wind. Engaging in cause marketing is having deep waters beneath you and a full sail on deck. The winds that will fill your sails will come from millennials, social business, social media, and mobile technology.

Trust me, you'll need all of them to reach your destination.

Joe Waters is one of the world's leading authorities on cause marketing. His blog at Selfishgiving.com is the number-one resource on the subject and he is the author of *Fundraising with Businesses: 40 New (and Improved!) Strategies for Nonprofits* and co-author of *Cause Marketing For Dummies*. Joe has written for *The Huffington Post, Forbes, The Nonprofit Quarterly*, and *The Chronicle of Philanthropy* and has been quoted in the *New York Times*, among other publications. Joe is a well-known speaker on topics of philanthropy, marketing, and new media. Previously, Joe was director of Cause & Event Marketing at Boston Medical Center, where he launched its cause marketing program in 2004.

Notes

1. "McDonald's and RMHC Celebrate 40 Years of Supporting Children and Families" (press release), October 7, 2014, http://news.mcdonalds.com/press-releases/mcdonald-s-and-rmhc-celebrate-40-years-of-supporting-children-and-families-nyse-mcd-1149583.
2. "St. Jude Thanks and Giving Campaign Raises More than $72 Million Toward Finding Cures and Saving Children" (press release), February 25, 2013, www.stjude.org/stjude/v/index.jsp?vgnextoid=e06319b764c0d310VgnVCM100000290115acRCRD.

3. Starbucks website, "(Starbucks) RED," www.starbucks.com/responsibility/community/starbucks-red.
4. From his keynote presentation at the 2014 Cause Marketing Forum conference, May 29, 2014, Chicago, IL.
5. Cone Communications, *2006 Millennial Cause Study*, www.conecomm.com/2006-millennial-cause-study.
6. Edelman, *Good Purpose 2012*, http://purpose.edelman.com/.
7. For more on Kellogg's "Breakfasts for Better Days," visit http://newsroom.kelloggcompany.com/2013-02-25-Kellogg-Company-Launches-Breakfasts-for-Better-Days-Hunger-Relief-Initiative.
8. The Giving USA Institute, *Giving USA 2013 Report*, store.givingusareports.org/Giving-USA-2013-Report-Highlights-P98.aspx.
9. Leon Kaye, "The World's Most Sustainable Retailer? Marks & Spencer's 2013 Plan A Report," TriplePundit, June 11, 2013, www.triplepundit.com/2013/06/marks-and-spencer-2013-plan-a-update/.
10. Alexa Valiente, "Sleeping-Bag Coats Warm, Employ Detroit Homeless," ABC News, May 9, 2013, http://abcnews.go.com/blogs/headlines/2013/05/sleeping-bag-coats-warm-employ-detroit-homeless/.
11. "Internet of Things," Wikipedia, http://en.wikipedia.org/wiki/Internet_of_Things.
12. Ipsos MediaCT, "Social Influence: Marketing's New Frontier," Crowdtap, http://go.crowdtap.com/socialinfluence.
13. Bobby Sisk, "Emerson College Students Raise Almost $1M Selling Boston Strong Shirts," CBS Boston, June 11, 2013, http://boston.cbslocal.com/2013/06/11/emerson-college-students-raise-almost-1m-selling-boston-strong-shirts/.
14. Karlene Lukovitz, "Dunkin' Launches National Fundraising Program," MediaPost, September 22, 2014, www.mediapost.com/publications/article/234529/dunkin-launches-national-fundraising-program.html.
15. "Ice Bucket Challenge," Wikipedia, http://en.wikipedia.org/wiki/Ice_Bucket_Challenge.
16. www.charitywater.org/blog.
17. Rob Schmitz, "Former Homeless Man's Videos Profile Life On Street," NPR.org, March 6, 2010, www.npr.org/templates/story/story.php?storyId=124356908.
18. National Center for Charitable Statistics, "Quick Facts About Nonprofits," http://nccs.urban.org/statistics/quickfacts.cfm.

PART FIVE

Changing Strategies

Chapter 20

Measuring the Volunteer Program

Beth Kanter
Author and Master Trainer

When my first book, *The Networked Nonprofit*, came out in 2010, a lot of people in the nonprofit world wondered how its ideas could ever be applied to volunteer engagement. Facebook and Twitter may make sense for fundraising campaigns and awareness building, I heard, but they don't quite fit with the needs of volunteer programs. Now, four years later, many of those naysayers use those exact tools to strengthen volunteer relationships and leverage connections for greater impact.

My second book, *Measuring The Networked Nonprofit*, which was awarded the Terry McAdam Nonprofit Book Award in 2013, focused on what nonprofits can do to measure and assess their social networking. Again, I heard from many nonprofit professionals in volunteering that these ideas didn't really apply to them. Yes, they were tracking and measuring key metrics such as volunteer hours worked, but those metrics were far removed from the insightful, social-media-oriented data points I was talking about.

In this case, although I see some changes happening, more remains to be done to help the volunteer engagement field adopt a culture of data-informed decision-making. Collecting data to measure success is essential—but often, we only see part of the equation done well. Sometimes they're not even collecting the right data!

Why Measure Your Volunteer Program?

According to the 2014 Volunteer Impact Report from Software Advice and VolunteerMatch, a bit more than half (55 percent) of all nonprofits[1] collect volunteer engagement data with the intention of measuring it. Many respondents reported that they didn't really have a formal process for collecting volunteering data. They might, for example, collect numbers such as how many people showed up for a volunteer event, but there was no way to get a sense of the specific social impact of an individual volunteer or group of volunteers.

But even *that* is better than not measuring at all. Which begs the question—why aren't more nonprofits focused on measurement? Here's why:

- Lack of resources and tools.
- Lack of skills or knowledge.
- Lack of time.
- And some just don't see the value of gathering data.

Before this chapter is over, I plan to combat each of the preceding items to show you what they actually are: limiting beliefs that have no place in an innovative volunteer program. In fact, insight always improves outcomes—and those improvements are directly proportional to the care taken when planning for, gathering, and evaluating volunteer program data. This chapter will help you understand what kind of information is persuasive based on the story you're trying to tell. And it will help you better understand and communicate impact.

More importantly, I'll also do my best to break through the misconception that data-informed decision-making may be "right" for some functions at a nonprofit . . . just not volunteering.

Measurement Helps You Understand Impact

No matter your role, understanding how to pull meaningful insight from your efforts helps your organization make smarter investments, achieve its mission with fewer resources, and helps *you* become just a little bit better at saving the world. And then there's this:

Measurement Helps You Understand Volunteer Impact

At a basic level, the right data can hone in on volunteer hours donated and the dollar value for that work, and help you make sense of the impact of their work, the cost per volunteer to run your program, and when it makes sense to change headcount.

Measurement Improves Your Volunteer Relations

Struggling to listen and engage with your volunteer community? Measurement helps you understand how your community perceives you, what they do with the information you send out to them, and where to direct your volunteers' efforts.

Measurement Helps You Exceed Expectations

Boards and senior management increasingly expect results expressed in the language of measurement—and funders require data to evaluate impact (and not just any data; they want to see standardized measurement criteria, because data without insight is just trivia). Communicating the actual value of volunteer engagement is one of the more difficult challenges that nonprofits face. Hours donated is an important metric, but other important metrics, like the amount of trees planted, meals served, or young minds opened, need to be quantified in a way that demonstrates the value of the work and impact on the community. Measurement offers that.

Measurement Recognizes Incremental Success

Some ideas simply don't work, others see dramatic results—but most find success with baby steps. Being able to measure even small changes will put your volunteer program on a steady climb.

Measurement Helps Tell Your Story

Insight breeds insight. Understanding how the big picture of your volunteer program breaks out into smaller, successful (and unsuccessful) chunks can result in additional funding and more staff to support your efforts. How? Because you'll be able to provide a data-informed story detailing your efforts.

Gathering the right data and then making sense of it *and applying it* requires a balance of "left brain" (number crunching) and "right brain" (creative thinking). And it's the first step toward becoming a data-informed organization.

Becoming a Data-Informed Organization

So what is a data-informed volunteer organization, specifically—and what are the skills required to become one?

First, a distinction: Being "data-informed" is very different from being "data-driven." Data-driven is relying on cold, hard data to make decisions. *Data-informed* takes that cold, hard data and combines it with information from multiple sources to make informed decisions.

Data-informed cultures assess, revise, and learn as they go. Every aspect of their work is tied tightly to the concept of continuous improvement. And their KPIs (Key Performance Indicators) reflect this commitment, offering mileposts that don't simply *reflect activity* (as many organizations' KPIs do), but *measure progress* toward a goal. Data-informed cultures design measurement into their projects; they do not just do it so they have measurable outcomes. They provide the data necessary to improve them over time.

And this brings us to the biggest challenge for organizations, and it is not collecting or organizing data (though that takes planning, too)—the biggest challenge is how to make measurement a part of your organization's DNA and encourage data literacy skills for your staff.

For example, one of my favorite data-informed nonprofits, DoSomething.org (whose millennial engagement ideas you can read about in Chapter 5), was only able to create such a data-friendly culture because it understood the need to get buy-in from the top first. If the CEO isn't onboard and supportive of making data-informed decisions, it won't happen.

Other key elements of DoSomething's success include:

Being transparent. Nancy Lublin, DoSomething's CEO, recognizes the value of "being "transparent about sharing our dashboards, [as] it generates feedback and discussion from our stakeholders that leads to improvement."

Listening to the data and experimenting. When things aren't working, Lublin isn't afraid to take action to change it. Her team will also frequently "state a specific hypothesis with a number and measure against that," relying on various methods like A/B testing to figure out what's working and where they can improve.

Embracing failure. DoSomething is fearless about failing. We'll speak to this more at the end of the chapter, but know that failure isn't the end of the world—and it can actually be inspirational.

How to Build Capacity and Gain Skills

You can't be a data-informed organization if your staff doesn't have skills to collect, organize, and make sense of data! Most nonprofits can't afford to hire their own data scientist, so the goal is to build this capability in-house. Being data-informed and data-literate must become part of your organization's DNA.

How does this look? First, it's an attitude of intense curiosity where leadership is always asking, "What does this data mean?" and using data to dig beneath the surface of a problem, hypothesize, formulate questions, and learn. But it's also shifting from ad-hoc analysis and simple (though detailed) recordkeeping to a systematic approach to improvement. And although this competency can't (shouldn't) be outsourced to consultants, you *can* seek additional help:

- Find experts through existing connections.
- Check out LinkedIn's Board Connect.
- Read blogs that cover data. Try Lucy Bernholz's Philanthropy 2173 Blog, MarketsForGood.org, and NTEN's Change Journal.
- Get online training. NTEN, Leap of Reason, and Ann K. Emery's free video tutorials are good places to start.
- Attend a data or measurement panel at your next conference.
- Explore free help options. The Analysis Exchange (web analytics), DataKind (pro bono data scientists), and the SumAll Foundation (data analysts) may be worth checking out.
- Engage a student volunteer. Nearby colleges may require capstone projects where students demonstrate skills in data and measurement.

Now you have some ways to master your data, so let's get a little granular and explore how to define outcomes.

The First Step: Defining and Getting Buy-In on Outcomes

Typically, volunteer programs share results that consist solely of numbers. These results would be much more telling if someone had asked this question: "So what?"

For example, if 10 volunteers put in 500 hours this quarter, and that's an increase of 5 percent over last year—so what? Why is this significant? What change did they accomplish?

When asking "So what?" you'll come up with answers that can be evaluated, measured, and used to build organizational capacity. These answers will speak to your volunteer program's vision, resources, actions, short-term results, and the sustained outcome and impact your efforts accomplished. And these answers will elevate the conversation by demonstrating powerful, data-informed, and results-oriented volunteer engagement that both inspires and informs ongoing strategy.

But how does asking "So what?" help you measure the impact of your efforts, specifically? You need to define a framework to follow, a set of outcomes and metrics designed to comprehensively measure this impact.

Expressing Your Results to Speak to Organizational Goals

You need to express your results clearly and powerfully, showing how your programs helped your organization achieve its mission. And it's important to share both successes and failures.

And you need to keep specific outcomes top of mind. Why? *Outcomes are important.* Activities help accomplish outcomes, but they are not end results to be measured on their own. Outcomes speak to long-term impact, with activities working to accomplish measurable milestones along the way. These outcomes should fall into two major buckets—volunteer outcomes and nonprofit outcomes:

1. *Volunteer Outcomes.* How are your volunteers benefiting personally and professionally? This will help encourage future participation—track it!
2. *Nonprofit Outcomes.* How efficient is your operation? Are you continuously improving your capabilities? And how is your program perceived? Map out separate outcomes and metrics for each.

Before you get to those outcomes, though, you need to develop a mindset of thinking strategically about your program from the start.

How to Think Strategically About Your Program

Have a clear vision of both short- and long-term results and how you'll measure success along the way. And don't just think in terms of tactics—know how your plan will create value for your organization. (One way to do this is listing your objectives and having your team brainstorm the ultimate value and work backward.)

Not everything will have a direct causal relationship to tangible or "hard results." Tangibles are pretty straightforward when it comes to measurement—they're objective, easy to quantify, and easy to assign money or time values to. Soft results (intangibles) can be difficult to measure, yet they are just as important when it comes to understanding impact. They're often measured with transformational metrics, like building awareness, increasing trust, generating new ideas, and deepening relationships. As you can imagine, these intangibles can be viewed as less credible—unless you can demonstrate a logical path of progression from intangible to tangible.

With those basics in mind, let's talk about how to express your results in a way that makes sense for your organization.

Theory of Change (Demonstrating the Value of Soft Results)

A theory of change is a conceptual map, often laid out visually, that identifies the steps toward a long-term goal with "soft" results. You can have a theory of change for a specific initiative, or for your organization overall. Either way, it forms the basis for ongoing decision-making, measurement, and learning.

The goal is to create an objective that answers "So what?" with clear "So that . . ." statements. "We will do *this* so that we will achieve *that* end."—and then defining the steps along the way toward results.

And whether tangible or intangible, the actual data you decide to collect in your organization makes all the difference in the world. It can mean the difference between stakeholder buy-in or volunteers merely going through the motions, unheard.

When stakeholders buy in they're also tuned in—and when they're not, you've got trouble. It is often easier for nonprofit staff to describe results and match a key performance indicator (KPI), but it can be much harder to get consensus, because your board, fundraising directors, and staff all may have different interpretations of the data based on what they'd like to see. This is dangerous because it can completely bottleneck a process.

You can avoid organizational politics by using consensus-building techniques to come to an agreement around defining these outcomes ahead of time. When facilitating this discussion, be sure to make use of tips from Sam Kaner's book, *The Facilitator's Guide to Participatory Decision-Making*, about facilitated listening. In some cases, it may be worth it to hire an outside facilitator to facilitate the meetings.

Now that you've made some decisions about what to measure, let's talk about how to measure.

A Simple Formula for Measuring Your Program

Proper measurement requires sticking to seven basic steps if you want valid and actionable results (and, of course, you do, or why bother?). These are the steps to measuring anything, whether it is your social media strategy or the outcomes of your volunteer program:

Step 1: Define your goals.

Ever heard of the "Fire, Ready, Aim" approach? It's very common unfortunately—and ultimately fatal to your efforts. Remember to always ask "To what end, and why?" If your planning doesn't include clearly defined time frames, audiences, and outcomes, you cannot objectively recognize success.

Once you've identified your outcomes or intent, translate them into SMART objectives (Specific, Measurable, Attainable, Realistic, and Timely). SMART thinking answers questions such as "How many?" and "By when?"

Step 2: Define your audience.

You will never be able to measure everything you want to measure, so you need to be selective and set priorities—and defining your audience is chief among them. Who are you are trying to reach and how will connecting with them help to achieve your goals?

List all the various groups that influence the success or failure of your volunteer program and ways in which having a good relationship with each contributes to that success or failure. Consider that list prioritized!

Step 3: Define your benchmarks.

Who or what will you compare your results to? Measurement is a comparative tool, so understanding whether a new number is bigger or smaller than the previous quarter's number (or, say, your opposition's number) is crucial. Decide who or what you are going to compare yourself to.

Peer organization comparisons are telling—or you can refer to your organization's past performance. Either can prove difficult initially, particularly if you don't have any stats (from your organization to start with as a baseline). Making a best guess works initially, if that's the case. You'll have more accurate results to compare against the next time around. And when comparing yourself to peer organizations, looking at share of volunteer hours or share of wallet, for example, is helpful with time—and becomes more informative with time! The most important benchmark is what matters to your organization—and your executive director.

Step 4: Define your metrics.

What are the Key Performance Indicators that you will use to judge your progress toward your goal(s)? (Remember, KPIs are meaningful, actionable, and relevant metrics used to chart progress toward your SMART objectives—and there are thousands you could potentially collect.)

After completing the first three steps, your KPIs should be apparent, though. You just need to translate your priorities and goals into a number you can calculate, such as:

- Percent increase in donations.
- Percent increase in new donors or members.
- Percent increase in number of conversations expressing support for the cause.
- Percent increase in conversations that contain your key messages.

Step 5: Define your time and costs.

What is your investment? It's important to identify the true costs involved in your programs. Most of the cost is going to be in staff time, so you'll need to find out how much time your volunteer program or specific campaign requires, and determine how much time you're going to invest. And then the kicker—are your expected results reasonable for the time investment?

Sometimes you'll have to manage either the time commitment or the expectations, if not both. And be sure to consider opportunity cost and whether potentially shifting resources to accommodate for a promising endeavor makes sense. There may also be alternative ways to achieve your goals. You're much better off being honest with yourself and sorting this out now than later!

Step 6: Select your data collection tool(s).

Tools are useless if they aren't helping you connect your activities, their impact on your audience, your progress toward objectives, and, ultimately, your goals. There are three general types of measurement tools:

- Content analysis of social or traditional media.
- Primary audience surveys via online, mail, or phone.
- Web and social media analytics.

Will you use Google or other web analytics, surveys, or content analysis maybe? To sort out which tool you need, consider your goals and your KPIs.

Step 7: Collect your data, analyze it, turn it into action, and repeat.

Continuous improvement can only happen when results are consistently assessed and changes are made depending on results. It's a never-ending process. Establish a regular reporting schedule and stick to it.

And do not give in to the temptation of focusing on the best results. Being proud of successes is one thing (and expected), but do not let it blind you to the big picture. Get rid of things that aren't working—even if they provided one flash-in-the-pan moment of awesome.

Measurement can be a tough sell. And the planning process can seem a bit overwhelming to organizations new to the process. So what can you do to ease your volunteer program into the land of hard and soft data?

Simple Tools

If you aren't fortunate enough to have a central database that can handle everything you need to track, you'll want to explore some auxiliary options like spreadsheets and custom databases:

Spreadsheets

The spreadsheet is your most powerful tool because it can capture strategy, outcomes, tactics, KPIs, and other metrics—and it is relatively easy to organize. Collecting data from free or paid measurement tools is the easy part—the tough stuff starts when you're sorting out how to work with the data. It just takes a little elbow grease!

But be careful: Making sure you're using your spreadsheet correctly is really important.

My colleague, David Geilhufe, points out that 85 percent of spreadsheets contain errors, so be sure to crosscheck totals and formulas.[2]

Custom Databases

Depending on your technological savvy, there are also custom database options that are relatively inexpensive and flexible, like Microsoft Access and Filemaker Pro—but you'll need to invest time to make sure everyone knows how to use these tools effectively.

There are also proactive data-gathering options, where you ask your community for feedback by way of surveys, apps, and texts.

Online Surveys

Surveys are certainly cost effective, but can be hit or miss as survey participation can be a tough sell unless your community is particularly engaged. To encourage higher levels of participation, make sure they're timely (sent immediately after an event, for example). There are lots of free or low-cost survey tools available like SurveyMonkey and PollDaddy.

Apps

Mobile apps can encourage community members to "check in" at your event or location (with the best offering a social share option to help spread the word) and provide data about who is participating. They can also be used to take attendance at events. Event Check-in from Constant Contact is one example of a popular attendance app.

Texts

SMS (text messaging) is a fantastic option for programs seeking to reach constituents immediately and they work very well for demographics that are text-friendly. Unfortunately, most nonprofits don't maintain robust lists of phone numbers anymore (but there's no time like the present to start, right?).

Data visualization tools are probably the most exciting of the pack. Data visualization is a fantastic way to make sense of data. I spend 30 percent of my measurement time collecting and organizing data and 70 percent thinking about what it means. Seeing it helps me—a lot.

Consolidating your insights with a DIY infographic requires some inspiration and a little bit of perspiration. For inspiration, check out Pinterest and search for infographics. Or learn some basic design skills! PiktoChart and Infigr.am both offer popular infographic-making tools for free. Microsoft PowerPoint and Microsoft Publisher are also both great data visualization options, because each has layout tools that make infographic or chart projects a snap.

The goal, ultimately, is to create an executive dashboard that pulls your metrics together to create a visually appealing, easy-to-understand snapshot of your efforts. Deciding which metrics to present is key—and it isn't as time-consuming as you'd think.

Keep Calm and Document

Capturing what actually happens as a volunteer event or initiative unfolds is important because it offers ways to reflect and debrief meaningfully afterwards. It can be as simple as keeping a journal and taking quick notes during the event. Dana Nelson from GiveMN, one of the most successful giving days, tells me her team is always "writing it down as they go." Here's how to capture relevant info for an "After Action Review:"

- Capture the lessons learned (big or small).
- Use a collaborative social site where all members of your team can add and access (a Google document works great for this).
- Ask team members to reflect on their lessons learned and to share stories from the event that speak to best practices as well as things they'd do differently.
- Review it together in a meeting and summarize into a series of "do, improve (say how), don't do."

With reflection comes the realization that you'd do some things differently, of course—and that is valuable info that should be celebrated, not feared. When you identify opportunities for improvement, it's time to take a failure bow!

Failing Forward

No one likes to make mistakes and placing blame is counterproductive, so smart organizations are finding ways to make failure productive and fun—one of my favorites being the "failure bow."

It was developed by Seattle-based improvisation teacher Matt Smith, and is transformative because it alters our physiological response to failure by removing the demons of self-doubt and self-judgment.[3]

You raise your hand, share your failure, take a bow, and move on. Trapeze artists, acrobats, and other athletes are trained to take a failure bow after a stumble because it releases them from the fear of making a mistake.

MomsRising, a grassroots organization that runs online campaigns to promote family-friendly policies, holds "joyful funerals" where they give unsuccessful initiatives a formal burial and eulogy during which they surface new ideas to improve future campaigns. Executive Director Kristin Rowe-Finkbeiner says removing the stigma from failed campaigns encourages people to take risks and try new things.[4]

People won't try out new ideas or approaches if failure is seen as a career-killer. But when it's treated like what it is—an opportunity to learn—it can be a fun and rewarding process.

Summary

As I said at the start of the chapter, many volunteer engagement teams say they don't measure because—like a lot of nonprofit staff—they don't believe they have time, resources, or training to measure. But if you've read this far, you can probably now see that the real barrier to effective measurement is simply not seeing the value of gathering data on what's working and what isn't.

Fortunately, I am meeting fewer and fewer nonprofit people who believe this every year. But while it's true that those who work with volunteers have tended to be some of the last to embrace a culture of collecting data, assessing programs, and failing forward, I firmly believe volunteer programs could see some of the biggest gains from shifting in the direction of measurement.

Just remember that measurement is not a one-time add-on to your planning process. Much like those ideas that are successful in small steps, so too is measurement—and it's an effort that builds social proof (and enhances your organization's credibility) with time.

And be sure to have time set aside to reflect and do something meaningful with what you discover. Make measurement your first measurable goal, in fact—and get ready to chart your success!

Beth Kanter is an international leader in nonprofits' use of social media. Her first book, *The Networked Nonprofit,* introduced a new way of thinking and operating in a connected world, and her follow-up, *Measuring the Networked Nonprofit,* is a practical guide for using measurement to achieve impact. She is the author of *Beth's Blog,* the go-to source for using networks and social media for social change. Beth has 30 years of experience in nonprofit technology, training, and capacity and has facilitated trainings on every continent in the world (except Antarctica). Named one of the most influential women in technology by Fast Company and one of *Business-Week's* Voices of Innovation for Social Media, Beth was visiting scholar at the David and Lucile Packard Foundation 2009–2013.

Notes

1. Software Advice and VolunteerMatch, "Volunteer Impact Report," 2014, www.softwareadvice.com/nonprofit/industryview/volunteer-impact-report-2014.
2. For spreadsheet examples, see: www.bethkanter.org/spreadsheet-sm_re.
3. Matt Smith has a great video on how to take a failure bow: http://tedxtalks.ted.com/video/The-Failure-Bow-Matt-Smith-at-T.
4. Beth Kanter, "Likes on Facebook Are Not a Victory: Results Are!," August 9, 2011, www.bethkanter.org/momsrising-key-results/.

Chapter 21

The New Volunteer Manager's Toolkit

Jennifer R. Bennett, CVA
Senior Manager, Education & Training, VolunteerMatch

Was working with volunteers a career you fell into? Or was it something you planned for? The former was definitely true in my case.

I was attracted to nonprofits because of the mission-driven focus, but as I became inspired by what volunteers were doing, I began to see how with just a little bit more training and support their impact could really be magnified. But despite working with volunteers every day, I still didn't consider myself a volunteer coordinator—mainly because I wasn't recruiting and screening them. Still, my work depended on them and they depended on me.

Finally I took time to really look closely at the role that volunteers were playing. Once I saw how critical they were to my success and the organization's mission, I finally found my inner *leader of volunteer engagement*!

Whether you chose intentionally to work with volunteers or you've found yourself to be an accidental volunteer manager in your organization, you also have a role as a leader of volunteer engagement. You have the opportunity to truly shape and guide the engagement of individuals who are passionate about a cause and who see your organization as the best way to act on their values. That's pretty important!

When starting up a volunteer engagement initiative or taking over an existing one, you'll definitely want to think about best practices and foundation components, which parts are working, and what might be outdated or putting your organization or volunteers at risk. These are the practical pieces of your job. As a volunteer manager, however, it is equally important to think about being *a leader of volunteer engagement*—to create meaningful opportunities for volunteers to make a difference in your organization.

Being a leader of volunteer engagement means having a vision for your role and for volunteers at your organization, and recognizing the transformative potential of working together to achieve high-impact outcomes. It means trusting that even a new volunteer manager can make a real difference.

Which Road Are You On?

To figure out where your program needs to go and what needs to change or evolve to meet the needs of your organization and your volunteers, you first need to know where you are. Imagine what your volunteer program feels like to your volunteers. If it were a road, what kind would it be?

The Cul-de-Sac

Does your program literally feel like a dead end, with limited roles for volunteers, and nowhere to go once you get there? Many traditional volunteer programs feel like this to today's volunteers. Volunteers are funneled into task-based work that can be done by almost anyone, with little or no opportunity to learn new skills, take on more responsibility, or deepen their relationship with the organization. Volunteers can feel like they aren't doing work that really matters, aren't contributing to the mission of the organization, and often leave as soon as they get bored of doing the same tasks over and over.

The Country Road

Country roads eventually take you where you want to go, but it doesn't happen quickly. If the work that volunteers do in your organization has evolved over time, without a clear vision of how volunteer engagement helps you meet your mission, your program may feel like this to volunteers. Volunteers in these organizations may eventually receive new opportunities to lead and learn new skills, but the process (and who gets to participate) can seem mysterious. These types of programs overemphasize longevity and volunteers "paying their dues." Volunteers who lack patience or want to see the impact of their work more quickly may become frustrated and move on to an organization that is better prepared to find a role that fits their skills and interests.

The Highway

Highways take you to new places. They have signs telling you where you're going (and how long it will take to get there.) It's easy to get on a highway and, if you need to take a break, it's easy to get off. A successful volunteer program understands what its volunteers want to accomplish and where they want to go. The work is important and there are clear position descriptions and training to ensure that every volunteer has the skills to do it. Volunteers receive regular help and are recognized and honored for their support. And the relationship has built-in flexibility so that a volunteer can grow into a leadership role or take a step back, if need be, without having to leave the organization entirely.

Obviously we want our programs to be a superhighway with a direct route to impact! So, what do you need to know to turn your program into that highway?

As people become more connected and busy—with immediate access to information and each other—how we approach volunteering and being a volunteer has changed. Everyone, including volunteers, wants to make good use of what little free time they have. (For more on the big trends that will impact the future of volunteering, see Chapter 1.)

Leading volunteers within an organization has gone from making sure that everyone is busy and happy to ensuring that the time and talent of each volunteer is being harnessed effectively to meet the mission of the organization. Volunteers and paid staff work with organization leadership to identify goals and outcomes, and a leader of volunteer engagement helps to make this collaboration successful. This is the shift from volunteer management to volunteer engagement.

What Engagement Means in Volunteering

If you've ever looked for resources to help you create a volunteer program, you may have come across the 3 Rs of volunteer management. The 3 Rs—recruitment, retention, and recognition—come from traditional volunteer management, and a good program certainly includes those activities and outcomes. But contemporary volunteer engagement is both simpler and more complex.

It sounds simple when the goal is stated as creating work that's meaningful to the volunteer and that meets the mission of the organization, but in practice this can be challenging. It was much easier when everyone was just quietly stuffing envelopes in a cul-de-sac.

The new model for volunteer engagement is far more collaborative. Everyone is on the same highway, going to the same place. Yet this model can challenge an organization's culture and the way staff thinks about what volunteers can accomplish. It can be perceived as, and, unfortunately, occasionally is, a threat to the job stability of paid staff if organization leadership see replacing paid staff with volunteers as a way to save money. The new model also pushes staff into new situations using new skills, which can be scary.

To be fair, though, volunteer management was *never* as simple as the 3 Rs made it seem. Building relationships and working with people is rarely simple. But if you look at Figure 21.1 and Figure 21.2, you can see how much more complex things are when the goal is engagement and collaboration.

In 2010, VolunteerMatch undertook a survey of thousands of volunteers who used our web service. Ninety percent said they'd be more (or much more) likely to volunteer for a cause if they cared about it—and 82 percent said they'd be more likely to embrace a volunteer opportunity if it gave them a chance to make an impact.[1]

At the same time, many respondents said they'd be much less likely to volunteer for an opportunity that didn't make an impact (30 percent), that wasn't

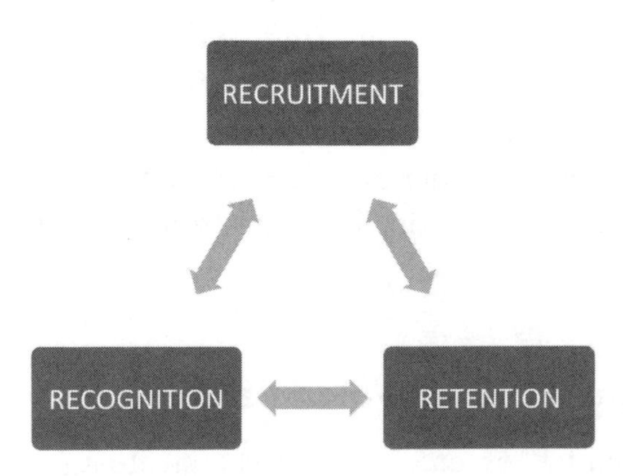

Figure 21.1 The 3 Rs of Volunteer Management
Source: VolunteerMatch.

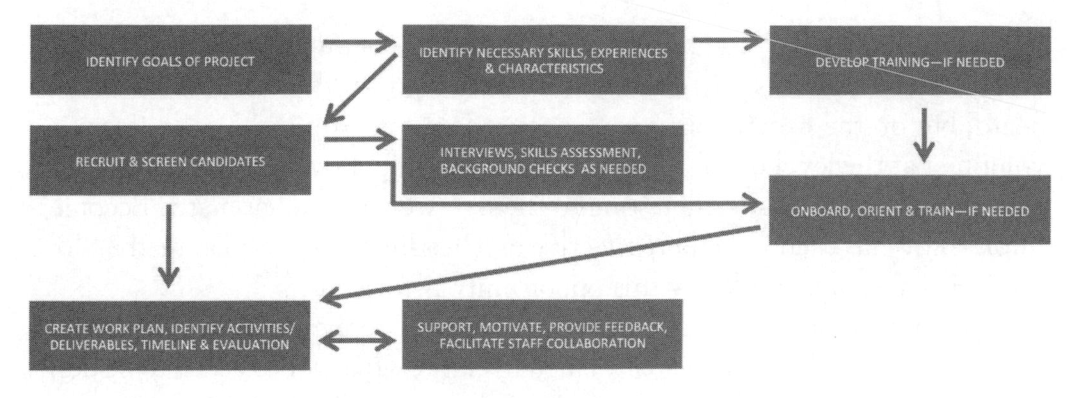

Figure 21.2 Volunteer Engagement Flowchart
Source: VolunteerMatch.

interesting, challenging, or engaging (45 percent), and that wasn't flexible (61 percent). Although this all may seem obvious, it's worth considering that for many previous generations the point of volunteering was to be helpful for the community—not necessarily to satisfy personal goals around purpose or meaning. Clearly there's huge opportunity to be had in adapting to these new generational realities!

Take a moment now to consider how volunteer involvement works at your organization. Is your volunteer program on a highway or on a cul-de sac?

Recruiting the New Volunteer

Creating work with impact—and that's interesting, challenging, and engaging—requires a shift in thinking about volunteer recruitment. When you shift to volunteer engagement, you want to move away from an "anyone can do this" attitude and start to create specific roles designed to attract volunteers with specific skills. You need to start thinking about finding the right person for the job, not create jobs that can be done by anyone. What does a volunteer need to know, do, or be to be the right volunteer?

To find that right volunteer you need to know what you want to accomplish and what your organization needs. When you're ready to begin recruiting, this information, along with the impact and the reason the work matters, becomes the bulk of your recruitment message.

Titles and headlines are just as important. When I first started at Volunteer-Match, I was amazed how many nonprofits titled their VolunteerMatch.org listings "Volunteers Needed." Of course you need volunteers; you're posting on VolunteerMatch! This might make sense for a flyer on the community bulletin board, but on the web it means you've missed an opportunity to connect with a volunteer at the level of engagement. They'll skip right over your generic title to land on something that's interesting to them. "Are you good at math? Become a tutor!" This has been incredibly effective as a headline. Not good at math? Move on. But if you are, you know this opportunity is for you.

As I looked into our listings, I also saw not only were many listings essentially just broad open calls for help, many failed to clarify what work needed to be done, who would be a good fit, or why that work matters—all missed opportunities to connect. Fortunately, most volunteer engagement staff get it now. In the 90,000 or so opportunities at VolunteerMatch.org today, I'd be hard-pressed to find one titled "Volunteers Needed"!

Consider how your organization is recruiting volunteers today. Are you communicating how your opportunities align with what volunteers are looking for and what they bring to the sector?

The New Thank You

Recognition, like recruitment, needs to change to meet a modern volunteer's needs and expectations. Don't assume that what's always worked still works. Volunteers who are motivated to make an impact or learn new skills may not be interested in your annual brunch. Successful recognition aligns with the work being done, includes the impact of that work, and matches the motivation of the volunteer. In many cases, a LinkedIn recommendation or a blog post recapping a project can be much more meaningful than a certificate of recognition—which is why you need to understand your volunteers. And, never overlook the power of a handwritten note, sent by mail. When was the last time you opened your mailbox and was excited by what was waiting for you?

Engaging the New Volunteer

With a traditional program, the role of the volunteer manager was to keep all the volunteers busy and happy. With a shift to engagement the old-fashioned goal of retention shifts as well. When we approach volunteering with the focus on impact, a volunteer leaving is not necessarily a bad outcome. If a volunteer finishes a project or completes his or her commitment and moves on, that is a success. A volunteer coming to your organization on Wednesday at 1 P.M. from now until the end of time isn't how volunteer engagement works anymore. Remember the highway—volunteers want to get to that impact, make a difference, and then change their engagement. That might mean a new project, working for a new organization, or taking a break from volunteering until they find the next cause they care about. Your responsibility becomes finding the right role for the right volunteer, rather than trying to keep everyone happy forever—a far more accomplishable goal!

The key to making that right match is screening. Screening is one of the most overlooked activities in volunteer engagement. But it's the only way to know if a volunteer could be the right fit, and it's instrumental in building a relationship with a prospective volunteer. The interview is where you learn what a volunteers want to accomplish with their time, what's motivating them to work with your organization, and how they want to help. Screening, particularly interviewing prospective volunteers, is one of the best ways to manage some of the risks associated with your volunteer engagement program. Criminal or background checks may also be appropriate for volunteers in your organization, but beware of "Swiss cheese" screening. Relying on just a background check, without an interview, can only tell you about a volunteer's previous activities—it leaves holes in your screening process and can't answer the question "Is this person the right volunteer for the job?"

Are you intimidated by the thought of interviewing all your prospective volunteers, trying to get to know them, and then making a decision on how to proceed in just a few minutes? You aren't alone. I hear all sorts of reasons that organizations don't always screen. Some organizations tell me they can support an unlimited number of volunteers, so they don't bother to screen them. Others say they place hundreds of volunteers each year—far more than they could possibly interview.

In the sidebar I've included an example I like to use about the power of screening. Though slightly simplified and somewhat exaggerated, it shows how relying just on the basics of paper matching doesn't always tell the whole story. In the engagement era, screening isn't necessarily about weeding people out—it's about finding the right fit for someone who cares about your cause. Often there may be a better opportunity available for someone who expresses interest—one that more closely matches his or her skills, habits, and interests.

Then again, not every prospective volunteer is a good fit. One of the most important skills a leader of volunteer engagement needs is the ability to say no.

Case Study: A Match for Mary

Mary applies as a volunteer on the information desk at a museum where you are the director of volunteer engagement. She provides her availability and her background check is clear. She's on time for her orientation and training. She's met with the shift supervisor, Jane, and successfully answered some test questions. She seems like the perfect volunteer. But after a couple of weeks Jane comes to you with concerns. It turns out Mary is often short-tempered with visitors, and sometimes even ignores them.

In a meeting you ask Mary how she thinks things are going. She admits that she may not be meeting expectations. She's been trying to do a good job, she explains, but since she's so shy she gets nervous talking to strangers. It's also hard for her to multitask—she likes to finish a project like restocking the pamphlet holder before turning to a waiting visitor. Actually, Mary says, volunteering isn't for her, and she's sorry she wasted everyone's time.

This is a bad outcome that didn't have to happen; all it would have taken is asking a few screening questions specifically related to the work Mary would be doing at the information desk. Learning about her preferred work style and ideal work environment would have made it clear that Mary would be a better fit serving as a volunteer on a special project for museum archivists.

The Art of Saying No

Not many people (except maybe toddlers) like saying no! Volunteer program managers tend to be problem solvers, people people. We want to find a place for everyone who is interested and it just feels wrong to say no to someone who wants to help. Your boss or executive director may even have told you that you can't say no to prospective volunteers.

When we evolve our programs to be a superhighway, we have to realize that we no longer have a place for everyone. People can ride their bikes on a country road, kids can play catch in a cul-de-sac, but those activities aren't safe on a highway. Not saying no, just like letting someone ride their bike on the highway, is risky. It may seem like finding a place for everyone would be the best outcome, but this actually opens up your program, and your organization, to risk.

Saying yes when you should say no means that you're placing volunteers who don't understand or aren't naturally suited to the work you're asking them to do. In the museum scenario Mary wasn't happy either and it had a negative effect on her and the other volunteers she worked with. It also had a negative impact on museum visitors and its overall reputation in the community.

What do you do when the volunteer who's not suited to their role is already a volunteer? If you can find a better opportunity for them to use their time and talent, try to make it happen. Mary is much happier—engaged and making an impact—working with that archivist!

But if there isn't a right role, you need to ask that volunteer to leave.

Leaving Your Comfort Zone

At the beginning of this chapter, I asked you to think about your responsibility as a leader of volunteer engagement and that you may need to step out of your comfort zone. This may be that step for you. If you've mastered the art of saying no, pat yourself on the back! Saying no to a prospective volunteer or asking a volunteer to leave are two of the hardest things you'll face on the job.

It's also important to learn how to hear no! Listen for phrases that sound like yes, but aren't, such as "Let me think about it," or "Maybe, but I have to check my schedule." These are nice ways of saying no.

Collaboration Doesn't Mean "No Rules"

If your organization has had a hard time saying no to volunteers in the past, I bet you have a thick volunteer policies manual or volunteer handbook on your desk. Many traditional volunteer engagement programs try to manage their volunteers into being the right volunteer, instead of screening for them in the first place.

All those policies weighing down your handbook can be confusing for volunteers and can actually prevent successful collaboration from happening. If you have a lot of historical policies that aren't enforced, volunteers can't know which policies are really important, which ones don't matter, and how to tell them apart.

As you are transitioning to a new model volunteer program built on engagement, not management, it may be time to reconsider these rules. Keep the policies that help volunteers, paid staff, and clients work together, and be sure to provide training and information on why these policies are in place. Invite volunteers to provide input and feedback on the policies as they're developed.

The policies you create need to be able to be enforced consistently and fairly. The rules need to apply to everyone, or to everyone with certain roles or responsibilities. By creating this strong framework for how your organization works together, creative, flexible, collaborative volunteer engagement can happen.

Although engaging volunteers in new ways can be exciting, don't overlook that framework. Recently the board chair of a small arts organization contacted me looking for advice. She had recently engaged Joe, a volunteer who'd been with the organization for years, to help her create the organization's website. She knew Joe well, so she didn't think there would be any problem just letting him run with the project. Joe built her a great website, and Joanne, not knowing much about websites, didn't ask many questions. Everything seemed fine.

Sure enough the organization suffered some financial setbacks. Some programs had to be cut and the future was looking uncertain. The program Joe usually volunteered to help was eliminated, and he felt angry and betrayed. During this time Joanne needed to get the website updated to reflect the changes and she found that Joe wouldn't respond to her phone calls or e-mails. Even worse, it turns out Joe had registered the website in his own name. She didn't know what to do. Most likely she'll need to hire an attorney.

This is a situation in which a policy about intellectual property and a short volunteer agreement letter would have eliminated any future problems.

What If . . . ? Planning for When Things Go Wrong

When working with volunteers, there are many things that can go wrong. If volunteers are working on tasks that most people can do or that don't have a direct impact on the mission of your organization, those risks can seem minimal. But as you move toward engaging volunteers in high-impact work, those risks can feel larger. What I've discussed so far are all best practices for creating a volunteer engagement program that helps mitigate risk. But there are also specific steps you can take to minimize risk and better respond to situations in which the success and safety of volunteers, clients, or the organization might be jeopardized.

It's important to have policies in place that help you create a framework for how everyone works together, but when you're developing specific policies around risky activities—or working with vulnerable populations—you need to involve your organization's leaders and legal counsel. Confidentiality agreements, DNAs, and waivers can help a volunteer understand the risks, but your organization can still be open to liability if volunteers are poorly trained, equipment is faulty, or volunteers are exposed to risk outside their defined role. Talk with a legal professional in your area to make sure you understand the laws in your jurisdiction and how they apply to the work volunteers are doing in your organization.

Often the big scary risk is the one we focus on—What if a volunteer crashes the van? But that's why you have insurance. Remember Mary? She opened your organization up to far more risk—misunderstandings, misperceptions, bad feelings in the community, loss of donors or supporters—than a fender bender ever could. You need to start identifying the less obvious risks and creating those policies and processes to help mitigate them. Accidents happen, that's outside of your control. You can control how volunteers are screened and trained, and how you create meaningful volunteer engagement in your organization.

Putting the Pieces Together

Thinking about changing how your organization engages volunteers—and being the one to lead that change—can be overwhelming. Where should you even start? Here are three principles to guide you in the process:

1. *Know the work/know your volunteers.*

   From designing opportunities with impact to building great relationships with volunteers, the more you know about what needs to be done and who should do it, the more successful you'll be. Create strong foundation components—position descriptions, agreement letters, and outcome and impact statements. Look to other organizations doing similar work, or other volunteer managers in your community so you don't have to start from scratch. Consider engaging an HR professional as a volunteer to help you create these components. Once you have them—use these resources to develop trainings and orientations. What do volunteers need to know? Do they already have those skills, or do they need to learn them? Which skills can only be learned on the job?

I've talked about the importance of initially getting to know volunteers, but it's just as important to build an ongoing relationship. Volunteer leaders and paid staff should also be involved in building these relationships and following up with volunteers to keep them motivated and engaged.

2. *Focus on success but plan for the worst.*

   Think big. What could your organization accomplish if it wasn't limited to the time and talent of paid staff? Develop opportunities for volunteers to contribute in meaningful ways to the success of your organization, and then share that impact! At the same time, put policies in place to help volunteers know what to do if something goes wrong. Accidents do happen.

3. *Get everyone on the same page.*

   Paid staff, volunteer staff, members, donors, clients, and organization leadership all have their own ideas of what successful volunteer engagement looks like. Clear goals and written policies help ensure that everyone can work together. And when problems arise, have procedures in place to resolve them.

Getting Started

Don't get lost on a country road! Make it easy for people to participate. Help them understand what their role is, and why it matters. The world is changing and volunteers' expectations are changing, too. No matter how hard you try, you can't manage or policy someone into being a different person! Instead focus on finding the right volunteer for the job.

VolunteerMatch Learning Center

You can find additional resources, templates, and samples, and free webinars on all of these topics in the VolunteerMatch Learning Center at http://learn.volunteermatch.org.

Making the shift from a traditional volunteer management model to one that focuses on engagement, impact, and collaboration can feel overwhelming. Changes don't have to happen all at once; you can focus on one component, launch a pilot program, or start by identifying the current culture or processes that keep your program from being as successful as possible. Become an advocate for incorporating impact into your organization's volunteer opportunities.

I encourage you to invest in your volunteering superhighway.

It doesn't happen overnight, but with some planning, building, and maybe knocking a few things down, you can create a direct route to impact and engagement!

Jennifer R. Bennett, CVA, joined VolunteerMatch to formalize and manage the organization's volunteer engagement program. She is a strong nonprofit generalist, with over 15 years of nonprofit management experience and working with volunteers. Jennifer shares her experience with VolunteerMatch's community of nonprofits to help them better recruit and engage volunteers through webinars found on the Learning Center, in newsletters and blog entries, and in person at conferences around the country. She's a strong believer in the importance of engaging volunteers in meaningful work and was certified in Volunteer Administration in 2009, and joined the Board of the Council for Certification in Volunteer Administration in 2012.

Note

1. "2010 Users Survey," VolunteerMatch/Hart Research Associates, 2010. (Unpublished research.)

Chapter 22

National Service for the Twenty-First Century

Wendy Spencer
Chief Executive Officer, Corporation for National and Community Service

Magnificent. Discovery. Matinee. Scolded. Hypnotist. Reading alone, a young child can easily struggle with such words. If the student does not comprehend even a few words in a paragraph or passage, all important clues, to context and meaning, will be missed. Before long, frustration sets in and reading can become, at best, a chore to be endured and, at worst, an obstacle to be avoided altogether. And the costs—both to the student and to her community—can be immense. Research shows that students who do not read on grade level by the end of the third grade are four times more likely to drop out of high school.

Enter a volunteer. Each Monday, I visit Washington, DC's Shaw Elementary where I spend 45 minutes tutoring a young student who needs extra help. We read together and when we come to words like the ones listed above, we sound them out, look them up, and discuss how a single word's definition can add meaning to the story as a whole. We also work together on a number of reading comprehension strategies, including understanding the concept of cause and effect. And although our tutoring sessions are one-on-one, my volunteering is not.

That is because I volunteer as part of a great youth literacy nonprofit called Reading Partners. Through Reading Partners' AmeriCorps program, more than 5,000 volunteers just like me work with more than 5,000 students, many of whom attend schools in traditionally underserved communities.[1] Drawing on strong partnerships with schools, corporations, civic groups, and clubs, AmeriCorps members serve as outreach and site coordinators who mobilize and manage volunteers drawn from the local community. They also train volunteers on the best ways to tutor and read to a student. And I know that having the guidance and support of the AmeriCorps members makes me a better volunteer and a better tutor.

I am just one volunteer whose time and talent are magnified by the reach, creativity, and commitment of national service. And just as I do not go into the classroom alone, there are 4 million other volunteers working in 60,000 sites across the country—recruited and managed by 75,000 AmeriCorps members or serving alongside 300,000 Senior Corps volunteers—who are similarly supported by the Corporation for National and Community Service (CNCS) to help tackle challenges in one of our agency's six focus areas: disaster services; economic opportunity; environmental stewardship; healthy futures; veterans and military families; and, of course, education.

How does national service help nonprofits fulfill their missions and engage more volunteers?

Volunteering Is in America's DNA

National service harnesses—and, importantly, makes effective use of—one of the American people's oldest, simplest, and most transformative impulses—the impulse to help our neighbors. In fact, this impulse is so strong that when we ask Americans as part of our "Volunteering and Civic Life in America" study if they help their neighbors or "informally volunteer" we find, year after year, that about two-thirds—or roughly 143 million of our fellow citizens—do.

It was this wellspring of compassion that President George H.W. Bush was determined to tap into when he renewed the federal government's focus on encouraging volunteering. President Bush said, "Ours should be a nation characterized by conspicuous compassion, generosity that is overflowing and abundant."

We see this compassion in the wake of devastating storms, like the aftermath of the 2011 Joplin, Missouri, tornado when 2,000 volunteers showed up on the first morning. Over the next year, AmeriCorps members helped manage some 75,000 volunteers to help the families of Joplin recover and rebuild.

We also see the compassion of neighbors helping neighbors when a community is in crisis. In 2003, Eastern Kentucky Congressman Hal Rogers founded the nonprofit organization Operation UNITE to tackle the scourge of drug abuse in his rural, economically distressed district. Operation UNITE was small but mighty, working tirelessly to do vital, lifesaving work. Because CNCS recognizes that fighting the drug epidemic in Appalachian Kentucky requires a concerted, coordinated effort, AmeriCorps partnered with Operation UNITE in 2007 to launch UNITE Service Corps. Since that time, CNCS has invested $1.6 million to deploy and support 125 AmeriCorps members who have, in turn, provided before and after school math tutoring, developed healthy choices programs to address drug prevention and nutritional education, served as sponsors for antidrug clubs, and recruited volunteers for school-based prevention programs and community service projects.

In just the 2012–2013 school year alone, our members' work meant one-on-one mentoring for nearly 3,300 students and math tutoring for more than 2,100 students. Those students' test scores increased by 34 percent during the year. The program has been so successful that Kentucky Governor Steve Beshear recognized UNITE Service Corps with the citation for outstanding service to the people of Kentucky two straight years.

UNITE Service Corps is a great example of how national service works because it supports a local solution to a local challenge. The program also leverages matching funding, making it more cost effective. And UNITE Service Corps successfully bolsters the "triple bottom line" by connecting thousands of young Kentuckians with quality tutors and mentors; by helping AmeriCorps members develop a range of skills, jumpstart their careers, and pay for college or graduate school; and by supporting the community of Eastern Kentucky to become safer, healthier, and more economically secure.

Maximizing the Volunteer Experience

Another great example of national service in action is our 20-year partnership with Habitat for Humanity. Each year, Habitat hosts more than 500 AmeriCorps members in communities across the country. And since 1994, 8,000 Habitat AmeriCorps members have mobilized 3.1 million volunteers who have, together, helped build or repair homes for 20,000 families.[2] Habitat AmeriCorps members have also raised tens of millions of dollars in cash and resources.

Our partnership with Habitat for Humanity exemplifies the second way that national service strengthens volunteering in our country: by increasing the number of volunteers serving and by expanding those volunteers' impact. And it does that by maximizing the volunteer experience.

When I served with Habitat years ago, I learned to tile a roof. It was unfamiliar work but with practice and the proper support, I was soon tiling well enough to consider launching a second career. Well, maybe I did not do quite that well. But the experience reminded me of something a dear friend and one of the godfathers of the modern service movement often says. Former U.S. Senator Harris Wofford frequently describes full-time national service and traditional volunteering as working in concert like "twin engines." By providing recruitment support, oversight, screening, training, and proper management to help nonprofits retain volunteers, national service enables nonprofits of all sizes to harness more value from each volunteer, thereby advancing their missions and strengthening their work over time.

And our research tells us that Senator Wofford is right. In our annual "Volunteering and Civic Life in America" study, we investigate all aspects of volunteering and service in our nation. As part of that research, we have also tallied the annual cost to organizations that lose volunteers.[3] And what we have found is alarming. Each year, organizations in the volunteer sector lose more than $35 billion through volunteer attrition alone.[4] We also know that all too often nonprofits and other organizations are unable to put proven best practices in place simply because they do not have a volunteer manager supporting their work.

Good volunteer management not only keeps volunteers engaged and coming back, it also can help an organization's bottom line. Our research has found that volunteers are almost twice as likely to donate to charity as nonvolunteers—on average, 8 in 10 volunteers donate to charity. That's compared to 4 in 10 nonvolunteers.[5]

And by maximizing the experience for volunteers, national service can do more than simply help organizations fulfill current goals; we can also help organizations develop new initiatives, as we did in 2013 when AmeriCorps and Habitat for Humanity launched Veterans Build, an initiative designed to provide simple, affordable housing specifically for military veterans and their families. Importantly, Veterans Build engages our returning heroes in this work, capitalizing on the many skills our military members gain during their service. The initiative also helps military members successfully transition to lives as civilians by providing access to financial literacy and homeownership education programs.

Opening the Door to Partnerships

Veterans Build is a great example of how national service works with nonprofits to help open the door to new partnerships. In fact, strengthening volunteering through partnerships is a core part of our mission.

When President Barack Obama launched the Task Force on Expanding National Service in the summer of 2013, the first line of the President's executive memorandum instructed the entire Cabinet to expand national service "through partnerships." As co-chair of the President's Task Force, I took that directive and ran with it. In just two years, we have launched partnerships with local and state governments to improve public safety; with financial institutions and nonprofits to expand economic opportunity; and with other federal agencies like the Justice Department to address humanitarian crises here at home.

I have been fortunate to travel the country and see much of this work firsthand. That includes a great partnership we launched with Michigan Governor Rick Snyder, then-Detroit Mayor Dave Bing, Detroit Police Chief James Craig, and Wayne State University to mobilize community members to help increase public safety and reduce blight in a number of high-need Detroit neighborhoods. The program is called the Urban Safety Corps and it uses the innovative management accountability process pioneered by the New York City Police Department, COMPSTAT. COMPSTAT permits AmeriCorps members and volunteers to create maps featuring crime "hotspots," which can then be targeted with focused area patrols—of both uniformed and plain-clothes officers—and other community policing methods. COMPSTAT also allows officials to develop "Safe Routes" for students who live in communities with high crime rates. These routes can then be protected by police officers at the start and end of the school day.

The Urban Safety Corps relies on strong community support and participation in block clubs, area patrols, lot clean-ups, vacant-home board-ups, and neighborhood watches. Since the program's launch, focus neighborhoods have seen crime decrease by a remarkable 44 percent—a reduction that local officials credit for saving Detroit $62 million.

I have also met with AmeriCorps VISTA members who are working to expand economic opportunity by connecting more low-income families to financial literacy education as part of the Financial Opportunity Corps, which we launched in 2013 with Bank of America and Points of Light, a national volunteering organization.

Financial Opportunity Corps members develop financial coaching programs and recruit and train volunteers who, through one-on-one or small group workshops, help low-income families in 10 communities across the country create strategies to reduce debt, improve credit to receive lower-interest loans, start saving for emergencies, access benefits, and build assets.

In just its first year, the program exceeded its target for volunteer recruitment and garnered the support of a number of organizations, including the New York Public Library, which provided space to host workshops; Clarifi in Philadelphia, which integrated the Corps' financial coaching model into its existing programs; and Sacred Heart Community Service in San Jose, which helped to recruit and train financial coaches.

Connecting People to Their Passion

Often we find that the most successful volunteer is someone whose service matches their passion. That is why we make data on volunteering—including opportunities to volunteer and guides that organizations and individuals can use to create their own service projects or events—available at Serve.gov, the online home of President Obama's nationwide service initiative, United We Serve.

As the President has said, "Ordinary people can come together and achieve extraordinary things when given the proper tools." So our agency encourages all of our partners and grantees to also share information on how Americans can get involved in their local communities and volunteer. The more information Americans have on opportunities to volunteer, the more likely they are to not only discover an opportunity that matches their passion; they are also more likely to make volunteering and service a lifelong tradition.

I have been fortunate to see that passion play out in dramatic and inspiring ways time and again.

Senior Corps, for example, fosters connections that often bridge barriers of language and culture. In 2014, I visited a number of Senior Corps programs in Nebraska. During my visit, I learned of a volunteer named Ezequiel serving in the Eastern Nebraska Office on Aging's Senior Companion Program who I will never forget.

In 2009, Ezequiel was assigned to work with a former engineer who was battling Alzheimer's. As Tom's Alzheimer's disease progressed, he left the house less often. And his friends' visits became fewer and farther between. So Tom's wife Kathy contacted her local Senior Companion Program in the hope that a regular companion for Tom would help brighten both their lives. Enter Ezequiel. For three days a week, Ezequiel visited Tom and Kathy's home, helped Tom work with tools again and build things by hand. Ezequiel and Tom gardened together. They laughed and joked together—and played a few practical jokes on Kathy. Ezequiel even modeled exercises for Tom so that he could increase his physical activity. Amazingly, their bond was forged even though Ezequiel, who was born in Mexico, was learning English as a second language. In fact, Kathy said that as Tom's language skills decreased, Ezequiel's English improved. Ezequiel and Tom's bond was so strong, that as Tom's long battle with Alzheimer's approached its end, Tom called out for Kathy to please get his "brother." Kathy called Ezequiel, who rushed to Tom's side and laughed with his "brother" one last time.

Senior Corps also fosters stronger partnerships with Native American communities. For example, the Zuni Nation in Western New Mexico and the Greater Lakes Inter-Tribal Council of Wisconsin are developing programs that bring different generations together in tribal community classrooms, helping to affirm students and show them that they have value because there is a Senior Corps volunteer in the classroom who speaks their native language. As Nelson Mandela said, "If you talk to a man in a language he understands, that goes to his head. If you talk to him in his language, that goes to his heart."

Senior Corps also provides mentoring opportunities for experienced professionals, allowing older Americans to impart first-rate guidance and pro bono instruction to small nonprofit organizations. One such program is Senior Corps' SOAR 55 (Service Opportunities After Reaching 55), operated in Newton, Massachusetts. SOAR 55 volunteers work directly with nonprofit clients, offering specialized support in areas such as Information Technology and Human Resources Management. SOAR 55 volunteers include highly skilled professionals like Jack, a former legal counsel for Apple and Reebok. These volunteers serve as pro bono consultants, providing management assistance to help nonprofits reassess their structure and, if necessary, reorganize to become stronger, more efficient, and more effective for the long term.

A number of Senior Corps programs also connect experienced professionals to students, as does the Retired and Senior Volunteer Program (RSVP) of Eastern Iowa and Western Illinois, which partners with Western Illinois University (WIU) to recruit and train mentors for students in WIU's School of Engineering. That includes mentors like Tom, a retired engineer and product manager for John Deere who was looking to "make a difference." The WIU Engineering School

Mentoring Project was a perfect fit for him. Tom now serves as lead mentor for the project. He plays an integral role in the program's development and provides ongoing assistance as an advisor in the school's Engineering Club, as well.

And, just as important, Senior Corps helps older Americans live longer, healthier lives. In fact, more than two decades of research shows an association between volunteering and mental and physical health benefits. In particular, older volunteers report lower mortality rates, lower rates of depression, fewer physical limitations, and higher levels of well-being. That is certainly the case with Foster Grandparent Virginia McLaurin, who has spent more than 25 years volunteering as a foster grandparent to children with special needs at the Melvin Sharpe Health School in Northwest DC. In 2014, the DC Commission for Women inducted Grandma Virginia into its Hall of Fame. The ceremony was something of a birthday celebration for Grandma Virginia because it took place on the day she turned 105.

Developing Leaders

National service participants like Grandma Virginia help schools, faith-based groups, and nonprofits build and improve their efficiency and strengthen their volunteer networks. And as they help make organizations stronger, AmeriCorps members are fortifying their networks and honing their job skills. All across the country, AmeriCorps members are learning valuable skills—from project management to fundraising, from interviewing to public speaking. Employers across the country have recognized this, too.

That includes many employers in the volunteer sector. Year after year, organizations that host AmeriCorps members go on to hire them once their year of service ends. In that way, national service strengthens the entire volunteer movement—by training the movement's next generation of leaders.

Our agency is committed to taking what has worked so well in the volunteer sector and expanding it throughout the nonprofit, public, and private sectors, too. And in 2014, we launched a new initiative that is going to strengthen the service-to-employment pipeline for the present and future workforce. It is called "Employers of National Service" and it encourages nonprofits, corporations, and local, state, and federal agencies to create recruitment, hiring, and advancement opportunities for AmeriCorps and Peace Corps alumni. For example, employers can add language to their job postings or add to their job applications a "checkbox" in which alumni can indicate national service experience.

Whether they are in small towns or big cities, employers are looking for qualified applicants. And "Employers of National Service" like Disney, Comcast, NBCUniversal, the American Red Cross, the City of Nashville, and others know we produce them.

Not only are AmeriCorps alumni hired by the nonprofits for which they work, they are also launching businesses and becoming employers themselves.

That is certainly the case for Blair, a former AmeriCorps VISTA member turned entrepreneur. After being exposed to the plight of refugee youth and their families during her service year, Blair—who was only 24 when she founded her nonprofit—now leads GirlForward, an organization that offers mentorship and educational opportunities for girls who have been uprooted from their war-torn countries.

Fostering Innovation

Blair is just one example of how national service participants—especially millennials—are bringing new energy and ingenuity to the volunteer sector and the broader service movement. By fostering programs developed with millennials in mind, national service provides a valuable incubator for young Americans to develop innovative solutions to our nation's challenges. That is yet another way that national service strengthens volunteering—and FEMA Corps, a partnership between AmeriCorps and the Federal Emergency Management Agency—is a prime example.

A unit of 1,200, FEMA Corps members travel to regions that have endured a natural or man-made disaster, working in Disaster Survivor Assistance Teams—or, as we affectionately call them, "D-SATs." And during one of the worst storms of the past century, our members' ingenuity—and willingness to ask those of us in charge to re-think some things—became a game-changer.

During the Hurricane Sandy recovery effort, FEMA Corps members asked a simple question: "Why can't we harness the power of technology to go to survivors rather than have families stand in line for hours to get help?"

FEMA loved the idea. CNCS loved the idea. And now, rather than families having to stand in line, FEMA Corps members equipped with iPads go to families and help them get critical assistance following a disaster.

Just as national service provides a platform for young Americans to "crowdsource" their ideas, we provide a national network for nonprofit partners—particularly small organizations—through which these groups can attract new investors. Becoming an AmeriCorps or Senior Corps grantee brings a broad range of benefits, including great brand and name recognition; it means garnering the support of the federal government; tapping into a proven accountability and oversight framework for your programs; loan forbearance and educational scholarships for the service members your organization hosts; and the infrastructure that will guarantee your program has impact in communities and helps to improve people's lives—which is what we all want.

A New Blueprint for the Twenty-First Century

In 2009, during the early days of the President's Administration, Congress came together and decided that in order for national service to continue serving its vital role in improving and strengthening our communities, our blueprint needed a reboot for the twenty-first century.

The result was one of the final—and greatest—legacies of American statesman U.S. Senator Edward M. Kennedy. The bipartisan Edward M. Kennedy Serve America Act, which was cowritten by Senator Kennedy's friend and colleague Senator Orrin Hatch, not only expanded opportunities for Americans of all ages to serve, the law also focused our efforts on outcomes, impact, and, for the first time, created our now six core priorities. Five years after its signing, we have only begun to see how the Serve America Act will alter the service landscape. But some important improvements are already evident. CNCS and our hundreds of partners and grantees have renewed our commitment to seeking innovative solutions to our nation's greatest challenges. We have also made a commitment to using federal and private resources more efficiently. And we have made a commitment to finding what works and then making it work for more Americans.

Both the Serve America Act and the President's Task Force on Expanding National Service have encouraged us to refashion these commitments as tools for enhancing our impact. And we have learned that measuring and recording our success is just as important as creating the success itself. CNCS has adopted standardized performance measures to ensure resources are being used to maximize results and better show the impact of national service on critical challenges. These measures cover a range of activities, from increasing student academic performance to improving housing to expanding the number of volunteers.

Performance measures are being implemented throughout the federal government and are increasingly being used in the nonprofit and philanthropic sector to ensure return on investment. Finding what works for your organization and recording your results allows for a better assessment of your strengths and highlights areas that need improvement. It also can be key to making the case for investment from funders, whether public or private.

From national and local nonprofits to schools, to faith-based organizations and Native American tribes, many of our existing partners and new friends-in-service apply for federal grants each year to add AmeriCorps members and Senior Corps volunteers to their teams. These grants help our programs recruit, train, and manage national service members and our grant applicants design service activities for a team of members who serve full or part-time for one year or during the summer. Both AmeriCorps and Senior Corps grant applicants must provide a work plan that clearly explains how members or volunteers will benefit the organization and do work that supports one of my agency's six focus areas. To further ensure we are using the taxpayers' dollars as efficiently as possible, our applicants must show that their organization's culture and mission aligns with ours. So what makes a strong application? One that identifies a problem the organization is poised to solve and then outlines how "people power"—in the form of a national service participant or volunteer—can be applied to solve it. And one more thing: great applications also detail how their program will impact lives and how they will measure their success.

Expanding Nonprofit Capacity Together

I often say that if you offer organizations a check or a volunteer, they will take the volunteer every time. Whether they are leading energy conservation projects, devising new ways to tutor students, or using technology to connect veterans to housing resources, AmeriCorps members and Senior Corps volunteers are strengthening volunteerism in America. They add tremendous value by recruiting and managing new volunteers for the organizations they serve and they reshape our communities with their time, energy, and talents. The national service family is breaking new ground every day, and we are eager to expand our work with nonprofits of all sizes to advance this work.

From America's classrooms to its boardrooms, volunteers advance the spirit of service in so many ways. We know we are at our strongest and our best when we serve others. And as President Obama reminds us, national service shows that "people who love their country can change it." Our nation faces some challenges, but if we keep working together we can transform the road ahead.

Wendy Spencer is the Senate-confirmed Chief Executive Officer of the Corporation for National and Community Service (CNCS), the federal agency that engages more than five million Americans in volunteering and service through AmeriCorps, Senior Corps, and other initiatives. As CEO, Wendy has spearheaded the creation of a number of innovative public-private partnerships to give more Americans the opportunity to give back to their communities. The first woman to serve in this role, Wendy has also renewed her agency's focus on research and innovation. Prior to joining CNCS, she served as CEO of the Florida Governor's Commission on Volunteerism, where she coordinated volunteer efforts in response to disasters, including eight record-breaking storms from 2004 to 2005.

Notes

1. Reading Partners, "2013-14 National Impact Report," http://readingpartners.org/wp-content/uploads/2015/01/National-Impact-Report.pdf.
2. Habitat for Humanity International website, AmeriCorps Impact page, http://www.habitat.org/node/302798.
3. Read more about the study at www.volunteeringinamerica.gov.
4. David Eisner, Robert T. Grimm Jr., Shannon Maynard, and Susannah Washburn, "The New Volunteer Workforce," *Stanford Social Innovation Review* (Winter 2009): 34.
5. Corporation for National and Community Service, "Volunteering Among Americans Hits Five-Year High," (press release), December 12, 2012, www.nationalservice.gov/newsroom/press-releases/2012/volunteering-among-americans-hits-five-year-high.

Chapter 23

Service Enterprises: Strategic Human Capital Engagement

Amy Smith
Chief Strategy Officer and President of Action Networks–Points of Light

Sue Carter Kahl
President, SMCK Consulting

> *The volunteer pool . . . looks different. . . . Adults of age sixty-five and over are a significantly larger percentage of the population. . . . Teenagers are involved in community agencies and families are seeking to volunteer together. Corporate volunteering is encouraged and work groups call community agencies to offer their services.*
>
> *We have more potential and actual volunteers available than ever before. . . . The problem is, how do we deal with them? And the answer, apparently, is not well enough.*
>
> *At the Heart: The New Volunteer Challenge to Community Agencies* by Nora Silver

It's been our privilege to work in the volunteer field for two decades. We have worked with incredibly passionate leaders, gifted volunteers, and impactful organizations. Some of the most critical work in our world is happening through community organizations and their volunteers' hard work, grit, and smarts.

And yet.

There is this sense that all is not well. Those of us in the field continually beat the drum about the value of volunteerism only to have it chalked up as something warm and fuzzy, nice, but not necessary. Many organizations that rely on volunteers struggle to make an internal case for volunteers as evidenced by their lack of funding for, or staffing of, volunteer support. Interest in pro bono service is up, but there is a big gap between this growing supply and organizational demand.

Moreover, it seems like many volunteerism conversations leave out important parts of what makes it possible. News articles talk about how valuable volunteers are without mentioning the volunteer managers and leaders who help unleash their power. Volunteer initiatives and employee volunteer programs encourage more people to serve without discussing the infrastructure needed to support their involvement. Many training programs offer volunteer-management tips and best practices without addressing the organizational culture needed to make those techniques successful.

Something is missing.

And so, we find ourselves stuck, as the quote from Dr. Nora Silver's book reveals. Her passage is relevant today and yet her book was written in 1988—more than a generation ago.

Our purpose in naming these challenges is to highlight the need for a transformation. We need to transform the way we talk about, train, support, and view volunteerism. We have an opportunity to engage our volunteer human capital with the same care and strategic intent that we treat our financial capital.

It's why we are so excited about the emergence of the Service Enterprise Initiative, an initiative inspired by Reimagining Service, developed by California-Volunteers, and now administered by Points of Light. The Service Enterprise Initiative provides a new lens through which to view our organizations and the volunteer field. Its concepts apply to any organization engaging volunteers whether or not they participate in the Service Enterprise Initiative.

What's a Service Enterprise?

A service enterprise is an organization that strategically integrates and leverages volunteers throughout its operations, thereby improving its ability to meet its mission and bottom line. Service enterprises translate the skills, expertise, connections, and passion of volunteers into meaningful service that meets the programmatic and operational needs of the organization. For every dollar these organizations invest in volunteer engagement, they can realize a return of up to $6.

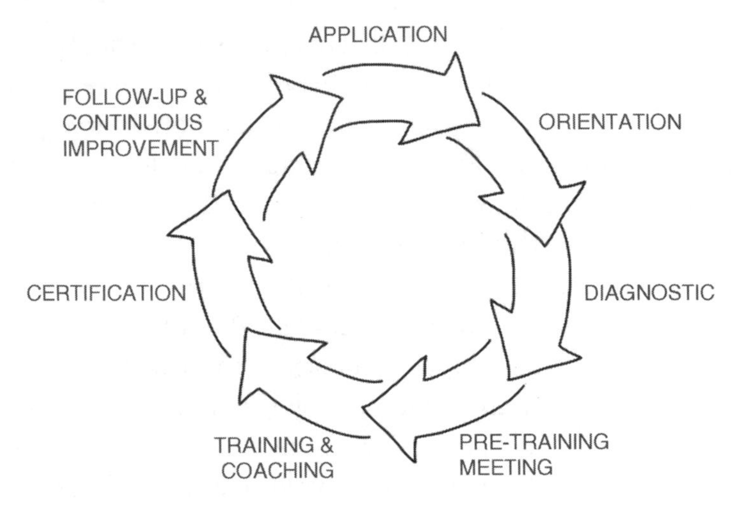

Figure 23.1 The Service Enterprise Model
Source: Points of Light.

The Service Enterprise Initiative is a holistic change-management process that helps organizations achieve these results through comprehensive assessment, training, coaching, and certification. Organizations that successfully complete the process earn designation as Service Enterprises, which helps distinguish them as organizations of excellence that offer quality volunteer experiences.

Service enterprise work is an acknowledgment that thoughtful and strategic investment in volunteerism—from board members to direct service and pro bono volunteers—helps provides the human capital needed to meet an organization's mission. What the volunteer field has known anecdotally is that organizations with strong volunteer practices don't happen by accident. We've seen how their intentional commitment to service flows throughout the entire organization and how their cultures create a readiness to engage volunteers strategically. Research from the TCC Group and Deloitte has since validated these anecdotes and observations leading to the development of the Service Enterprise characteristics.[1,2]

Service Enterprise Characteristics

The Service Enterprise (SE) characteristics are behaviors of organizations demonstrating excellent volunteer engagement. These behaviors help them better serve their constituents while meeting financial goals.

- *Planning and development*—SEs develop strategies and infrastructure for mission-driven volunteer engagement.

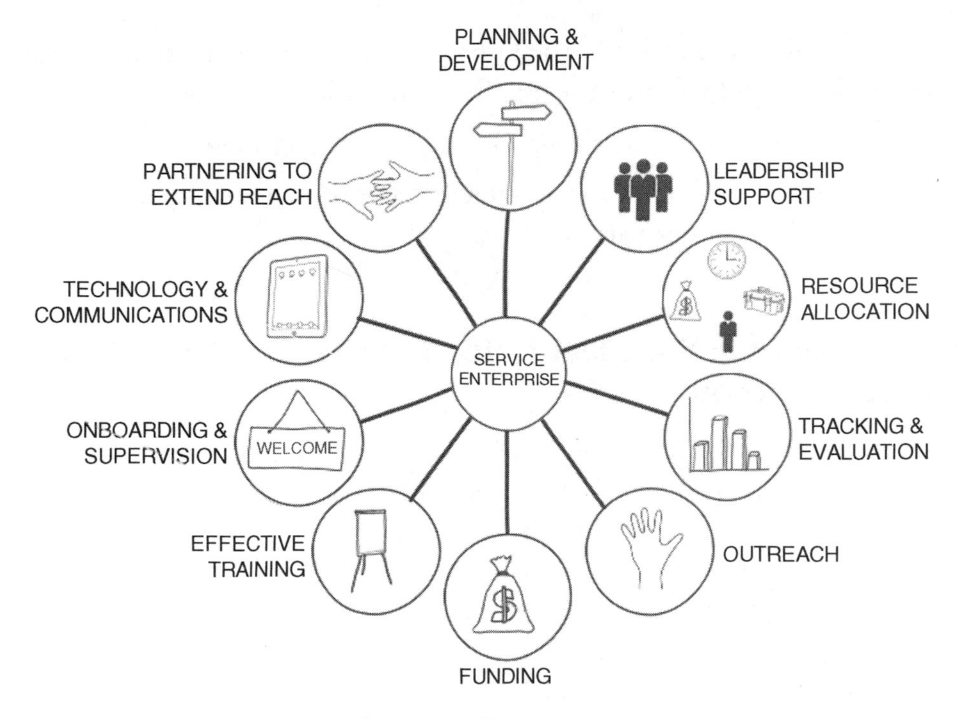

Figure 23.2 The Characteristics of a Service Enterprise
Source: Points of Light.

- *Leadership support*—SEs demonstrate executive commitment to volunteer engagement.
- *Effective training*—SEs train volunteers and staff on their respective roles and equip them to successfully work with each other.
- *Outreach*—SEs conduct outreach to recruit volunteers for programmatic and operational roles.
- *Onboarding and supervision*—SEs match volunteers to appropriate positions, clarify their roles, and orient and support them throughout their service tenure.
- *Partnering*—SEs cultivate a mutually beneficial relationship with service groups, funders, and other community partners to increase engagement and reach.
- *Technology and communication*—SEs implement supportive technology, invite dialogue with volunteers, and articulate volunteer contributions and impact.

- *Tracking and evaluation*—SEs track the outputs and outcomes of volunteer contributions and monitor the quality of the volunteer experience.
- *Funding*—SEs raise funds to support volunteer engagement.
- *Resource allocation*—SEs allocate sufficient resources (time, money, people, tools) to volunteer engagement.

Reinvigorating the Volunteer Field—How Service Enterprises Advance Our Work

The Service Enterprise Initiative (SEI) uses a learning approach that marries practice and research, broadens the focus from the volunteer manager to the entire organization, expands our notions of volunteer value, and enhances the partnerships between corporations and volunteer host organizations. Each of these aspects has its roots in how we have traditionally done business at our organizations, but brings a fresh, and sometimes challenging, framework to how we want to do our work in the future.

Bridging Research and Practice: A Learning Approach

Though many studies on volunteerism have been conducted in the last two decades, they tend to not make it out of the academic realm and into practitioners' hands. Furthermore, the topics studied are rarely packaged for practitioner consumption and application.

The SEI is different in that it blends practice and research. It's a smart approach that includes a variety of professionals and perspectives. Feedback is built into each element of the initiative. It all adds up to a program that is continually evolving and improving.

The research began with support from the TCC Group, a national consulting firm that had been assessing nonprofit organizational effectiveness for years with its Core Capacity Assessment Tool (CCAT). It wasn't until one of the researchers, Pete York, got involved with the Reimagining Service collaboration that he considered applying a volunteer lens to the results. The outcome was compelling. York found that organizations that engaged 50 or more volunteers and demonstrated good practices in doing so performed better on other core indicators of organizational effectiveness[3] than their peers that didn't engage volunteers. Although this correlation was not the same as causation, it established a real relationship between volunteer engagement and organizational effectiveness, providing an impetus for additional study.

Deloitte picked up the baton next to identify and examine the characteristics that are present in organizations operating as service enterprises.[4] These characteristics informed the first service enterprise model and provided the foundation for the original Service Enterprise Diagnostic (SED). The SED combined the CCAT's organizational effectiveness questions with those from the Volunteer and Community Engagement Capacity instrument developed by the RGK Center for Philanthropy at the University of Texas at Austin. These two tools provided a robust assessment of an organization's practices and capacity. As more organizations completed the diagnostic, researchers from the RGK Center for Philanthropy and Algorhythm, York's consulting firm, gained new insight and data, which then translated into the enhanced Service Enterprise model that is used today.

These updates have led to the refinement of the service enterprise characteristics. The original 8 characteristics were expanded to 10 to better reflect the practices that matter most to operating as a service enterprise. For example, planning and development and outreach have been separated from onboarding and supervision to highlight their importance as distinct practices. The researchers also discovered that not all characteristics are created equal: Planning and development, leadership support, and effective training are especially important practices for service enterprises to demonstrate. The research team continues to explore and fine-tune the service enterprise model and is now focusing on how the characteristics may vary at service enterprises of different sizes and missions.

Creating Feedback Loops: A Voice for and Beyond the Volunteer Field

The ongoing study of service enterprises is distinct from a lot of research in its blend of people involved. The SEI team includes academics, data experts, and practitioners, all of whom bring unique expertise and perspective on the volunteer field. The SEI model itself was designed by a team of volunteer centers in California the members of whom combined their expertise in volunteer engagement with their experience in supporting meaningful change in organizations. Their field-testing revealed the need to supplement training with coaching support.

Facilitators and coaches, who serve as an important link between the curriculum and the field, deliver the Service Enterprise training. They offer feedback about how the SEI Model aligns with participant needs. In addition, SEI participants share their experiences through their pre- and postassessments and training evaluations, giving us a picture of what volunteer engagement looks like at organizations of different sizes and missions. These multiple feedback loops and the researcher-practitioner connection make for more insightful learnings and impact the volunteer field in more relevant ways.

The structure of the SEI curriculum also reflects this belief in a learning approach through its use of a cohort model. The training facilitators are experts in their own right, but they know that some of the best wisdom about what works (and doesn't) comes from the participants. After all, practitioners engage volunteers day in and day out, testing ideas, and learning what volunteers and their organizations need.

It's a rare case of blending lessons learned in the field with lessons learned through research. At the core of the SEI is an underlying assumption that ongoing evaluation and thoughtful consideration of the results will help us enhance volunteer engagement and the ways that we train organizations to improve their practices. This collaborative learning approach is generating rich data and gives our field an opportunity to assess—and validate—its work beyond anecdotal evidence.

Focusing on Organizational Culture: Why Volunteer Management Training Is Not Enough

The SEI is confirming that good volunteer-engagement practices are important, but they are not the whole solution. Volunteer management professionals have known this and been flummoxed by it for decades. They create the scaffolding for incredible volunteer strategies and watch in frustration as they seem to be the only ones in the organization who "get it" when it comes to volunteers.

This disconnect suggests that volunteer management training alone is insufficient for making significant organizational progress on engaging volunteers as strategic assets. Instead, an organizational development approach broadens volunteer engagement from something that the volunteer manager (or whoever is tasked with those duties) does to something that warrants attention and investment from the entire staff, including the CEO. In fact, involving the whole team often means transforming the role of the volunteer department.

The volunteer manager at an SE food bank shared: "The SEI process transformed how I see my department's role in the organization. I realized we had so much more potential to engage people beyond food sorting and office volunteers.

"We needed volunteers involved in our whole organization. To do that meant I had to shift from just working directly with volunteers to supporting the entire team in their work with volunteers.

"I now teach others how to make volunteer engagement more accessible and successful. And when a team member has problems with a volunteer, I don't fix it; I work with him or her to determine the best approach for resolution."

The organization where this took place had sophisticated practices in place and a volunteer-friendly culture. They had a high "get it" factor. Yet, even they were able to identify areas for improvement after the training and experienced a profound shift in their thinking about how they engage volunteers at all levels of the organization.

Engaging the Team: It Starts at the Top

Senior leadership buy-in is particularly crucial to be an SE. Leadership buy-in translates to support for building a volunteer-friendly culture, to allocating staff time to engage and deploy volunteers, and for funds to support the technology and other infrastructure needed to track and evaluate volunteer efforts. This leadership involvement is often left out of volunteer-management training, yet it can mean the difference between policies that collect dust in a binder and a robust culture that strategically engages and deploys all of an organization's human capital to serve the cause.

An executive at an organization that helped connect volunteers to organizations that needed them realized that his own organization did not engage many volunteers outside of its volunteer board members. He discovered that many of the staff assumed they didn't need volunteer help or could do the work faster on their own. The executive initiated conversations about ways that volunteers could get involved and challenged the staff to do so, too. As the team broadened their thinking about where volunteers could partner with the staff, they created new roles that were meaningful to the volunteers and the organization's bottom line. The process took time, but it's moving the entire organization closer to its mission and financial goals.

The SEI addresses the reality that volunteer engagement is not a volunteer-manager issue; it's an organizational issue. That's why leadership involvement and change-management principles are built into the process. Each organizatio designates a team that includes the CEO, senior leaders, and other key positions to attend trainings. The curriculum utilizes organizational development and change-management materials that address how to cultivate and sustain a culture of volunteerism. Agency teams work together to flesh out action plans and also share lessons and challenges with the cohort. It's a collaborative environment that draws on the strengths of the group and helps each agency leave with actionable ideas and strategies.

Valuing Volunteers: The Return on Volunteer Investment (ROVI)

For most organizations, the Independent Sector's annual estimate of the value of a volunteer hour is the start and end of how they measure volunteer impact. Impressive as this figure and our volunteer numbers and hours may be, they don't get at the value that volunteers bring to our organizations, our missions, and the broader community.

One challenge is that the Independent Sector value doesn't take costs into account, which may help contribute to the myth that volunteers are free. Yet, a robust volunteer engagement strategy takes time, expertise, and money to implement well. Those investments come back to the organization in many ways. Service enterprises realize up to a 6:1 return on every dollar spent on volunteer engagement. Moreover, they operate at almost half the median budget of their peers that do not engage volunteers.

The SEI helps organizations further define their Return on Volunteer Investment (ROVI). The ROVI is a more rigorous method for calculating volunteer value than multiplying volunteer hours by an hourly rate. It uses a formula that accounts for the costs and value associated with volunteers to generate a dollar figure of what the organization receives in return for its investment.

However, it's not a matter of determining the one right way to define volunteer value any more than there is one right way to define the value a nonprofit provides to its community. Organizations have an opportunity to be creative with how they value volunteers and select the approaches that make sense for them. Some nonprofits are translating volunteer time into the number of full-time-equivalent staff members they represent. Others are tracking the amount of in-kind and cash donations their volunteers give and help raise. Still others feature clients and communities they serve and special projects they complete because of volunteer time and expertise. These valuations of volunteer time give us stronger metrics that appeal to different audiences and help us articulate the many ways that volunteers contribute to our causes.

Addressing the Elephants in the Room

There is a tendency to talk in glowing terms about volunteers and hold them up as model citizens. But the truth is that many staff members have not had a good experience with volunteers. For every rock star volunteer an agency touts, there is another who has been screened, trained, oriented, and placed—never to show up for a second shift. With all that staff have been tasked to do, who can blame them for not wanting to invest time in someone who isn't committed to the cause?

In some cases, we've set ourselves up for this. The lack of a good process to find and onboard the *right* volunteer means that people who are not a good fit are brought on in hopes that they will work out. Or perhaps the volunteer was a good fit, but none of the paid staff knew how to work with or support him or her. We have contributed to a vicious cycle where we underinvest in volunteers and are then surprised when they don't work out.

One SE participant shared that they had a problem with volunteers not showing up for their shifts at a program that supported youth. She was hesitant to give volunteers more responsibility for fear they wouldn't meet expectations. Her co-worker then pointed out that a staff member was always at the program site and led the youth activities. From the volunteers' perspectives, it didn't matter if they showed up or not since they didn't have a key role in the programming. The staff realized they had an opportunity to invite fuller volunteer participation in leading the programs. However, they also needed to provide clearer expectations about what that required and ways to support volunteers when scheduling conflicts arose.

The SEI challenges us to plan our volunteer engagement thoughtfully and intentionally and to thus increase the chances that more of our volunteers will work out. The SEI training sessions offer an opportunity to have real conversations about working with volunteers –the good, the bad, and the ugly. It validates the experiences of participants and empowers them to make changes to their volunteer strategies that benefit the organization, the community, and the volunteers. It also provides tools for having these kinds of discussions with the rest of their teams.

As a result, participants realize the importance of setting expectations upfront and then realizing that it's okay to explore options with a volunteer prospect who is not a good fit for a particular role. In some cases, the volunteer prospect can move to a different position that is a better match for their talents and availability. In other cases, a referral to another organization may be the best course of action. Ultimately, the disappointment of not finding a match is outweighed by the knowledge that a poor fit doesn't serve the volunteer prospect, the staff, or the organization's clients.

Changing the Conversation with Corporate Partners

This strategic engagement of volunteers is garnering the attention of corporations. Volunteerism has become a mainstay of many corporate philanthropy models. Businesses are seeking quality service opportunities for their employees individually and as teams. In many cases, it is hard for them to decipher if a service project will be well-run, organized, and rewarding until employees are already on site. The service enterprise certification is one way to distinguish an organization as a good partner for corporate and employee engagement.

The SE designation means an organization has been strategic about the ways that corporations can support their work. It considers what the company employees are uniquely positioned to contribute. Perhaps the corporate training department could offer professional development sessions for nonprofit staff and volunteers, the finance staff could develop cash flow spreadsheets, or the human resources team could help update employee handbooks. Oftentimes, these pro bono and skills-based projects have a significant impact on the organization. What they lack in photo opportunities, they make up for as meaningful projects that meet a real need.

Operating as an SE means that an organization shows up as a full partner in the relationship with corporations. Though the business brings to the relationship resources in the form of employee volunteers and sometimes cash or in-kind donations, the host organization contributes knowledge of and access to community needs and the expertise to meet those needs. This helps put the host organization on more equal footing with the corporate group so they can help craft a volunteer opportunity that makes the best use of everyone's time.

Strong partnerships begin with a conversation about what a host organization needs and what a corporation has to offer. This may require a bit of creativity because the volunteer opportunity may not yet exist. In one case, a corporate volunteer prospect approached an executive director with the suggestion of starting a podcast in the early days of social media. The executive found the idea intriguing but didn't have the expertise or equipment to implement it. The volunteer prospect, a self-described gadget guy, offered to purchase the equipment, record and edit the podcasts, and develop possible topics. The executive committed to supporting the effort with staff interviews, introductions to volunteers for interviews, and suggestions for episodes. Six months later, the podcasts had great reviews and a growing following, all from a volunteer opportunity that had never existed before.

Sometimes, there isn't a fit between what the corporation wants and what is available, even with some creative thinking. Though it's especially difficult to turn away corporate volunteer prospects, occasionally the best answer is "no, thanks" or "not now." Most companies respect that the host organization is strategic in volunteer engagement and wants to honor employees' time and talents. Equipped with knowledge of what the host organization needs, the corporate group may come back when it has the ability to meet those needs, or the organization may be better prepared to reapproach a particular company when their needs evolve and better align with what that company has to offer.

Engaging corporate groups as partners, articulating volunteer value in diverse ways, and taking an organizational approach to volunteer engagement represent ways to advance and elevate our field. When combined with the latest research, these strategies can help educate those outside volunteerism to better understand what it takes to support effective, meaningful, and relevant service.

Our Evolving Field—A Call to Action

The Service Enterprise Initiative is not a panacea that solves all of volunteerism's challenges—nor will an SE designation eliminate the headaches that trouble a nonprofit. But it does address many of those challenges and gives us language and examples that will help move our field in the right direction. It shines a light on organizations that are engaging volunteers in strategic and worthwhile ways that help them meet their missions and financial goals more effectively.

One SE participant experienced a greater appreciation for volunteer engagement throughout her organization: "We moved from a reactive and siloed approach to volunteering to a proactive and collaborative model that elevates our mission," observed the director of development. "We realized that our goals for serving more clients weren't feasible without leveraging the community in smart and strategic ways, including volunteerism."

In the past, the volunteer function within organizations has often gone unnoticed and underappreciated despite the critical work that it made possible. Everyone in the volunteer field owes it to volunteers and their host organizations to build on and share the research, best practices, and transformation that is coming from SEs and other organizations engaging volunteers well.[5]

In this way, we will be able to change the dialogue about the value and importance of volunteerism and the resources needed to realize its promise. That dialogue won't change unless all of us in the volunteer field, the experts on service, begin to direct and focus attention on the aspects of volunteerism that matter most. Then, and only then, will we find that others can understand and support volunteer engagement more effectively, too.

In the words of a new SE, "We expected the initiative to help transform volunteerism at our organization. We didn't know it would transform our organization through volunteers."

Amy Smith is the Chief Strategy Officer and President of Action Networks for Points of Light, the world's largest organization dedicated to volunteer service. At Points of Light, Amy is responsible for more than 250 HandsOn Action Centers worldwide; 200 AmeriCorps Alums chapters; the Corporate Institute that helps hundreds of Fortune 500 companies engage employees and customer; and generation On, Points of Light's youth service division. Amy serves on the national Reimagining Service Council and has also served as a member of the White House Future of Service Working Group.

Sue Carter Kahl is a consultant, writer, and facilitator who infuses her work with lessons learned as a nonprofit executive, board member, and researcher. She is a Senior Consultant with Points of Light and a Courage & Renewal® Facilitator. Carter Kahl is pursuing a doctorate in leadership at the University of San Diego where she is a Research Associate in the Caster Center for Nonprofit and Philanthropic Research. She has a Master's in Social Work Administration. She volunteers as a state commissioner for California Volunteers and as a coach for nonprofit executives through the Fieldstone Leadership Network.

Notes

1. Deloitte, "Nonprofit Service Enterprise Research Summary," April 2010, http://reimaginingservice.org/sites/default/files/u17/Researchsummary_Deloitte_2010.pdf.
2. TCC Group, "'Positive Deviants' in Volunteerism and Service," December 2009, http://reimaginingservice.org/sites/default/files/u2/TCC%20Group%20Positive%20Deviant%20Research.pdf.
3. Ibid.
4. Deloitte, "Nonprofit Service Enterprise Research Summary."
5. Points of Light offers a number of Service Enterprise resources. Check out the site for the latest list of certified Service Enterprises, research, and training opportunities: www.pointsoflight.org/service-enterprise-initiative.

Chapter 24

Leading Big Volunteer Operations

Carla Campbell Lehn, CVA
Library Programs Consultant, California State Library

The California State Library, in addition to being the library for California's legislature and state government, works in partnership with 183 municipal, county, and special district libraries who manage more than 1,100 library buildings serving 38 million Californians. It provides technical assistance and support to libraries, and federal funds are distributed to focus on enhanced library services and innovation. As a library programs consultant, my job, in addition to managing the statewide library literacy program serving 22,000 adults with 12,000 volunteers annually, is to develop new ideas and resources for libraries across the state.

All that is just one way of saying that the California State Library (CSL) is a big volunteer operation. This is the story of what happens when a big volunteer operation meets a big idea—and how transformation is possible even with the maximum of moving parts to plan for and stakeholders to engage.

In the mid-2000s, a clear societal shift in generational interests and expectations of volunteers presented a unique opportunity to capitalize on a growing resource to bring to the library table. Our idea was to help libraries across the state to truly engage community members' time and skills as volunteers, introduce them to what's new at today's library, and further connect them as advocates and supporters.

We began work on the new initiative "Get Involved: Powered by Your Library" in late 2008. At the time, California's annual library survey reflected 1,351 full-time equivalent volunteers—or 2,702,000 volunteer hours. Our path ahead seemed clear. And then came the worst recession since the Great Depression.

For libraries, as for most public and not-for-profit agencies, the greater economic disaster meant catastrophe within our programs—much less staff and funding, yet more demand for services. California was hit especially hard. Our staff was stretched daily to serve hundreds of new library users: providing Internet access to those who could no longer afford it; helping people who had never touched a mouse apply for a job online; and checking out significantly more children's books, DVDs, e-books, and other materials for families whose shrinking budgets kept them from making those purchases as they had in the past.

This is the story of how, despite the downturn, we successfully wrangled 183 separate library organizations and convinced them to embrace a concept of skilled volunteerism that would require big changes in their practices. In it you'll find many of the complex challenges and opportunities that big volunteer operations face. And, hopefully, you'll come away with new insights you can apply at your organization whether you have 500 volunteers or 50.

Stepping Outside the Vacuum

The best plan for change begins with an assessment of potential barriers and probable success factors. And a surefire way to hinder that assessment is to do it in a vacuum. Designing a plan for change without the input of the target audience will overlook critical issues that must be addressed.

Start with Your Biggest Barriers

Once an advisory committee of library staff working with volunteers throughout the state was established for our "Get Involved: Powered by Your Library" initiative, we asked for the volunteers' thoughts about the biggest potential barriers to success. By an overwhelming margin, the resulting consensus was unanimous that two things could stop us in our tracks: "union issues" and "staff resistance."

Staff resistance will no doubt be a familiar theme for you, but only some readers will face the union issue. As public entities, most libraries in California have collective bargaining agreements with their employees, and as a result, some fairly intense regulatory, contractual, and public relations challenges can pop up in discussions about change. And these agreements vary from library to library. Regardless of whether these are the same barriers facing your organization, how we addressed both concerns might hold some lessons for other nonprofits.

Busting the Union Myth

Let's start with the union issue. We began by conducting telephone interviews with library leaders from seven representative library jurisdictions. And guess what: It didn't take long for us to discover that there existed an urban legend about unions and library volunteers!

Our calls confirmed that there really wasn't, in fact, specific language limiting the use of volunteers in their collective bargaining agreements. True, many libraries had unwritten understandings that volunteers will not supplant employees, and some had even created mission statements for their volunteer programs to specifically state that volunteers will supplement, not supplant, the work of paid staff. But the more we asked about union rules, the more we discovered that most of what people assumed about the unions was just that—assumptions.

After hearing that we were exploring skilled volunteer engagement strategies, the library leaders highly recommended that libraries engage union leadership early on. This approach, plus committing to a supplement not supplant policy, ended up being the key to avoiding problems.

Transforming Fear and Resentment

Staff resistance, on the other hand, is driven by real fears of job replacement, decrease in quality, and loss of control, as well as resentment of additional workload and unclear roles for volunteers. Many staff also have previous bad experiences with volunteers. Although these can often be traced to past sloppy recruitment and other poor volunteer engagement practices, staff members don't really care—they only know they had a bad experience, and aren't looking forward to having another one. Add the emphasis on using skilled volunteers in new roles, and we were bound to get some "Are you kidding? This won't work!" responses.

So we approached the staff resistance dilemma in several ways. Most importantly, we started talking about it differently—instead of bemoaning how resistant staff were going to be to this idea, we started talking about how we would go about "gaining staff buy-in for skilled volunteers." This pivot, although it may seem modest, was crucial to help implementation staff see that despite our recognition that it was a problem, it was one that could be overcome, and was not the intractable barrier they had assumed.

Piloting Success

We provided the opportunity for libraries to apply to become pilot sites for the Get Involved initiative. The six libraries selected from the applications got extra training up front—mostly via webinars. Our goal was to eventually have real, live, skilled library volunteer success stories to share, and enthusiastic library staff to speak to other libraries from their own experience as we rolled out the statewide initiative. The only way to get there was to have some initial libraries onboard as key early partners.

We encouraged these pilot partners to not try to implement this new volunteer engagement concept library-wide, but to start with the low-hanging fruit. Which staff members or department heads already "get it?" Start with them. Helping them to create a successful skilled volunteer implementation and then have them share it will help others begin to see the possibilities and want to try it, too.

Save Story Time!

Story Time is the holy grail of children's librarianship. No matter how they feel about the rest of their tasks—return books to the shelves where they belong, wipe snotty noses, help parents find the perfect age-appropriate books, and so forth—children's librarians always have story time to look forward to!

So when the director of one of our pilot Get Involved libraries surveyed volunteers and saw that nearly every volunteer also wanted to "read stories to children," she was a little concerned about how staff would react. Indeed, in a meeting with her children's librarians, she wasn't surprised to find them less than enthusiastic about giving up their favorite part of the job to volunteers.

The director persisted, however, sharing how involving volunteers could free up time for staff to do previously out-of-reach new and exciting projects. Eventually, she was able to engage them in developing a volunteer job description, commitment "contract," and training process for volunteer storytellers. Within the year, the library was receiving accolades for expanding story times beyond the library as volunteers began reading to groups of children at local shopping malls and grocery stores.

This library director showed how staff could overcome their resistance to an expanded volunteer engagement program when their needs, interests, and concerns are taken into consideration. By engaging the librarians in designing the volunteer selection process and delivering the training, their fears about being able to maintain a high quality of service were allayed, and they got to build additional services that had been on the back burner for their clientele. And of course, new library volunteers are now able to do what they are interested in doing.

Incentivizing Training (for Staff and Management)

A major strategy of the Get Involved initiative was training of library staff about this new concept of skilled volunteering, and helping them to make the shift from traditional volunteer *management* practices to the new volunteer *engagement* strategy. Instead of implementing a training program the traditional way—just providing it to the volunteer coordinator—we knew that any real change would require management understanding and support, as well.

We developed a multiday Get Involved Training Institute and invited libraries to send a team. Each three- to five-person team had to include a senior manager, a volunteer engagement staffer, and a key volunteer. And in order to attend, libraries had to go through an application process.

The application process turned out to be pivotal. The selective nature of the procedure to attend the training heightened interest, and generated some excitement and buzz around the project. And, while we initially worried if we would get enough responses, in the end there were actually twice as many team applications than we could handle. Consequently, a second Institute was scheduled!

What We Learned That Works

During the first five years of the Get Involved initiative, we've hit upon some key implementation strategies that we believe are the keys to our success. We now use them in orientating and engaging new library staff in the volunteer engagement effort, and we think that readers attempting to make broad scale change in their organization, regardless of the organization's size, can use them.

Seek Input

Form an advisory committee or task force of those in a position to help you determine what the issues and potential barriers will be. Then, listen to what they have to say.

Show People the Vision

Don't ask everyone to just take a blind leap of faith. Identify your "champions"—the people who want to go there with you—and help them create a couple of successful pilot tests that can be shared with others.

Get Management Support as Early as Possible

Engage management from the beginning with the goals and positive end results for their organizations of embracing skilled-volunteer engagement. In our case, now that we have concrete outcomes to share, it's getting easier to bring new managers aboard than it was in the beginning.

Make Training Systematic

Don't just train one person and expect that to make an organization-wide difference. Train an organizational team to work on this critical function. And if you have "chapters," "branches," or other offices to engage in this work like we did, engage and train teams in multiple locations. By the way, not surprisingly, the Institute libraries that had the most success implementing the project back home were those who used some of the Institute training materials to train their staff and get them excited about implementation of a skilled volunteer engagement strategy.

There's No Substitute for Assigned Volunteer Engagement Staff

There's no question that the libraries having the most success with their volunteer engagement programs are the ones who have assigned paid volunteer engagement staff. Although few have a full-time volunteer coordinator, many have created a part-time volunteer coordinator position, or have re-organized a staff member's workload to include a portion of their time in this role.

Establish Clear and Meaningful Volunteer Roles

Written volunteer job descriptions that clearly outline time, tasks, skills required, and training delineated not only help the potential volunteer make an informed decision, but also help staff members understand their roles in relation to the volunteer's to avoid confusion. Use the development of the volunteer job description as a planning tool to help staff think through what the need is and what skills will be required. This is also a great approach for getting staff buy-in.

Today's volunteer also wants to know what the impact of their work will have on the organization's mission. Draft that right into the job description along with the list of tasks and requirements.

Cast a Wider Recruitment Net

Libraries are notorious for posting "Volunteer Here" signs on the check-out desk, and calling their recruitment quits. But a key goal of the Get Involved initiative has been to attract people to the library who may not be aware of the library's modern role, get them as volunteers, and eventually develop them into strong library supporters and advocates. For this, we needed to recruit outside the library, but convincing staff that outsiders would care about the library was a big initial challenge.

To streamline recruiting and also ensure we were getting the insights we needed to keep making the case for external recruiting, we formed a statewide partnership with VolunteerMatch.org that gave libraries access to all of VolunteerMatch's tools, training, and support.

The arrangement has been a real success—and not just for recruiting volunteers but also for letting us know how we're doing. For example, anecdotally we heard from libraries that they were successfully reaching a younger, highly skilled volunteer audience, and we also have hard numbers that prove our goals are being met.

Importantly, we also can show beyond a doubt that we are reaching new volunteers. Based on two years of surveying our VolunteerMatch volunteers, around 80 percent of volunteers say this was their first experience volunteering for a library. So we know we're reaching new people.

Measure Your Results

The annual statewide library survey that was already in place has been used as a credible source of data showing improvements in the amount of volunteer time given to libraries. We can show that over the course of the project, we've increased library volunteerism in California by 52 percent—from 1,351 full-time equivalent (2,702,000 annual volunteer hours) to 2,084 full-time equivalent five years later (4,168,000 annual volunteer hours).

Of course, there are other important outcomes that are much harder to capture. Whether the new volunteers have become donors too, whether they've told friends about the organization, and whether they've told friends about volunteering at the organization are all great questions to get a handle on, and, in so doing, shore up executive support for a new or renewed round of funding.

But getting to these answers only seems hard. *Just ask*. Each quarter we send out a SurveyMonkey invitation to anyone who refers themselves to a library opportunity on VolunteerMatch. The results show us that not only are we getting new and more volunteers, we are successfully turning them into library advocates and supporters in the community. In two years of reporting, we found, for example, that 68 percent and 70 percent told friends about what the library has to offer, and 40 percent and 26 percent have introduced friends to our volunteer opportunities. We're also learning how some volunteers are talking with public officials about how important the library is in their lives.

Share Your Results

Each year we've designed a one-page annual report that's shared with all 183 library directors, as well as the 500-plus members of the Get Involved listserv. We host periodic training webinars, and take the time to include our successes, and we volunteer to present at every library conference that will have us.

Your Role as the Volunteer-Engagement Project Leader

Whether you lead a big volunteer operation like our statewide Get Involved initiative, or a smaller volunteer engagement effort just in your office, there are a number of key roles I've learned the leader must play in order to sustain success. Although it seems like a long list, you can actually just instinctively add them into your daily routine. And some of them are strategies that recruit help for you with the sustainability process so that success doesn't rest solely on your shoulders.

Cheerleader—Be enthusiastic. Give recognition. Showcase success stories. And, practice what you preach . . . If you don't walk the talk by having skilled volunteers assigned to help you, how will you ever convince others that it's a good idea?

Engager of Additional Leaders—Like many of you, designing and managing this project is only a portion of my job. I couldn't possibly have the "reach" I need alone to make this statewide effort successful. So, I've identified region leaders—successful library staff in various parts of the state who are willing to lead and feel great about being asked. They organize regional meetings, attend conference calls, assist with future planning, and represent the program where necessary.

Training Champion—Understand the importance of training and exposure to success, and create opportunities for it at all levels. There will probably be a training event to kick off your effort, like our Institute, but more must be done to sustain change over time. We've held and archived a number of webinars. Five years into the initiative, this year we have a team of regional leaders working on two additional statewide training projects.

Communicator-in-Chief—Regular communication is a key element of success—it helps to keep the volunteerism strategy in the forefront for those who have additional distracting work assignments, and it also minimizes the effect of staff turnover. We've maintained a listserv for five years, which now includes over 500 people. We schedule periodic conference calls and online meetings to address particular topics or innovation. I also hold periodic online coaching sessions on how to get the most from VolunteerMatch—not everyone learns everything by just reading or listening.

Resource Provider—When it became clear that libraries were developing great stuff that others could benefit from—volunteer job descriptions, policies, procedures, training materials, and handbooks—we gathered them onto a website with a searchable database. This serves the dual purpose of sharing resources and giving recognition to those who developed the materials.

Reporter-in-Chief—Another key resource development role of the volunteer-engagement leader is reporting. We produce a colorful one-page annual report detailing key successes, and we volunteer to offer programs at regional, statewide, and national conferences to reach new audiences and increase our credibility factor.

Investment Manager—We've had a source of funds from supportive state librarians that allowed this to be done on a fairly large scale. But you can scale it to your organization—even if you don't have a large budget, acting on many of these ideas won't cost much.

Key Takeaways

Listening to your audience's issues and concerns, and then actively addressing them will help you gain the trust of staff and volunteers who, as human beings, often instinctively resist change. Helping them then see the possibilities by providing relevant success stories from their peers will engage them in the process and leave them wanting more.

Get Involved Resources

Here are links to a few of the resources we've developed that you are welcome to use, share, and/or replicate:

Get Involved Website (getinvolved.library.ca.gov)

Here you'll find resources on "Hot Topics" like getting staff buy-in and union issues. It also includes some video clips and a "Resource and Training Center" link to our Get Involved Clearinghouse.

Get Involved Clearinghouse (www.getinvolvedca.org)
This is a searchable database we built to store materials developed by libraries during the initiative: volunteer position descriptions; training materials; photos of library volunteers in action; and management tools like policies, forms, and volunteer handbooks.

Once the effort is off and running, you can't stop there. Providing continuous helpful communication, offering additional training opportunities, and sharing successful outcomes are what ensure sustainability.

Whether your program is large or small, well- or poorly funded, and regardless of whether this is your full-time job or just a piece of a full workload, you can scale these activities to your resources. Don't forget to recruit the additional leadership of successful early adopters. Their support will ensure more activities than you could hope to do alone, and they will feel great about being recognized as leaders.

And finally, we need to practice what we preach. If we think providing volunteers to work with staff in other parts of the organization is a great idea, then we need to model it in our own offices. I successfully recruited a volunteer to serve as "Assistant Volunteer Coordinator." For a few hours each week, she works with our VolunteerMatch account, posting volunteer opportunities and responding to interested volunteers. She also gathers monthly timesheets and enters them into our tracking system, and because of her personnel background, her role has expanded to scheduling interviews and checking volunteer references.

Having help like this frees time for me to focus on being the Cheerleader, while demonstrating to others that I don't just *talk* about the advantages of expanding volunteer engagement, I *live* it.

The payoff is awesome—we continue to enjoy growing statistics, more success stories, support of library leadership, and even the engagement of more states! After seeing a Get Involved presentation at a national library conference, the Idaho state library joined as a partner, and now provides a similar initiative for libraries there. As of this writing we've received a national planning grant to create and share scalable Get Involved: Powered by Your Library models for adoption by other states.

Carla Campbell Lehn, CVA, is library programs consultant for the California State Library, where she manages California's volunteer-based Library Literacy Service, which involves more than 12,000 volunteers in 500 locations each year, and leads the statewide volunteerism initiative "Get Involved: Powered by Your Library." Carla is author of *The California State Library's Volunteer Involvement in California Libraries: Best Practices*. She earned her MS in Community Development from the University of California at Davis. Carla began her career as a VISTA volunteer and today is an active volunteer for Girl Scouts.

Chapter 25

Taking Charge of Your Professional Development

Katherine H. Campbell, CVA
Executive Director of the Council for Certification in Volunteer Administration

What comes to mind when you hear the phrase "professional development"? The comments I've heard from colleagues over the years range from the reluctant to the reticent to the PD junkie!

"I do it because my organization requires it."

"It's not a priority, given everything else I have to do."

"I'll do it as long as my employer pays for it."

"I know it is important for my staff, but we have no money in the budget for it."

"I am not sure this will ever be my profession, so is it really worth the money and time to learn more?"

"Bring it on! I wish I could read and take classes all the time."

"I'll read anything I can get my hands on."

You may be surprised to see this topic in a book about volunteering. After all, isn't our work all about the volunteers themselves? Aren't we supposed to be focused on enabling and *supporting others?* Yes—but there's more to it than that.

As competent leaders of volunteer engagement we certainly ensure that volunteers have the best possible experience and that the work of the organization gets done as effectively as possible. We bend over backwards to give credit to others, and to build strong volunteer-staff teams. But if we completely ignore the development of *ourselves* as individuals and professionals, it limits our ability to be community mobilizers in the fullest sense of the role. The more we embrace a journey of professional development, the more we strengthen our own adaptive capacity to support and strengthen citizen engagement.

My Journey

My first job in this field was soon after college. I was hired to help start a brand new volunteer program in a large urban juvenile court system. At the conclusion of my hiring interview, I meekly asked the court administrator, "Can you tell me the salary for this position?"

He didn't gift wrap his response: "I'm not sure exactly, but I can tell you this—it's more than you're worth."

Clearly, he did not regard my role as "professional"! But then again, neither did I.

Back then, if you had asked me what *professional development* meant, I would have answered "training." I defined the term very narrowly, largely because I believed my options were very limited.

Now, after decades of career experience, I understand that professional development can be—and must be—much, much more.

Perhaps the most significant leap in my own professional growth occurred when I agreed to serve on the local host committee planning the national conference for leaders of volunteers. I took on the role largely to help a close friend and colleague who was already serving. I enjoyed the logistical details of conferences, and felt I could adequately manage the task.

I doubt it ever entered my mind that this experience was "professional development," yet that is exactly what it was. The chain of events it triggered was life-changing:

- I was later recruited to fill the vacant role of treasurer on the board of the national professional association. I knew very little about how to read financial statements and prepare a budget, but figured I needed to learn these skills in order to advance in my career. To support my learning, I asked a friend who was an accountant to tutor me in the basics and advise as needed.
- I was then nominated for the position of vice president. After four months in that role, the president resigned suddenly and I was then elected president. Did I feel ready for that leadership role? No way! But my mentors told me I could do it and they stood by me with support, so I took the plunge.
- After leaving the board I remained active with the national professional association. A few years later I was hired as the executive director, which opened the doors to many new opportunities to advocate, educate, and further build our field at the national and international levels.

Saying "yes" to this invitation to serve on a committee—an important but often overlooked form of professional development—was the first step of an amazing personal and professional journey.

Thinking Broadly

As mobilizers of citizen engagement, we are often focused on complex social issues and efforts to create social change. Our role inherently demands that we be many things to many people—inspirational leaders, project managers, evaluators, policy analysts, relationship builders, recruiters, strategic thinkers, and community advocates. This means our professional development can and should come from everywhere and anywhere.

According to Wikipedia, workplace professional development is "the acquisition of skills and knowledge, both for personal development and for career advancement."[1] Every profession requires certain knowledge, skills, and abilities. Structured professional development allows us the opportunity to reground ourselves in the knowledge of the collective group while learning from others in the fields that directly and indirectly relate to our work.

Although formal learning such as college courses, conferences, workshops, and online webinars immediately comes to mind, I now realize that informal activities are equally valuable, such as coaching, communities of practice, reflective reading, and mentoring. These experiential options provide testing grounds for us to explore, experiment, and engage with others about new ideas and approaches.

As you contemplate the role that professional development plays in *your* life, don't get stuck in a limited view—think broadly! Join me in adopting a definition that includes less formal experiences like deepening current knowledge and skills; venturing into new subjects, roles, or related fields; keeping current on trends and changes affecting your industry; and experimenting with innovative practices and models.

For Once It's About You—and Your Power

I believe that everyone deserves access to professional development. I also believe that employers have an obligation to offer opportunities to their workers—any textbook on human-resource management will stress the ways in which this yields a significant return on investment. But individual staff need not passively accept what is offered, or go without if the resources are not provided.

Today's collaborative and interactive world has largely eliminated many of the previous barriers to continuous learning. No longer can we use the old excuses "My boss won't pay for it" or "It takes too much time." We live in a time that offers unlimited ways to access information, networks of people, and new experiences—in small bits and large doses. This is not the rigid, expensive professional development of the past—it is a bountiful smorgasbord of gifts we can give to ourselves anytime we choose.

Reflecting back on my own experience, I now see clearly how pursuing professional development can yield many personal benefits, including:

- Increased self-awareness of strengths and weaknesses.
- Increased confidence.
- Proof of skills and abilities.
- Opportunities to practice and apply new knowledge.

- Affirmation from others.
- Exposure to diverse people and settings beyond my comfort zone.
- Fresh challenges when the current job has become stale.
- Changes in how others perceive us.
- A job promotion, pay raise, or repositioning in the organization.
- Meaningful, enduring relationships.

But the benefits don't stop with you; the ripple effect of your learning and self-growth is huge. As leaders in the field of volunteer engagement, we have permission to dream, to be pioneers, to make things happen that would otherwise go undone. Our role is inherently powerful, if we choose to exercise that power. As you gain a wider and deeper perspective on your role and the overall work of your organization, the social impact of your day-to-day actions increases. As you move forward into the realm of new ideas and innovation, your community becomes stronger.

Regardless of where you sit or what job title you hold, the world of work is moving and changing much too fast to ignore your own professional development. Let's not be among those who sit and wait for others to do things for them. Professional development is personal, and each of us must take ownership. Thus, my challenge to you: proactively use professional development as a *strategic tool* to move your own passion and your organization's mission where *you* want it to go.

Tips for Getting Started

The notion of being more strategic about your professional development may feel daunting—the choices can be overwhelming, and your to-do list is full of more urgent tasks. All the more reason to carve out a bit of time to focus your thinking and gain some clarity about where you are and where you want to go.

Find Your Direction

Do some exploratory thinking about various aspects of your current situation. Ask yourself questions like these to dig deeper into the potential for skill development, relationship building, reduced stress, and new roles.

"I'm really curious about . . ."

"I wonder if I could . . ."

"I wish I was better at . . ."

"I wish others regarded me as more . . ."

"To what extent are my personal goals aligned with my organization's goals?"

"How do I feel about my work now? Would I like to feel differently in the future?"

Name Your Fears

Identify the barriers to moving forward so you can better understand why change may be difficult. Naming our fears or obstacles is the first step toward overcoming them.

"What is holding me back from taking a step to grow or learn?"

"What am I nervous/stressed about changing? Why?"

"Is fear of failure keeping me stuck? Why?"

"If I don't do anything to improve my competence, what might happen?"

Know What's Available

Research options and resources, based on the thinking you've done and the barriers you've identified.

"What else do I need to know before I make a decision to act?"

"What do I need in order to move in the direction I want to go?" (This should be a specific skill or knowledge, a credential, an ally, membership in a professional group, etc.)

"Who might have advice to offer, or help me find what I need?"

Maximize the Power of Colleagues

In recent years the concept of networking has been abused to the point of losing its meaning. And yet, networking remains one of the most highly valued benefits of many membership organizations. Certainly, there is no denying that some of the best professional development can happen through structured interaction with peers.

Volunteer Engagement Associations

Local networks of volunteer engagement professionals exist in many communities, and several countries have established national networks such as the Association of Volunteer Management Professionals in Canada, the U.S. Association for Leaders of Volunteer Engagement, Managers of Volunteer Effort in Singapore, and the Australasian Association of Managers of Volunteers.

Similarly, you may be part of a regional or national affinity group of individuals who hold a similar role in a similar setting—for example, leaders of volunteers in national parks, museums, or hospice programs. These groups usually offer a regular schedule of workshops or webinars for their members, but often overlooked is the huge potential of member-to-member interaction. Listen for potential job openings, ask others to share what books or classes they've taken, and schedule one-on-one conversations to help you problem-solve. Maximize the benefits you gain from your membership by proactively tapping into the minds and experiences of others!

A more formal way to do this is to seek a mentor or coach. Ask someone you respect and admire or someone who has expertise you want to gain. This type of relationship involves fairly regular conversations, in-person or long-distance. You may hesitate to try this, thinking that the person you seek as a mentor is too busy or not interested. Don't let this stop you! Any prospective mentor would be complimented to be asked. You have nothing to lose but the potential of a rewarding relationship.

Yet another option is to identify a peer career coach. Unlike mentoring, a peer coaching relationship is a partnership of equals among two people who are on the same professional level and in the same arena of work. They can identify with each other's roles, yet each brings fresh perspective, knowledge, and experience to the other. You might find it helpful to pursue this type of collegial relationship if you want to:

- Grow your skills in any element of volunteer management.
- Develop a strategy to "educate up."
- Plan out your career path, moving up in the field.
- Become more comfortable working with new types of volunteers.
- Maintain a learning regimen and schedule.

In an e-Volunteerism article, Sheri Wilensky Burke and Gerald Pannozzo described how they teamed up for mutual benefit to discuss career goals, share frustrations, and work through obstacles.[2] They have a schedule of monthly phone calls where they discuss each other's situation and wrestle with related questions. Then they hold each other accountable for "assignments" between calls. The two are careful to maintain a balance of time spent on each person's needs, and to be supportive rather than judgmental.

Burke and Pannozzo stress that there are no hard and fast rules about how this type of relationship should be structured. Rather, the key is to mutually agree on a time frame and process for regular communication, and then stick to it. As volunteer management practitioners, we are naturally inclined to help others and generously share information with colleagues. Peer career coaching builds on these innate characteristics and channels them to yield powerful results.

Create a Plan

There are lots of templates out there for professional development plans, though many are intended for employers to use. Choose a format that works for you. The most important thing is to capture the results of your exploratory thinking and research, and create a pathway for moving forward. Putting it on paper starts to convert your abstract thoughts into action, and also provides a way to share it with others.

When your thoughts are clearer and you've decided on a few goals and steps toward those goals, you can create a more structured action plan. Consider including: short- and long-term goals; big steps broken into smaller actions; an estimated time frame or deadline; who else will be involved; resources needed (materials, information, tools, money, etc.).

One caveat: As helpful as it is to have an initial plan, I am not suggesting it is necessary to map out your entire life's journey! Just as with any long trip we take, the exact route we follow will most likely change over time as new circumstances arise and we find out more about each destination. As one colleague says, "I would characterize my professional development as more organic than planned. Not that I wasn't intentional—I simply responded to situations as they arose or that I anticipated." Create a plan that has an intentional opening to expect the unexpected.

Record and Celebrate Your Journey

Even if no one is requiring you to do so, keeping a written record of all your professional development activities is worthwhile. Documenting your investment in your own professional development provides quick access to information you can use on your resume, online profiles, or job interviews. And on those days when you feel undervalued or taken for granted, pull it up and celebrate all the ways you've directed your own continuing competence.

Recording your journey can be as simple as creating a spreadsheet that includes what you did, when you did it, why you did it, evidence of completion/achievement, and any reflections you may have on how you benefited.

A Foundational Resource

Certificate versus Certification

The terms *certificate* and *certification* are often confused. Each refers to a specific type of professional development. The Institute for Credentialing Excellence provides these definitions:[3]

> The primary focus of a *professional/personnel certification program* is on providing an independent assessment of the knowledge, skills, and/or competencies required for competent performance of an occupational or professional role or specific work-related tasks and responsibilities. Certification is intended to measure or enhance continued competence through recertification or renewal requirements.

The primary focus of an *assessment-based certificate program* is on facilitating the accomplishment of intended learning outcomes. Although assessment is an integral part of the certificate program, the primary purpose is to provide education and training that supports the accomplishment of the intended learning outcomes. The certificate designates that participants have completed the required training and demonstrated accomplishment of the intended learning outcomes.

The CVA credential is a certification. Certificate programs are usually offered by colleges or universities.

One resource that may be helpful as you start mapping your professional development journey is the Council for Certification in Volunteer Administration. CCVA delivers professional certification and advocates ethical practice so organizations can maximize the impact of volunteer involvement to achieve their missions. A visit to the CCVA website at www.cvacert.org may inform and stimulate your thinking.

Competency Framework

This articulates the full range of knowledge and skills needed to do this work effectively. Based on a job analysis survey of the field, the content is updated periodically to ensure its relevance and validity.

Self-assessment Tools

Use these practical tools to assess your own level of knowledge and experience against the competencies. This can be a quick way to zero in on specific topics for learning or skill development.

CVA Certification

Getting certified makes sense if you have at least three years of experience leading and managing volunteers and want to signal your professionalism with the CVA designation after your name. Candidates must successfully complete a multiple-choice exam and a written portfolio in order to document they have the knowledge and application skills to do this work with competency.

Continued Competence

Take a look at the CVA Renewal Guidelines[4] for specific ideas for pursuing continued competence. This list of ways with which CVA certificants may earn Professional Development Units (PDUs) includes both "head learning" and experiential activities:

- Attendance at workshops, seminars, conferences, and so on
- Self-study through online webinars, self-instruction modules, and virtual conferences
- Applied readings (read a book or article and write a brief essay about how the content is relevant to your work and will influence your actions)
- Postsecondary education: undergraduate courses, leadership program certificate, professional certification, or graduate degree in a related field
- Publishing: blogs, articles, research reports, website content, newsletters (beyond the normal requirements of your job)
- Public speaking, teaching, or consulting
- Volunteer leadership: serving on a nonprofit board of directors, chairing a committee, mentoring a colleague, leading a community initiative
- Volunteer activity (direct service or advocacy)
- Volunteer service with CCVA

Stories from Your Peers

Table 25.1 has a few real examples of managers of volunteers who have taken charge of their own professional development.

Table 25.1 Stories of Professional Development

	Outcome	*Activity*
Dan	To help his organization benefit from engaging more volunteers with disabilities.	Volunteered for projects with a local brain injury services program to become more comfortable interacting with individuals with disabilities.
Alison	To grow her understanding of adult education, enable herself to get better at something she really enjoys, and move toward a long-term goal of training on the national level.	Co-taught local classes with an experienced instructor.
James	To help others benefit from his experience with an innovative program model.	Despite always struggling with writing, he wrote an article for a well-known national publication.
Kate	To demonstrate to her employer that she is a competent leader.	Though not yet comfortable thinking of herself as a leader, she served on the board of her local professional association.
Rachel	To gather new information and ideas that would benefit her employer, and grow her own diverse network of peers and leaders.	Negotiated with her boss to attend a national conference and offered to cover her own travel expenses if the organization paid the registration fee.
Nikki	To get up to speed on new topics and earn credibility as an expert and leader in the field.	Delivers training and workshops as a volunteer in her local community.
Julie	To stay in touch with her community and the diverse world beyond her own organization.	Attends all the meetings of her local professional association.

Where to Find Professional Development in Volunteer Engagement

As you explore the landscape of potential ways to keep learning and growing, here are a few resources worth visiting:

52 Free Development Opportunities for Nonprofit Staff

Bridgespan maintains a fantastic list of suggestions of how nonprofit leaders can engage promising staff members in critical skill development areas without sending them to formal external trainings. Identify which opportunities best fit with your staff's or your own personal development needs, and put a few into action.

www.bridgespan.org

Energize, Inc.—This is probably the most comprehensive web portal especially for leaders of volunteers. It offers a wealth of information about educational courses, training, local networks of leaders, free articles, publications, etc. Sign up to receive free tips and regular updates:

www.energizeinc.com

VolunteerMatch—Offers free one-hour webinars on every conceivable topic related to volunteer engagement, as well as a resource list and monthly blog. I've found it to be just-in-time information that can easily fit into your busy schedule:

www.volunteermatch.org/nonprofits/

Nonprofit Hub—Keep up to date by visiting this site's "Guide to the Best Free Nonprofit Webinars":

www.nonprofithub.org

CVA Certification—If you have at least three years of experience, you can become Certified in Volunteer Administration and put the initials "CVA" after your name. This is an affordable option that demonstrates your knowledge and application of effective volunteer management principles. This international program involves an online exam and a written portfolio, and takes about a year to complete.

www.cvacert.org

Invest in Yourself

Several years ago I heard a leading trainer and author in our field, Nancy Macduff, talking about our role as leaders of volunteer engagement. She challenged us to be like the "canary in the mine"—alerting those around us to subtle changes in the atmosphere that might be harmful. This powerful analogy highlights an aspect of our work that connects back to the concept of professional development. Like the canary, we naturally sing a song of optimism and belief in the potential of people to solve problems and create change. And like the canary, we must remain vigilant and ready to signal the need for adaptation and innovation—hence the responsibility to attend to our own learning and evolution.

Do you regard your role as a leader and manager of volunteers as your job function, your career path, or your profession? Regardless of the answer, professional development is a critical tool for influencing your *personal journey*. Like the rudder of a ship, it will help you avoid aimless drifting; like the wind, it will fill your sails and power you toward your desired destination.

Equally compelling is the potential for professional development to steer the future of your *organization*. If done well, it yields a continual infusion of fresh thinking, updated expertise, renewed energy, and willingness to innovate—all of which are essential for sustainability in today's world. As individual practitioners, we must partner with our employers to embrace multiple approaches to quality improvement.

Seize the initiative and invest in yourself. Your future depends on it. And our volunteers, our organizations, and our communities deserve no less.

Katherine H. Campbell, CVA, has worked in nonprofit and volunteer management for over 30 years as practitioner, trainer, and leader. She is Executive Director of the Council for Certification in Volunteer Administration (CCVA), managing professional credentialing programs for leaders of volunteers. Her career began in 1973 at the Philadelphia Family Court where she helped develop an extensive volunteer program. For 14 years she worked at the Virginia Office of Volunteerism, eventually becoming Director. From 1997 to 2003 she served as Executive Director of the Association for Volunteer Administration (AVA). Katie also does independent consulting

(*continued*)

(*Continued*)

and has taught as adjunct faculty at several colleges. Katie earned a BA at Earlham College and holds the Certified in Volunteer Administration credential.

Notes

1. http://en.wikipedia.org/wiki/Professional_development.
2. Sheri Wilensky Burke and Gerald Pannozzo, "Peer Career Coaching: Investing in Your Professional Development," *e-Volunteerism* XII, no. 3 (April 2012).
3. www.credentialingexcellence.org/.
4. CVA certification renewal guidelines: www.cvacert.org/current-cvas/renewal.

Afterword

Robert Egger
Founder and President of L.A. Kitchen and CForward

Wow . . . quite a book, huh?

By now, you realize that the potential of volunteerism in America borders on a once-in-a-millennium opportunity.

"Whoa, Robert," you might be thinking. "Sure, there's lots to work with here, and the writers totally opened my eyes to a mountain of major opportunity . . . . But *once in a millennium?* Dude, reel it back in."

I totally stand by that comment. Here's why:

Every morning, 10,000 American baby boomers wake up either retired or one step closer to it—and that's going to keep happening, every day, for the next 18 years.

But despite being feted as a unique generation and being told that they'd one day have it all, many boomers actually feel at odds with what they've become, versus what they thought they'd be—when they were young and dreamed of changing the world.

This is a generation that grew up with people like John Lennon, Marvin Gaye, Cesar Chavez, Barbara Jordan, Martin Luther King, Jr., Gloria Steinem, and Malcolm X. They danced in the streets, saw men walk on the moon, marched to demand equal pay for women and equal rights for people of color.

They were the biggest, most educated, freest, and richest generation ever and they represent the deepest well of life experience in the history of the world.

And now I bet a bunch of them are wondering, "Could I, *should* I, have done more with my life?"

Let's look at the other end of the timeline, and the 100 million strong Millennial Generation. They're even more diverse and technologically advanced than boomers—and they've been raised in service. They too, long to change the world.

What if these two generations discovered that they actually want the same things? Sure, one is coming from a place of redemption, and another from a desire to walk a different road . . . but theirs is a mutual journey to a once-in-a-millennium opportunity. Can you imagine what they could create together? This is just one example of the possibilities for transforming your volunteer engagement as the world turns and changes. The book you just read is filled with many more.

In my experience there are three kinds of nonprofit leaders. Most just have their heads down. They work hard to make payroll and keep things moving. They might read this book, and consider putting out a few listings, but for the most part, they think things are rolling along nicely, so why rock the boat.

The second leader reads a book like this and a light goes off. They see the opportunity to amp up their daily mission and expand their impact. They might even hire new staff to bring volunteers in, get them signed up for some projects and lists, and help them learn, firsthand, about the issues they are confronting, together. That's cool.

But you, I can tell, are one of the third type. You see the future coming and you know the world is changing. You sense the moment, and rather than wait for it to come to you, *you* march out to meet it. You aren't going to *hope* volunteers show up, get engaged, and join the march forward; *you are going to make it happen*.

That's why this book is so important, and why you are the key.

You see that moment—where you can help build your organizational strength, guide volunteers to a deeper understanding of your cause, *and* send them out into the world with eyes opened, ears tuned, spirit elevated, and brain engaged, so that they see countless other ways to have an impact.

Imagine 100 million people thinking, "Wow, I get it. I can volunteer on Saturday, but what about the rest of the week?" Picture them thinking, "I don't have to just be a set of extra hands; I can use my brain, my heart, my skills, and *my life* to make a difference, too."

I've seen this light bulb go off countless times in my 25-year history at the DC Central Kitchen, where volunteers worked side-by-side with men and women enrolled in our culinary arts training program. Volunteers as diverse as 10-year-old school kids, corporate leaders, movie stars, and U.S. presidents, all working together, as citizens of a shared city. We demonstrated that everyone has a skill, a gift, a role to play as we prepared 5,000 meals together—meals that nourished people physically but, more importantly, fed the soul of the city and opened countless eyes to the way simple acts can have profound impact for both the giver and receiver.

The powerful ideas this book exposed you to can change the world, but only if you make it happen. There's an army out there, young and old, some laden with degrees, others hard-working hourly workers, but each with a skill to contribute, each with a desire to be part of the ongoing, universal quest to have their lives mean something.

All they need is a guide, an opportunity, and leadership. And that's exactly what your organization—and you—can do.

So what are you waiting for? *Go get them.*

Robert Egger founded the L.A. Kitchen, a nonprofit social enterprise modeled on the work he pioneered as the president of the DC Central Kitchen, the country's first "community kitchen," where food donated by hospitality businesses and farms fuels a nationally recognized culinary training program. Robert also founded the Campus Kitchens Project, which empowers students and recycles food in 40 university and high school cafeterias, and is the Founder and President of CForward, an advocacy organization that educates candidates about nonprofit issues. Robert has received numerous awards for his leadership. His book, *Begging for Change: The Dollars and Sense of Making Nonprofits Responsive, Efficient and Rewarding for All,* received the 2005 McAdam Book Award for Best Nonprofit Management Book.

About the Editor

Robert J. Rosenthal created the concept of *Volunteer Engagement 2.0: Insights and Ideas Changing the World*. He works at the intersection of causes, communications, and technology and is inspired every day by those who work in social change.

For seven years, Robert headed communications and audience engagement for VolunteerMatch, the web's largest volunteer engagement network, where he helped grow the organization's social impact to over $900 million in equivalent value generated for the nonprofit sector. Since then, he has worked independently while living and traveling abroad.

Prior to joining VolunteerMatch, Robert consulted for nonprofits in the San Francisco Bay Area including the Jewish Federation of San Francisco, Earth Island Institute, Taproot Foundation, Center for Volunteer and Nonprofit Leadership, Ecology Center, and Independent Press Association. In 2014, he produced GlobalGiving's first Summit on Social Media & Online Giving in New Delhi while serving as the organization's South Asian field representative.

Robert is an active writer and teacher, and frequently speaks to audiences on the subjects of branding, content, public relations, cause marketing, social media, and corporate social responsibility. He is on Twitter at @socialgoodR.

Index